Seeker Churches

Seeker Churches

Promoting Traditional Religion in a Nontraditional Way

Kimon Howland Sargeant

Rutgers University Press

New Brunswick, New Jersey, and London

Excerpts from "Let the Lord Love You," "From Here on out," "Only by
Grace," and "Man of God" cited with permission of Willow Creek Associa-
tion, Barnington, Ill. "Let the Lord Love You" and "Only by Grace"
Word/Maranatha! © Ever Devoted Music (ASCAP), Nashville, Tenn.

Library of Congress Cataloging-in-Publication Data
Sargeant, Kimon Howland, 1964–
Seeker churches : promoting traditional religion in a nontraditional way /
Kimon Howland Sargeant
p.   cm.
Includes bibliographical references and index.
ISBN 0-8135-2786-4 (cloth : alk. paper) — ISBN 0-8135-2787-2 (pbk. : alk.
paper)
1. Evangelicalism—United States.   2.   Church renewal.   I. Title.

BR1640 .S27 2000
280'.4'097309049—dc21   99-049852

British Cataloging-in-Publication data for this book is available from the
British Library

Manufactured in the United States of America

To Carol

Contents

Preface and Acknowledgments

This book is for those who are interested in the dynamic, and at times, puzzling world of American religion. It is written not just for scholars who study the sociology of religion but also for the reader who wants to learn more about one of the most significant new movements in American religion, evangelical seeker churches. These churches have emerged in response to profound changes in the American religious environment and will be an increasingly influential type of Protestant church life in the twenty-first century.

Although seeker churches are the main topic of this book, the larger question this project considers is: What does it mean to be religious, especially to be an evangelical, at this moment in history? As an entrepreneurial and innovative yet also traditional and conservative movement, evangelicalism provides an excellent window onto how religious groups negotiate the tensions between social change—particularly the cultural shifts that the baby boomer generation has spearheaded—and preserving traditional belief. I especially hope this book helps pastors and other religious leaders navigate the tensions between translation and tradition.

This project would not have been possible without James Davison Hunter's steadfast support and intellectual engagement. From initial conception to final product, his advice has been invaluable. The Lilly Endowment, through its support of the Religion and Power Project at the

University of Virginia, provided the financial support for the survey of seeker church pastors and the early stages of the research. In addition, the generous financial support of the University of Virginia's Institute for Advanced Studies in Culture allowed me to complete my research and spend an additional year in Charlottesville revising the manuscript.

I also owe several other faculty members at the University of Virginia a great debt. Sarah Corse unfailingly provided her enthusiasm, sociological knowledge of culture and organizations, and encouraging reassurance that this project was of interest to sociologists who do not specialize in religion. Tom Guterbock's survey research expertise was invaluable in the design and distribution of the seeker church pastor survey. The quality of his contribution is reflected in the remarkably high response rate to the survey. He also provided a humorous launch to the research design when he queried me about how I planned to investigate the growth of *secret* churches.

David Bromley of Virginia Commonwealth University gave valuable professional advice on presenting and publishing the findings of this research. Randall Balmer, Don Miller, Robert Wuthnow, and one anonymous reviewer graciously offered their considerable expertise on the manuscript. Joe Davis, Beth Eck, Jack Elsner, Jim Nolan, and Richard Horner have all paid me the highest tribute any scholar can receive by devoting their critical attention to a work in progress. Robert Loftin was an invaluable assistant on some research as well. Other friendly advisors include John Seel, who generously shared with me many of the materials on seeker churches that he had collected, and Ken Myers, whose writings and insights into the dynamics of popular culture helped me to engage issues that I might have overlooked. Luis Lugo of The Pew Charitable Trusts gave me the gift of time to complete the final stages of this book.

Several pastors generously agreed to examine a draft of the survey instrument. To John Hall of Trinity Presbyterian Church, Dr. Keith Smith of University Baptist Church, and George Ainsworth of Christ Community Church, all of Charlottesville, Virginia, my gratitude for their suggestions on how to improve—and especially to trim down—the survey. This project would not have been possible without the hundreds of pastors who returned the survey, as well as the two dozen pastors who agreed to speak with me about their churches. Furthermore, Jim Mellado of the Willow Creek Association assisted this research, especially by introducing me to pastors of seeker churches. I extend my thanks to the many pastors who agreed to be interviewed for this research. I hope the final product provides a valuable and balanced perspective on their remarkable movement.

Since this project began, the Sargeant family has more than doubled in size. My three sons—Alexi, Jadon, and Ellis—have been able to complete their own book projects in a much more timely fashion. I can only hope that this research may someday help them understand and find their own place in the dynamic world of American Christianity.

My greatest debt is to my wife, Carol. In her role as editor, "Slasher" has been relentless in her commitment to purging this book of scholarly obfuscation, unnecessary passive voice, and, especially, split infinitives. Where this manuscript fails to live up to her impeccable standards, the blame lies squarely on my shoulders. Just as important as Carol's considerable editorial assistance has been her gracious willingness to allow me to disappear for the lonely hours necessary to complete this project. I can never repay her love and encouragement. I can, however, thankfully acknowledge that this book would not have been possible without her help and that this project—as in everything else in my life—is immeasurably improved by her efforts and companionship.

Seeker Churches

Introduction

What is our business?
Who are our customers?
What are their needs?[1]

Throwing out Tradition

Spirituality is booming in America, as any review of best-seller lists or even public television specials will show. Spiritual seekers are no longer found only among the rare free spirits but represent a growing proportion of the population, especially among members of the baby-boom generation. One reason for this is that the increase of religious pluralism in our society since changes in the immigration laws in 1965 has expanded the cafeteria of religious choices greatly. As a result, the religious landscape of America is not the same as it was a generation ago.

In this dynamic environment, evangelical churches are finding creative ways to attract seekers to churches with a conservative theology by packaging that theology in an innovative, contemporary form. Of course, religious dynamism and vitality are not new in American life; they have characterized American religion from the eighteenth-century Great Awakening to contemporary figures such as Billy Graham and the innovative evangelical churches that are the subject of this book. What is new, according to many observers of the American religious scene, is a very different cultural environment in which these religious innovators must operate. Put simply, consumerism has become a predominant characteristic of American religion.

Consider Mill Pond Fellowship. Pastor John Nelson was raised in a Free Methodist church and now is head pastor of Mill Pond Fellowship, a rapidly

1

growing Free Methodist church in the suburbs of a city in the Pacific Northwest. While Nelson has remained faithful to the denomination of his youth, his church is drastically different from the one in which he was raised. Although certain aspects of the Free Methodist tradition—in particular an emphasis on small groups—play an important role at Mill Pond Fellowship, Nelson finds that, in general, the traditional Free Methodist church is unsuitable in today's religious environment. "The church I grew up in," asserts Nelson, "was small, legalistic, and dogmatic." When he decided in the late 1980s to start a church, Nelson's vision was to design a service that would appeal to those who were not attending church. His goal was "to throw out tradition [and] stay tuned to the unconvinced."[2] Mill Pond Fellowship was therefore intentionally designed to be radically different in style and form—but not in message—from the church of Nelson's youth. The result is an unconventional, and very popular, format. The church features contemporary music, a live band, dramas, and an informal and theatrical style that attracts people who might not otherwise attend. At a communion service, for example, Mill Pond's band played the Rod Stewart song "Have I Told You that I Love You"; on Easter, it played the Eagles' song "Desperado." Such informal and contemporary services have met with an enthusiastic response. In 1989, seven families founded the church. By 1999, over one thousand people attended each weekend. Despite its Free Methodist affiliation, Mill Pond Fellowship has more in common with the large, primarily nondenominational churches that are emerging across the country than with the small, denominational, neighborhood church of Nelson's youth.

Mill Pond Fellowship is an example of an influential trend within evangelical Protestantism: the emergence of the seeker church. A seeker church is one that tailors its programs and services to attract people who are not church attenders. The most prominent seeker church is the United States is Willow Creek Community Church, the self-proclaimed "largest church in America," which attracts more than fifteen thousand people from suburban Chicago to its services every weekend. This "modern American cathedral"—so described by ABC News anchor Peter Jennings—features an attractive winding drive around a picturesque lake, and a forty-five-hundred-seat theater offering a concert-quality "seeker service" complete with live band, professional lighting and sound, dramatic presentations, and topical messages on practical concerns. Large, contemporary churches such as Willow Creek represent one of the most influential movements within American Protestantism. They also offer the hope to many pastors that churches that revise their traditional outreach strategies can grow dramatically.

Across the country, hundreds and even thousands of pastors are flocking to seminars to learn more about the seeker church approach to ministry, which has led prominent seeker churches to boast impressive growth rates that inspire awe among pastors and breed confidence among evangelicals regarding the church's mission to American society. In fact, many pastors believe that the seeker model holds great promise for reinvigorating American church life. What is not promising, say seeker church leaders, is the use of old forms to reach a new generation of seekers. Yale philosopher Nicholas Wolterstorff provides an example of the old forms that seeker church leaders reject in his recollections of growing up in the Dutch Reformed Church:

> We "dressed up" on the Lord's Day, dressed up *for* the Lord's Day, and entered church well in advance of the beginning of the service to collect ourselves in silence, silence so intense it could be touched. . . . We faced forward, looking at the Communion table front center, and behind that the raised pulpit. Before I understood a word of what was said, I was inducted by [the church's] architecture into the tradition. Every service included psalms, always sung, often to the Genevan tunes. There was no fear of repetition. The view that only the fresh and innovative is meaningful had not invaded this transplant of the Dutch Reformed tradition in Bigelow, Minnesota. Through repetition, elements of the liturgy and of Scripture sank their roots so deep into consciousness that nothing thereafter, short of senility, could remove them. During the liturgy as a whole, but especially in the sermon and most of all in the Lord's Supper, I was confronted by the speech and actions of an awesome, majestic God.[3]

It is this kind of repetition, the hallmark of the traditional Protestant (and Catholic) service—this cycle of liturgy, and silence, and chant; this encounter with symbolic action and architecture—that pastors such as John Nelson want to "throw out."

Throwing Out Tradition

Innovative, customer-sensitive church programming is blossoming in evangelical churches across America. Saddleback Valley Community Church, for example, has grown to more than nine thousand attenders in the fifteen years since it was founded in Orange County, California; the church only recently completed its first building. Weekly services were held for many years in a large tent located on land the church had purchased. When it first sought to attract attenders, Saddleback mailed invitations to local residents, informing them, "We're a group of happy, friendly people who have discovered the joy of the Christian lifestyle." Saddleback's services are lively, upbeat, and contemporary—remarkably similar in feel to the worship style at Willow Creek. Saddleback's messages focus on applying Christianity to daily life; the church even provides fill-in-the-blank outlines to help attenders follow the sermon. Saddleback calls itself a "purpose-driven church" and it now sponsors seminars at the church and across the country that teach other pastors the principles that are the basis for its success. Senior Pastor Rick Warren confidently instructs seminar participants that "when the church is balanced around the five New Testament principles (worship, ministry, evangelism, fellowship, and discipleship), then growth is automatic." He also adds that the more pastors "target [their] community, the more effective [they] will be."[4] Along with Bill Hybels, Warren is one of the most influential—and in-demand—seeker church pastors in the country. Warren was prominently featured as a speaker at Willow Creek's 1997 "Leadership Summit" conference.

Another innovative church is Houston's twenty-two-thousand-member Second Baptist, known as "Exciting Second," which was profiled on National Public Radio. Second Baptist Senior Pastor Dr. H. Edwin Young has instructed his staff to find ways to make the church more "user-friendly" by studying the strategies of theme parks like Disney World. Young is not apologetic about his unabashed borrowing from successful secular models. "I take what is worldly," says Dr. Young, "and baptize it."[5] Exciting Second's marketing efforts are clearly paying off: the church has an annual budget of over sixteen million dollars. It sponsors sixty-four softball teams and forty-eight basketball teams and fields eighty-four teams in other sports such as volleyball, soccer, and flag football. The locus for all this excitement is the church's Family Life Center, which includes six bowling lanes, two basketball courts, an indoor jogging track, racquetball courts, and weight and aerobics rooms, as well as a music wing for its orchestra and five-hundred-member choir. Despite some criticisms of its marketing-based approach to outreach, Second Baptist is unapologetic. "People think because we're a church, maybe we shouldn't market," says Gary Moore, Second Baptist's music minister. "But any organization, secular or otherwise, if [it's] going to grow, [it's] got to get people to buy into the product."[6]

In Michigan, Kensington Community Church advertised its services by mailing out glossy advertising flyers, which featured a picture of the senior pastor in hunting paraphernalia. The caption read: "Is a guy who shoots ducks worthy of your time on Sunday?" This quirky ad campaign garnered local media attention, and within two years Kensington Community Church had more than thirteen hundred people attending its weekend seeker services. CrossWinds Church in northern California has grown phenomenally as well. By incorporating the musical style of the area's most popular radio station into a seeker-friendly format, CrossWinds has attracted more than fifteen hundred attenders to a refurbished old warehouse, the site of its weekend seeker service.

The extraordinary success of these new churches has even inspired other, more traditional churches to modify their basic format. First Baptist Church of Van Nuys, California, changed its name to Shepherd of the Hills Church, dropping the word "Baptist" from its official title. Why? "People just don't like denominational tags anymore. All they want to know is, 'What's in it for me?'" says the Reverend Jess Moody. A new six-million-dollar building features beamed ceilings, a stained-glass "hayloft" over the entrance, and a giant stone fireplace equipped for cooking breakfasts. Meanwhile, the Reverend Moody has renovated his teaching style, banishing all references to hellfire and damnation from his preaching. Also missing are many of the standard terms of Christian theology. "If we use the words redemption or conversion," Moody says, "they think we're talking about bonds." Moody sells a special version of the Bible called "Kwikscan" which highlights essential passages in boldface and requires no more than thirty half-hour sittings to read from Genesis to Revelation.[7]

Community Church of Joy in suburban Phoenix beckons to passersby with its immense front sign that reads "Welcome to Joy." The church features electric guitars instead of organs and offers worship services to fit a variety of tastes: a Saturday night country music service; a traditional Sunday morning service with a large choir; and a contemporary service with upbeat popstyle music. What the Community Church of Joy does not proclaim too loudly is its religious heritage. As one attender admitted, "We probably came here for a year before we knew it was Lutheran."[8] Like the Community Church of Joy, the Discovery Church in Orlando, Florida, also wanted to become more inviting to seekers. To this end, it not only changed its name but also dropped its affiliation with the Southern Baptist Convention.

Innovation that pays attention to what attracts today's religious customer—and where that customer shops—is becoming more commonplace. In Minneapolis, the three-thousand-member Wooddale Church of Eden Prairie has taken church to the consumer by initiating a special service in the rotunda between Bloomingdale's and Sears at the Mall of America, the largest mall in the world. Other seeker congregations attempt to draw in the crowds by emphasizing just how different they are from traditional churches. For example, at Shiloh Crossing Community Church ("A Celebrating United Methodist Church for Contemporary People") outside Indianapolis, visitors are given ten reasons to "check out" the service. This list includes:

Great upbeat music;

Casual dress (no ties, please!);

Professional multi-media and video presentations;

Practical encouraging messages that relate to life in the real world; and You'll get a lift for your week.[9]

Another church offers reasons why you would *not* want to attend a typical church service. At Daybreak Community Church in Michigan, for example, one seeker service featured a David Letterman–style "Top Ten List of Things to Do During a Boring Sermon." The inventory included picking a scab, learning a foreign language, and, at the top, "mining for nose noogies." The implicit message of this irreverent skit was that the pastors of Daybreak would never deliver a boring sermon.

Other churches are likewise aware of the dangers of dull preaching and the benefits of humor. Heartland Community Church in Kansas, for example, once dedicated a service to the "Real World Series," during which a local baseball announcer teamed up with the pastor to do the "play-by-play" for the Team of Faith, starring Enoch as pitcher and Abraham behind the plate. Discovery United Methodist Church in Richmond, Virginia, promises its visitors that they will experience "the most refreshing hour of [their] week." For younger visitors, Discovery has also developed an extensive collection of live animals, which regularly appear in church. The Sunday before Thanksgiving, for example, "Tom Turkey" was the guest of honor.

New Methods for a New Millennium

What these and hundreds of other churches across the country have in common is that they are all committed to using innovative methods, frequently drawn from marketing principles, to reach those who currently do not attend church. This broad movement, unlike previous movements within Protestantism that were associated with a particular theology (such as neo-Orthodoxy or fundamentalism or the Social Gospel), is not defined by doctrine or denominational affiliation. Instead, the seeker church movement is distinguished by its emphasis on a particular methodology. The "tradition" that seeker church pastors want to throw out is not the belief in the authority of the Bible or the divinity of Christ, but the form of the church in which they were raised.

Although traditional in their theology, many seeker church pastors are discovering that new methods often succeed in attracting to church people who otherwise might not come to a traditional church. These methods include an emphasis on contemporary music and on practical messages; providing excellent child care; featuring a wide variety of choice in small groups and other ministries; creating an informal atmosphere; and deemphasizing denominational identity. Pastors are not inventing these new approaches on their own. They receive training from the many conferences, books, and resource materials available today. These resources are overwhelmingly concerned with methods and programs that have proven successful in attracting baby boomers to church. Thus, when pastors flock to conferences at Willow Creek or Saddleback, they are interested primarily in methodology, not theology. They are looking for practical marketing suggestions, not theological justifications.

What do churches such as Willow Creek, Saddleback, and Mill Pond Fellowship have in common? In addition to their respective commitments to helping the church reach people more effectively, they share certain assumptions about the role of the church in society, such as: a commitment to Christian renewal through the local church (often a megachurch) rather than through politics, the culture, the denomination, or even parachurch organizations; a commitment to evangelism as the primary mission of the church; and finally, a commitment to "using the insights and tools of the behavioral sciences to aid effective evangelism."[10]

This movement to revamp the church's form and methods is both diffuse and diverse. Numerous large churches, consultants, marketing experts, denominational leaders, parachurch organizations, and representatives from specific churches (especially Willow Creek) all participate. While there is not *one* single model that the various proponents of the "new paradigm" church recommend, many church growth analogies draw from the marketplace where large, specialized institutions compete to meet customers' needs. Thus, seeker church experts often proclaim the shopping mall, Disney, and other customer-sensitive companies as models for the twenty-first-century church.

In order to offer the services that attract seekers, many church growth consultants advise pastors to build big churches. One such consultant, Lyle Schaller, claims that the rise of megachurches (generally defined as churches with more than two thousand attenders) is one of the "most significant changes taking place in American Protestantism in the second half of the twentieth century." Schaller estimates that "between 1950 and 1990, the number of Protestant congregations averaging more than eight hundred at worship has at least tripled and perhaps quintupled."[11]

Some seeker church leaders emphasize the importance of having a distinct seeker service, while others claim that a clear vision for the church and how it intends to assimilate newcomers is essential. Almost all stress the importance of using contemporary music and other forms of modern communication technology. Additionally, all seeker churches and their leaders share one common understanding—the church in American society today is facing a crisis so fundamental that, unless it radically alters its approach to those outside its doors, it will become increasingly irrelevant. The proper response to this crisis, say seeker church leaders, is to initiate a "paradigm shift" in the church's philosophy of ministry. Congregations, many pastors claim, must abandon traditional methods and aggressively recast themselves in ways that are more inviting to today's religious seekers. Simply tinkering with the traditional methods will not do. The new millennium requires new forms of church. And leading the way in propagating new forms is Willow Creek Community Church.

The Pivotal Role of Willow Creek

Willow Creek, and those seeker churches inspired by Willow Creek's example, provide the empirical basis for this study of the "paradigm shift" within evangelical circles regarding new forms and methods of outreach. I focus on Willow Creek and those seeker churches influenced by Willow Creek for several important reasons. First, churches such as these are distinctive in their efforts to design services, programs, messages, and ministries that will appeal to unchurched individuals. By changing the form in which Sunday message are delivered, seeker churches offer religious consumers a product that might not have been inviting in its traditional packaging. While an emphasis on evangelism always has been a part of the evangelical tradition (hence its name), the form of evangelism that seeker churches practice is significantly different from previous evangelistic efforts.

A second reason why Willow Creek is a primary example of innovation among evangelical churches and, therefore, is the basis for this study, is that its influence extends far beyond the suburbs of Chicago and the evangelical community. Church consultant George Barna claims that since Willow Creek was founded, "the seeker approach has grown to more than ten thousand churches nationwide" and "as many as one-fifth of all churches claim they have some kind of seeker service."[12] The national media have clearly taken notice of the Willow Creek's success. It has been prominently featured in *Time*, *Newsweek*, *Fortune*, and the *Harvard Business Review*, as well as in a host of Christian publications. In the public television series about evangelicalism, *Mine Eyes Have Seen the Glory*, Willow Creek was the first church profiled. *In the Name of God*, an ABC News special about religion in America, prominently featured Willow Creek, and the *New York Times* 1995 Easter week series on megachurches in America highlighted Willow Creek. *Guideposts* magazine named Willow Creek its 1989 Church of the Year for meeting "the needs of the 1990s by presenting timeless truths in a contemporary way."[13] Even Mainline Protestantism is taking a careful look at Willow Creek's success. Paula Kadel, chairwoman of the marketing support group for the National Council of Churches, led a group of about thirty church leaders from across the country on a week long 'field-trip' to Willow Creek to study first-hand the secret of its success.[14] Willow Creek's leaders are attracting interest even from the nation's highest office. One paper reported that Willow Creek's Bill Hybels met with President Clinton on a monthly basis for over a year.[15]

In addition to this national media attention, Willow Creek is making its own effort to publicize its success and instruct other churches to follow in its footsteps. It has, in fact, institutionalized its strategy through the formation of an association. The Willow Creek Association (WCA), founded in 1992, helps interested churches devise strategies to appeal to seekers. It has grown to over five thousand member churches internationally and provides conferences, seminars, regional round tables, consulting services, membership lists, newsletters, employment exchanges, and resource materials to its members. WCA conferences disseminate the principles of church growth and instruct pastors in how to apply these principles in their own churches. In 1985, WCA held its first conference; only thirty pastors attended. By 1990 more than two thousand attended, and in 1999 more than seventy-five thousand visitors came to Willow Creek's expanded conference series, which includes several different conferences. According to one satisfied participant, "These conferences are essential to the viability of the church." Another attender admitted, "I truly believe the future of our church depends on what our people do with all we've learned here at Willow Creek."[16] Through the Willow Creek Association, Willow Creek has formalized a network of seeker churches and, most interestingly, assumed some of the training responsibilities normally ascribed to a denomination. Thus, the third and most important reason to use the Willow Creek Association as the basis for this study is that, by institutionalizing the strategy and vision of Willow Creek, the Association has embraced the mantle of leadership for the seeker church movement.

New Forms of Church

Why are seeker churches like Willow Creek emerging now? Seeker church pastors claim that the old models or forms of church are no longer effective, primarily because of significant cultural changes within American society. These changes have created an environment in which religious leaders can no longer take for granted the loyalty of their congregations—especially their children. While there is a growing interest among Americans in spirituality, this interest does not necessarily mean that baby boomers are turning to traditional churches. Instead, this "generation of seekers" chooses freely from an increasingly diverse cafeteria of spiritual options, not only in religion but also in other institutions such as the family and interest-based associations. There is a broad movement in American society "toward de-centralization and a reshaping of structures to fit the needs of individuals. . . . [T]oday's culture of choice . . . [empowers people] to create new types of communities and ways of mobilizing."[17] We are observing, to use sociological terms, the shift from religion as an ascriptive identity based on birth to an achieved identity based on choice. This shift is at the core of the emergence of consumerism as a primary characteristic of American religious practice. The seeker church movement, I would argue, is an effective institutional response to today's consumerist ethos.

This book provides the first sociological mapping of the seeker church movement, whose ambitious goal is to re-form the Protestant church.[18] Although there have been a variety of popular media accounts of Willow Creek, Phoenix's Community Church of Joy, Houston's Exciting Second, and other fast-growing churches, the seeker church remains largely unexplored from a sociological perspective. This book offers a comprehensive national study of Willow Creek and the movement of like-minded seeker churches that are committed to adapting the style and idiom of contemporary culture into their services. This book also includes information from in-depth interviews with pastors across the country. These interviews help document how seeker churches appeal to the needs and interests of many non-churchgoers.

The focus here is on religious institutions, their leaders, and how they are adapting their message and methods to an uncertain environment. It is not a how-to manual of church growth. I will not suggest an ideal process for assimilating members or creating an "effective" worship service. Furthermore, this research does not rank programs by effectiveness; it will not measure which churches are growing the fastest or which seminar provides the most information. It will not even suggest which church has an optimal design strategy. These are the tasks of the practitioners.

My purpose, instead, is thoroughly sociological. My concern is not with which churches are most effective, but with the sociological pressures that lead to a heightened concern with effectiveness. I will examine the understandings and symbols of the Christian faith that are stressed by seeker churches, as well as those that are comparatively de-emphasized. I will study the strategic and institutional changes that seeker churches are implementing in order to reach today's "generation of seekers."

Although both church leaders and attenders are important, this book focuses particularly on institutions and their leaders, using the theoretical insights from the production of culture. This research approach highlights how actors and institutions actively shape cultural products whether "high art," such as sculpture; popular products, such as country music; or even religious products, such as contemporary worship. Robert Wuthnow's *Producing the Sacred* provides an excellent example of the utility of this approach. Chapter 1 focuses on what the producers of religion— in this case, seeker church pastors and their churches—are offering to seekers. In it, I first examine Willow Creek's remarkable success in detail, discussing the church's history and innovations. Second, using data from my Seeker Church Pastor (SCP) survey, I document the practices and strategies that characterize the seeker church movement. The critical question raised in chapter 1 is whether the emergence of seeker churches might constitute a revival—a powerful movement of both religious and cultural significance. Although the data allow only a speculative answer to this question, I argue that the seeker church movement is best understood as a re-*form* of evangelicalism.

Why this emphasis on new forms? It is the form of the seeker church, particularly its embrace of innovative services, that makes the seeker church movement distinctive—and controversial. Forms of organization are not simply neutral carriers that achieve a given end; they embody assumptions and values in and of themselves. Consider Marshall McLuhan's famous phrase, "The medium is the message." The form of communication is as important—as loaded with information—as the actual message itself.

After the review of the changes in the American religious environment since the 1960s in chapter 2, the discussion moves outward with each successive chapter, from a visitor's first encounter with a seeker church in chapter 3 to the broader issue of the movement's denominational role in chapter 6 and theories of religion, such as secularization, in chapter 7. Chapter 3 examines the rituals of seeker churches—modern liturgies for the unconvinced. I argue that the deliberate absence of religious symbols and denominational affiliation, as well as the contemporary style of music and the informality of dress and address, suggest that seeker churches depict the sacred primarily as an internal presence. External representations of the sacred (for example, crosses) are considered "offensive." Chapter 4 extends my analysis of seeker services to their weekly messages. Based on an analysis of a year's worth of messages at Willow Creek, I demonstrate how seeker messages are both traditional in their theology and innovative in their stress on the satisfactions and psychological fulfillment that Christian faith offers.

Chapter 5 discusses the strategies that seeker churches use, first to attract visitors to their services and then, more importantly, to incorporate people into the life of the church. While the marketing techniques of these churches may have received the most attention and criticism, "shopping mall churches" do not succeed simply because of marketing. They carefully plan to meet the "felt needs" of seekers by offering choice in programming, flexibility in scheduling, creativity in connecting people to service opportunities, and a plethora of small groups to promote intimate relationships and lasting friendships.

Perhaps the most remarkable evidence of the influence of the seeker church movement is the growth of the Willow Creek Association (WCA) to more than five thousand member churches in less than eight years. Chapter 6 presents my argument that the WCA represents a new kind of denomination—a postmodern denomination that stresses flexibility, specialization, and flat authority structures. Just as Mainline Protestant denominations formed large bureaucracies in an age of vertical integration in the corporate world, the WCA embodies the kind of flexibility that technology allows—and that low levels of denominational loyalty require.

Chapter 7 considers the sociological and religious significance of the seeker church movement. In particular, how does the production of culture perspective relate to today's contested notions of secularization? Given the rapid growth of seeker churches, it is clear that religion is *not* disappearing from the modern world. This book, however, does provide considerable evidence that institutional change mirrors cultural change. More specifically, religious institutions such as seeker churches thrive primarily within the private realm by offering meaning and fulfillment to spiritually searching baby boomers. Meanwhile, some of the other social roles of religion—providing for the poor, building schools and hospitals—seem to be diminishing as the social function and location of religion is increasingly privatized. Nevertheless, religion still is an important force in American life, particularly in the voluntary sector and the private realm. Seeker church leaders are creating innovative institutions that may successfully engage many Americans in religious and social involvement that they might not otherwise have considered. Yet, despite seeker churches' remarkable success, the public significance of religion seems likely to diminish in the midst of an increasingly therapy-oriented and consumerist culture.

One

There are really two types of churches today: business as usual churches and "new tribe" churches.[1]

A New Reformation?

On a typical weekend at Willow Creek Community Church, more than fifteen thousand people attend one of the church's four services. What is remarkable here is not simply the sheer number of attendees but that these Sunday services are not church services, at least not in the traditional sense. Willow Creek, which is located in an affluent suburb of Chicago, describes its weekend service as a seeker service—a polished, one-hour, professionally produced show designed for those who are *not* members of the church or even professing Christians. The seeker service is the linchpin of Willow Creek's carefully developed strategy to reach its target market of "Unchurched Harrys," twenty-five- to forty-five-year-old, white-collar professional men who do not attend church. The seeker service is held in a forty-five-hundred-seat auditorium, complete with plush movie theater–style seats, a curtain and stage, and technical equipment rivaling that of any professional theater company. There are no crosses or religious symbols of any sort on display in Willow Creek's auditorium. Instead of stained-glass windows, two sides of the auditorium are made of clear glass, providing visitors a view of a lake filled with geese and ducks, as well as a view of a stream of cars winding its way to the church's gigantic parking lot. Before services, police officers and traffic teams clad in orange safety vests stand at the entrance to the church campus (as it is called) and direct cars to available parking spaces, which are arranged alphabetically in rows just as they are at airports and large shopping malls.

Visitors will notice immediately that Willow Creek, nestled along the border of a small lake, does not look like a church. In fact, even the exterior has no crosses or other religious symbols on display. Willow Creek's extensive complex of dark-brick-and-smoked-glass buildings resembles a modern community college or corporate training center. (Actually, Willow Creek is so large that finding the auditorium can be a challenge.) Willow Creek's facilities include a conference center, a cafeteria food court and atrium dining area, three basketball courts, an entire wing of offices, a chapel the size of many churches, a bookstore, and endless hallways of Sunday school rooms and immaculate nurseries that rival the most expensive private day care centers.

Despite this maze of facilities, visitors clearly do find the auditorium. What draws thousands of visitors to Willow Creek each week is its innovative seeker service. To attend this service, a visitor first enters what looks like the lobby of a theater. There are skylights in the ceiling, tall trees surrounded by benches, and conspicuously placed informational booths with brochures available for the taking. A half hour before the Saturday night seeker service, teenagers gather excitedly in front of the closed doors, hoping to get the good seats right up in front, much as at a concert. Once the doors open, greeters distribute bulletins without asking for names or attempting to seat anyone. Visitors are free to take a seat inside the spacious theater, enjoy the soft jazz/pop background music, and read the bulletin. This is not a standard one-page photocopy of the service order. It is a professionally printed brochure. Only one of the six panels is used as a guide to the service; most of the bulletin is devoted to announcements, events, updates, requests, listings of meetings during the week, and a card on which people can request more information on Willow Creek. When the service is about to begin, the house lights dim, the recorded music ends, and the curtain draws open to reveal a large stage with a band located in the rear and a set for the day's drama presentation.

On the evening of my first visit, the stage was set with a large executive desk, matching chair, and two additional chairs. As soon as the lights had dimmed, the five-member band at the rear of the stage launched into a lively, upbeat instrumental piece, the "prelude" according to the bulletin.

Once the song was finished, four young women strode onto center stage and began singing a soft-rock number entitled "He Won't Let Me Down." The audience responded with applause and was then directed by a man dressed in jacket and tie to rise and sing "You Satisfy My Soul." (Such formal attire in a church where most people are dressed casually indicates that this individual is a pastor.) This was not a difficult song. Three lines of lyrics were printed in the bulletin and, if you still needed a little prompting, were projected onto large screens on either side of the stage. Singing a few songs is the only participation requested of visitors. Following the song, a woman in a business suit entered the stage and sat in the executive chair that was positioned front and center. Two men sat to her right. In this week's drama presentation, titled "Conversations" in the brochure, a man asked his boss (the woman behind the desk) for more responsibility in his job. The second man on stage represented the voice of doubt inside the promotion seeker's head. Humorously, the actors portrayed the confusion that developed when the promotion seeker answered his doubting voice aloud, leading his boss to conclude that he needed a break, not a promotion.

Following this drama came a segment of the service that the brochure called "Scripture." At first, this seemed to be a misnomer. One of the church's pastors walked onto the stage (again sporting a jacket and tie) and began to tell the story of how his car was stolen from a Chicago garage. The point of his story was that he was angry at himself for leaving his briefcase in the trunk. At the end of the story, the pastor briefly mentioned a Bible verse relevant to the problem of self-anger: Ephesians 4:26—"In your anger do not sin; do not let the sun go down on your anger." The pastor read the verse aloud. No one was expected to look it up—it was not listed in the bulletin and there were no Bibles under the seats. Following this Scripture reading, one of the singers from earlier in the service performed "Let the Lord Love You," a contemporary pop-style song. At the conclusion of the song, the pastor returned, made a few announcements, offered a short prayer of thanks for everyone who had attended, and then requested that visitors not contribute to the offering since they are guests of the church.

The second half of the seeker service was devoted to the message. Pastor Lee Stroebel took his place behind the clear Plexiglas podium, prayed briefly, and then spent the next forty minutes using personal reflections, vignettes, and the story of the prodigal son to illustrate three different types of self-anger: (1) exaggerated anger over everyday errors; (2) simmering anger over past wrongs; and (3) a growing regret over life's missed opportunities. Stroebel's message was simple: "There's wisdom in the Bible to help us recover from self-anger." His style was far from the "fire and brimstone" preaching one might expect to encounter at an evangelical church that stresses the need for personal conversion in order to avoid eternal damnation. Instead, Stroebel reminded me of Tom Peters, the business consultant and author of *In Search of Excellence*, whose popular speaking brims with enthusiasm while he promotes successful management strategies. Stroebel was effusive about the Bible's relevance to our daily lives. His main theological point was that we cannot truly forgive ourselves until we realize that God has forgiven us first. Before closing with a prayer, Stroebel encouraged the audience to come hear next week's message, "When I'm Mad at God." He also reminded everyone that the morning's message would be available for a nominal fee on cassette tape in the church lobby immediately after the service. When Stroebel had finished, the lights were raised, background music was immediately pumped into the auditorium, and people began streaming toward the exits.

Although there is some variety in the format of Willow Creek's seeker services, each one is arranged around a single theme. The songs, dramas, stories, and Scripture passages are coordinated to highlight that week's theme, which is expressed in the title of the message. Message titles include "Enriching Your Relationships," "The Power of Money," "Fanning the Flames of Marriage," "Discovering the Way God Wired You Up," "Energy Management," "Authenticity," "The Art of Decision Making," "Maintaining a Healthy Attitude," and so on. The entire service is carefully designed to meet the "felt needs" of the attenders; that is, Willow Creek strives to address questions that people are asking in their daily lives, not theological matters that they may never have considered. To this end, the seeker service strategy is based on the premise that visitors need time to consider the claims of Christianity and prefer anonymity while they do so. In contrast to other evangelical events such as crusades, which place an emphasis on one distinct moment of conversion, Willow Creek expects people to consider the church's claims over time. At Willow Creek, seekers are allowed to observe anonymously. They are encouraged to investigate the church's religious claims at their own pace. The anonymity of the seeker service emulates other activities common in our mass society, such as going to a mall, attending a sporting event, or relaxing at a movie.

Using this innovative strategy, Willow Creek has become one of the nation's largest and most influential Protestant congregations. This phenomenal growth is all the more impressive given that the church is only twenty-five years old. Today, the church's annual budget exceeds $12 million and the physical plant, located on 141 landscaped acres, is valued at over $15 million. Willow Creek's buildings contain some 352,000 square feet, the size of a small shopping mall. But Willow Creek is not only big, it is also beautiful. Its grounds are immaculate, its hallways clean, and its posted signs eye-catching. Every aspect of the church's facilities emulates the best of corporate America in quality, design, and style. These similarities are intentional. Willow Creek's aim is to reduce or minimize any cognitive distance between the religious realm and the working and shopping world of suburban middle-class Americans. Willow Creek describes its design strategy: "Music, facilities, and the use of the arts should all reflect the culture within which we live." To this end, "[W]hen leaders of Willow Creek designed their buildings and campus, they didn't visit other churches for inspiration; they visited the sites frequented by those they hoped to reach, like corporate offices, malls, and civic centers."[2]

Underlying all of Willow Creek's specific strategies is a deliberate commitment to market the church's message in ways that make sense to its target audience, namely "Unchurched Harry." The origins of this untraditional approach date back to 1975 when Bill Hybels, who was then working as a youth minister, decided to found a church that would appeal to the unchurched parents of teenagers. Hybels and some friends surveyed local neighborhoods to find out why people did not attend church. The survey yielded five reasons. Many people thought that churches always ask for money or that church services are boring and lifeless. Others suggested that church services are predictable and that the sermons are irrelevant to daily life in the "real world." Finally, respondents complained that pastors often make people feel guilty and ignorant so that people leave the church feeling worse than when they arrived. The founders of Willow Creek determined that they would avoid these pitfalls by designing a new form of service based in part on the survey results. What they came up with was an amazingly successful strategy, one that *Fortune* magazine praised in 1989 as "the paradigm of customer orientation."[3]

Willow Creek's format is a model for evangelical churches both across the country and internationally. Willow Creek's influence is evident in the rapid growth of its membership association; the prominence of the media publicity it has garnered; and, most important, the thousands of pastors and church leaders who have attended Willow Creek conferences, purchased Willow Creek products and materials, and now downloaded resources from *Willow Net*, Willow Creek's Web site. Before examining these developments, I will take a closer look at the theological convictions of these pastors. To put it simply, are these innovative leaders also theologically conservative?

Theology of Pastors

Data from my Seeker Church Pastor (SCP) survey confirms that seeker church pastors are traditional in their theological commitments. According to the SCP survey, seeker church pastors are quite conservative and orthodox theologically. The vast majority (98 percent) say that "evangelical" describes their theological/doctrinal preference "very well." In fact, "evangelical" was the only category that a majority of pastors said described their views "very well" or "fairly well." The next largest category was "fundamental," which slightly more than one out of three pastors (37 percent) said described their views "very well" or "fairly well." In contrast, most pastors (89 percent) said the term "liberal" described their views "not well at all." This strong pastoral identification with the term "evangelical" is mirrored in the pastors' descriptions of their seeker churches. When asked to choose one term that best describes their church's doctrinal views, most pastors (80 percent) chose "evangelical." The other most common responses were "traditional/confessional" (8 percent), "fundamental" (5 percent), and "other" (3 percent).

Seeker church pastors consider themselves evangelicals and their responses to specific doctrinal questions clearly confirm this. Virtually every pastor (99 percent) agreed that "the Bible is the inspired Word of God, true in all its teachings." The major division was between pastors who thought the Bible was "to be taken literally, word for word" (70 percent) and those who thought that the Bible "is not always to be taken literally in its statements concerning matters of science, historical reporting, etc." (29 percent). No pastor agreed with the statement that "the Bible is an ancient book of legends, history, and moral precepts recorded by men."

On other key issues of evangelical theology, such as the divinity of Christ and the nature of the afterlife, the responses of seeker church pastors were in general theologically orthodox. Almost all (99.6 percent) agreed with the statement "Jesus Christ is both fully God and fully man." (Only two pastors chose instead the statement "Jesus Christ was a man but divine in the sense that God worked through him.") Questions about the afterlife and the relationship of Christianity to other religions solicited a little more variation. While three out of four (76 percent) seeker church pastors agreed with the statement "Other religions are merely human attempts at understanding God and are untrue," most of the remaining pastors (23 percent) selected instead the statement "Other religions contain some truth and should not be seen as completely wrong."[4] In a different question on the nature of salvation, most pastors (81 percent) indicated that the statement "The only hope for heaven is through personal faith in Jesus Christ" comes closest to their own views. About one in five pastors (19 percent) chose the more open-ended response ("The only hope for heaven is through personal faith in Jesus Christ *except* for those who have not had the opportunity to hear of Jesus Christ"). When asked to evaluate human nature on a seven-point scale on which one represented "Human nature is basically good" and seven represented "Human nature is fundamentally perverse and corrupt," two out of every three seeker church pastors (67 percent) selected the most pessimistic view of human nature. Overall, the vast majority of pastors (88 percent) selected the two responses closest to the view that human nature is perverse and corrupt. None of the other five possible responses received more than 5 percent of the total. This emphasis on the total depravity of human nature is consistent with Reformed teaching about the desperate need sinners have for redemption via God's plan of salvation. (In evangelical theology, the depravity of human nature is the "bad news" that precedes the "good news" of the Gospel.) In sum, seeker church pastors are firmly evangelical in their theological commitments.

The Growth of Seeker Churches

Now that it is clear that the pastors of seeker churches are evangelical, what do we know about the churches themselves? For starters, the number of seeker churches has been growing steadily, as represented by the growth of the Willow Creek Association (WCA). In order to grow, most churches target the "generation of seekers," many of whom were raised in Roman Catholic or Mainline Protestant churches, that Roof has documented as searching for meaningful religious or spiritual involvement. What is the current religious background of these seekers? Put differently, how unchurched is "Unchurched Harry"? To answer that, I will turn first to the founding and growth of WCA churches.

In 1992, Willow Creek founded the WCA in response to the growing demand for training from churches seeking to emulate Willow Creek's tremendous success. By September of that year (the date marking the first publication of the *Willow Creek Association Monthly* newsletter), 186 churches were members of the association. In just over three years, its membership increased 750 percent to include almost 1,400 churches in the United States and internationally. By early 2000, the WCA had grown to over five thousand members. The WCA has grown so rapidly that it is now comparable in size (in terms of the number of churches that are members) to many denominations in the United States. In fact, it already has more member churches than the Baptist General Convention and is similar in size (in terms of participating member churches) to the American Baptist Churches in the U.S.A., the Church of the Nazarene, and Lutheran Church-Missouri Synod. Overall, the WCA is already larger (in terms of the number of its member churches) than 85 percent of the denominations in the United States.[5]

Not only is the Willow Creek Association growing, but so are its member churches. According to the SCP survey, the average attendance at seeker church weekend services has increased steadily in the five-year period from 1990 to 1995. In 1993, the median attendance at seeker church services was between 150 and 300; by 1995, the median had risen to between 301 to 500. These data show that the average size of a seeker church is larger than the national average. One church growth expert notes that half the churches in the United States have an attendance of less than 75 on a typical Sunday morning. Although most churches may be small, most churchgoers attend larger churches. Another church consultant suggests that half the churchgoers in the United States attend 14 percent of the churches. The large church is clearly a growing trend within American Protestantism.

This growth in the average size of services is not simply the result of a few extremely large churches inflating the averages. Instead, this growth is the result of widespread increases in attendance among seeker churches. From 1990 to 1995, three out of four (75 percent) WCA churches grew in their average weekend attendance, while 23 percent remained at the same level, and only 2 percent of churches declined in attendance. Even in the shorter period from 1993 to 1995, almost two out of three (64 percent) WCA churches increased in their average weekend attendance, while 36 percent remained at the same level, and only 2 percent declined in attendance. This growth is all the more remarkable when compared to trends for all U.S. churches. According to the WCA, four out of five U.S. churches (80 percent) are either stagnant or declining. No wonder pastors are flocking to Willow Creek to learn the secrets of its success.

This widespread growth in seeker church attendance contributes to a related trend—that seeker services are, on average, growing larger. According to the SCP survey, in 1990, only six percent of seeker churches surveyed averaged more than one thousand total attenders on a weekend. By 1993, 10 percent of seeker churches averaged more than one thousand total attenders on a weekend. In five years, the number of churches averaging more than one thousand attenders more than doubled, with 16 percent of seeker churches surveyed reporting more than one thousand attenders on average in 1995. A similar trend emerges from an examination of the growth in churches with an average weekend attendance between five hundred and one thousand. The percentage of churches averaging between five hundred and one thousand attenders nearly doubled between 1990 (10 percent) and 1995 (19 percent). This is good news for seeker churches, where bigger is better because the programming and production of the weekly seeker services require a large pool of talented and dedicated people.

What kinds of churches are most likely to have large weekend services? Older churches are more likely to have larger weekend attendance than younger churches. Eighty-four percent of the churches averaging more than 750 attenders on weekends are more than ten years old, while 94 percent of the churches averaging fewer than 100 attenders on weekends are five years old or less. This makes sense given that older churches have had more time to build attendance at their services.

While older churches are more likely to have large weekend services than are younger churches, younger churches are more likely than are older churches to be growing (see table 1.1). Seventy-three percent of churches less than five years old are growing; 75 percent of churches six to ten years old are growing; 66 percent of churches ten to twenty-five years old are growing; and, in contrast, only 45 percent of churches more than twenty-five years old are growing. Even in the shorter period from 1993 to 1995, most seeker churches (60 percent) less than five years old grew in their weekend attendance, while the majority of churches more than five years old did not grow during this time.[6] Churches that offer separate seeker services are more likely to grow than churches that do not. Sixty-nine percent of the churches that offer weekly seeker services grew from 1990 to 1995. The data are somewhat ambiguous, however, because a majority of churches (51 percent) that *never* offered a seeker service grew from 1990 to 1995. In the shorter period from 1993 to 1995, half of all churches (50 percent) that offered separate seeker services grew in their weekend attendance, while only about three out of ten (32 percent) churches grew during this period. This suggests that churches

_____ *Table 1.1* _____
Seeker Church Growth, 1990–1995, by Number of Years Established (N)

	Less than 5 years	6 to 10 years	11 to 25 years	More than 25 years	Total
Growth	73.3%	75.4%	66.1%	45.2%	57.1%
	(11)	(46)	(37)	(71)	(165)
No growth	26.7%	24.6%	33.9%	54.8%	42.9%
	(4)	(15)	(19)	(86)	(124)
Total	100%	100%	100%	100%	100%
	(15)	(61)	(56)	(157)	(289)

that offer separate seeker services may grow faster than those that do not.

The trends in attendance are not as clear for those churches that hold separate services for believing Christians. The mean size of believers' services has dropped slightly since 1990. Furthermore, the number and percentage of churches with an attendance of more than five hundred at believers' services has remained relatively constant since 1990. The main area of growth has been in the number of churches that offer separate services. In 1990, 76 churches offered separate services for seekers and believers. By 1993 this total increased to 120, and by 1995 the total reached 176. One distinguishable trend is that seeker churches that are less than five years old are more likely than not to have separate services. As table 1.2 indicates, more than half of seeker churches (53 percent) less than five years old have separate services, while only one out of four (24 percent) seeker churches more than ten years old have separate services. Thus, the "pure" Willow Creek model of holding separate services for seekers and believers is more popular among newer churches and is therefore likely to become more prevalent in the future as more seeker churches are founded.

Overall, seeker churches are relatively young churches. Half of the seeker churches surveyed are less than eleven years old, and one quarter of the churches surveyed are less than four years old. The year of founding alone does not always tell the whole story, however. Some of the older

_____ *Table 1.2* _____
Separate Seeker Services by Number of Years Established (N)

	Less than 5 years	6 to 10 years	11 to 25 years	More than 25 years	Total
Separate seeker service	52.6% (80)	50.0% (31)	16.1% (9)	26.8% (44)	37.8% (164)
No separate service	47.4% (72)	50.0% (31)	83.9% (47)	73.2% (120)	62.2% (270)
	35.0% (152)	14.3% (62)	12.9% (56)	37.8% (164)	100.0% (434)

churches have undergone profound transformations in their organization and worship practices. For example, the 171-year-old Shiloh United Methodist Church near Indianapolis recently instituted a new seeker service in 1995. This change was accompanied by a change in name to Shiloh Crossing Community Church. In many ways, it is more accurate to consider Shiloh Crossing a new seeker church built upon an older Methodist foundation than to consider it an old Methodist church with a seeker-sensitive facelift. While this is only one example, there surely are numerous other instances of older churches that have drastically revised their strategy of ministry as a result of their contact with seeker churches.

Denominational Diversity

One of the most interesting features of the seeker church movement is its denominational diversity. In fact, the rosters of the WCA gradually have come to include a remarkable variety of denominations—although there is also a marked increase in the proportion of nondenominational churches among the newer WCA churches. Evangelicalism is not defined by any one denomination (although some denominations are more likely to include evangelicals than others), and thus it has a transdenominational quality. In order to compare the distribution of denominations within the seeker church movement to the distribution of denominations within evangelicalism in general, I will compare the SCP survey data with data from the 1992 National Election Survey, which includes some new questions that increase our ability to measure evangelical presence and denominational affiliation in the United States.[7]

Using the NES data, I combined several questions in order to create a broad measure of evangelicals in the U.S. population. The NES data provide a general view of Americans who identify with particular denominations. Let us now turn to the data. Baptist churches are by far the most prevalent in the Willow Creek Association. Three out of every ten WCA churches (31 percent) are Baptist, and of these Baptist churches, two out of three belong to the Southern Baptist Convention (21 percent of the total). The second-largest denomination within the seeker church movement is, ironically, not really a denomination at all. Independent and nondenominational churches make up the second most prevalent category—after all types of Baptists—

of seeker church affiliation. The third-largest denominational group represented among seeker churches is Presbyterian or Reformed. Slightly more than one out of every ten (11 percent) seeker churches is Presbyterian or Reformed. After Holiness churches, which comprise 7 percent of WCA members, no other denomination claims more than 5 percent of the total WCA membership. The largest remaining denominational groups are United Methodist, Churches of Christ, Evangelical Free, Pentecostal, and Lutheran. These data indicate that the seeker church movement draws most of its membership from the Baptist and Reformed traditions within evangelicalism.

According to my research, one of the most significant trends within the seeker church movement is the growing predominance of nondenominationalism. But the data on denominational affiliation only begin to reveal the importance of this trend. When I compared the denominational affiliation of seeker churches with the year of their founding, the trend toward nondenominationalism was indisputable. Table 1.3 shows that nondenominational churches represent the smallest category (12 percent) of seeker churches more than twenty-five years old and the largest category (35 percent) of seeker churches five years old or less. In contrast, the distribution of Baptist and conservative Protestant churches has remained relatively stable

Table 1.3

Denominational Affiliation by Number of Years Established (N)

Denomination	Less than 5 years	6 to 10 years	11 to 25 years	More than 25 years	Total
Baptist	31.6%	30.6%	21.4%	31.7%	30.2%
	(48)	(19)	(12)	(52)	(151)
Nondenominational	34.9%	33.9%	35.7%	12.2%	26.3%
	(53)	(21)	(20)	(20)	(114)
Conservative	30.3%	27.4%	28.6%	38.4%	32.7%
Protestant	(46)	(17)	(16)	(63)	(142)
Mainline Protestant	3.3%	8.1%	14.3%	17.7%	10.8%
	(5)	(5)	(8)	(29)	(47)
Total	35.0%	14.3%	12.9%	164%	100.0%
	(152)	(62)	(56)	(37.8)	(434)

over time. Meanwhile, Mainline Protestant churches have steadily declined in influence in the movement. Mainline Protestant seeker churches are most likely to be found among churches more than twenty-five years old. In contrast, Mainline Protestant churches represent the smallest proportion of seeker churches (3 percent) less than five years old. If these trends continue, the future of the seeker church movement will rest largely upon nondenominational churches.

More recent data from the Willow Creek Association confirms the increasingly nondenominational character of the member churches. The WCA reports that, in 1996, 35 percent of its member churches are nondenominational (up from 26 percent in 1995) and that 24 percent of its member churches are Baptist (down from 31 percent in 1995). Clearly, nondenominational churches will play a more prominent role in the seeker church movement.[8]

One notable trend is that many seeker churches choose to de-emphasize their denominational identity. This trend seems to go hand in hand with the rise in nondenominational churches. In the SCP survey, pastors were asked to indicate whether they included their church's denominational affiliation on their church's main sign. Close to half of all denominational seeker churches (44 percent) answered that they did *not* include their affiliation on the church's main sign. When all seeker churches (denominational and nondenominational) are taken together, more than half (57 percent) appear to be nondenominational to visitors. The clear trend is toward deemphasizing denominational identity.

This growing trend toward de-emphasizing denominational identity is most pronounced when we consider the ages of the churches. Denominational seeker churches that are less than five years old are three times more likely not to display their affiliation on their main sign. In contrast, denominational seeker churches that are more than twenty-five years old are six times more likely to list their denomination than not. More than three out of four (77 percent) seeker churches that are older than twenty-five years list denominational affiliation. This pattern is reversed for churches younger than five years. Among these younger churches, close to nine out of ten (85 percent) do not list any denominational affiliation.

It is clear that seeker churches are growing, especially the younger, nondenominational members of the WCA. But who is coming to these churches? Is it "Unchurched Harry," the defined target for the innovations, or is it "Churched Larry," a transfer from another local church?

The Religious Background of Unchurched Harry

If seeker churches are reaching many people who have no religious background whatsoever, it suggests that they are at least extending their influence outside the religious sector. If most of the attenders, however, are coming from other churches, it suggests that their influence primarily comes at the expense of other churches. Put in seeker church terminology, how unchurched is "Unchurched Harry"? The evidence is not conclusive, largely because the data are based on seeker church pastors' assessments of the religious backgrounds of church newcomers rather than on actual attendance data. Even though these data are not conclusive, they nevertheless are highly suggestive. The SCP survey asked pastors to gauge what percentage of people who started attending their church in the last year previously had been attending other churches and what types of churches those were (conservative Protestant, Mainline Protestant, or Catholic). The survey also asked pastors to estimate the percentage of people who started attending their church in the last year who had previously been unchurched (the term of choice in the seeker church movement) and the religious traditions (conservative Protestant, Mainline Protestant, Catholic, or unchurched), if any, in which these new attenders had been raised.

The SCP survey data suggest that seeker churches are more likely to attract people who have attended another church in the previous year than to attract people who had no previous involvement with a church. Three out of every ten pastors (30 percent) claimed that more than half of their new attenders came from other churches, and almost two out of every five pastors (38 percent) said that one-quarter to one-half of their new attenders came from other churches. While attenders with a history of church involvement make up the largest segment of visitors to seeker churches, individuals without any recent religious participation make up the smallest. Three out of ten seeker church pastors (31 percent) claim that 10 to 25 percent of their new attenders in the last year came from unchurched backgrounds and about the same percentage of pastors (31 percent) claim that fewer than 10 percent of new attenders came from unchurched backgrounds. In sum, new attenders who moved from other churches contributed to the two largest categories of seeker churches' growth, while new attenders with no religious background contributed to the two smallest categories of seeker churches' growth.

This suggests that the growth of seeker churches may have more to do with the "circulation of the saints" than with the conversion of the unchurched.[9] Although every church is likely to emphasize its success in converting the lost (such as the account of Lee Stroebel who first visited Willow Creek as a highly skeptical journalist and is now a teaching pastor on staff), these data raise the question of whether seeker churches are actually reaching Unchurched Harry or mostly attracting Churched Larry from the more traditional churches in the vicinity. To the extent that seeker churches are attracting churchgoers from neighboring congregations, the success of seeker churches has less to do with converting secular people than with providing people who have a tenuous denominational loyalty and an unclear religious identity (though likely some type of Christian identity) a connection to institutional religion.

One example of this is the extent to which people raised in the Catholic Church are coming to seeker churches. Willow Creek, for instance, draws a substantial number of seekers from people who were raised in the Catholic Church. In a newspaper interview, Bill Hybels claimed that ex-Catholics, who had avoided church prior to coming to Willow Creek, now account for 40 percent of Willow Creek's congregation. The magazine *U.S. Catholic* corroborates this claim by reporting that "by conservative estimates, 12,000 of the 25,000 persons who identify themselves as Willow Creek Community Church members are former Catholics."[10]

Why are so many church attenders leaving their former places of worship (presumably more traditional churches) for seeker churches? There are many practical reasons why people might choose to switch to seeker churches. Many seeker churches provide good nurseries and children's education programs, which are appealing to parents. Many people may also prefer the contemporary music or the more casual style of seeker churches. Some Christians may choose to join seeker churches because, as Christians, they are committed to reaching out to seekers and seeker churches provide an opportunity to do just that. Certainly, every successful seeker church must have a core group of Christians who are committed to evangelism in order for the church to survive and grow. Yet the reasons why seekers attend a church may be quite different from why many Christians devote themselves to this new model of church. People might attend seeker churches because they are more entertaining and less demanding than smaller, traditional churches. The creative talents of the seeker church staff assure that there will never be a dull moment (and, as a matter of policy, never a silent moment) during the service, something to which many traditional churches do not aspire. If the seeker church is large, it is easier for attenders to avoid volunteering for programs or committees.

There are other reasons why seeker churches are attracting large crowds and great interest. Put simply, seeker churches present a more plausible model of Christianity—a model that fits with pervasive cultural understandings about choice, individualism, autonomy, the importance of the self, therapeutic sensibilities, and an anti-institutional inclination common today. In other words, it is not just convenience or even a rational cost-benefit calculation of the advantages of participation that contribute to the success of seeker churches. Instead, their success is due to their creative synthesis of traditional and contemporary ideas and forms, to their mix of evangelical insistence on the divinity of Christ, grace, and atonement along with a stress on authenticity, fulfillment, choice, and relevance.

A Second Reformation?

Is the success of the seeker church strategy leading to a second Reformation, one based not on a new doctrine but on a new way of organizing the church?[11] Put somewhat differently, are we witnessing a major evangelical revival in American society? Certainly many seeker church leaders make bold claims for the significance of their movement. For example, Willow Creek's Bill Hybels often declares that "we're making kingdom history." Similarly, Robert Schuller of the Crystal Cathedral confidently proclaims that his insights amount to a "new reformation" of the church.[12] As subsequent chapters of this book will show, seeker churches offer pastors more than just the pragmatic details on how to design innovative services; they also provide the hope of yet another evangelical revival.

Revivals have a long history in America, and in fact extend back to England before the settlement of the Colonies. After the Puritan Awakening in Britain in the early seventeenth century, which provided the ideological fervor behind Puritanism's mission to found "a city upon a hill," revivals have had significant cultural and social consequences upon American society. The First Great Awakening of the mid-eighteenth century, most closely associated with Jonathan Edwards, contributed to the creation of the American Republic. The Second Great Awakening, in the early nineteenth century, helped solidify the Union and fostered the rise of Jacksonian participatory democracy. Early in the twentieth century, the Social Gospel movement challenged unregulated capitalism and contributed to the beginnings of the welfare state. During the civil rights movement of the 1960s, the churches played a critical role in providing both moral arguments and physical resources for the civil rights movement—and against it as well. Religion has long had public significance in American life.

From the extravagant Billy Sunday to the widely respected Billy Graham, revivals and revivalists have occupied a particularly prominent place in evangelicalism. Of course, to some the term "revival" may bring to mind unfavorable images of religious hucksters hawking their wares in a carnival-like atmosphere. Sinclair Lewis's *Elmer Gantry* and the comparatively recent travails of Jimmy Swaggart and Jim and Tammy Bakker certainly offer unflattering portraits of soul-saving. But to many evangelicals, revivals are a sign of God's action in history, of hope for the renewal of the church—and even the nation, given evangelicals' predisposition to conflate America's status with God's providential purposes. In fact, the revival is perhaps *the* evangelical method for saving not only souls but also the country, given evangelicals' predisposition toward a strategy of personal influence in which converting enough people will result in conversion, or at least, changes, in the nation itself.[13]

While evangelicals agree that revival is a good thing, historically there have been some major disagreements about what legitimately constitutes a revival. Jonathan Edwards, the great eighteenth-century minister, believed that revival was "a surprising work of God," while Charles Finney, the nineteenth century's foremost evangelist, declared that revival was "a work of man." There clearly is a broad chasm between the understanding that revival is an unplanned divine gift and that it is a rationally planned, human effort. Both models nevertheless assume the centrality of individual conversion or awareness of grace. In fact, evangelicalism's emphasis on the importance of making a personal commitment to Christ—of turning away from the old life of sin and turning toward the new life of grace and re-demption—draws largely on a revivalistic model of conversion. George Thomas's book *Revivalism and Cultural Change* analyzes the social signifi-cance of revivals. According to Thomas, a revival is a new social movement that reshapes cultural codes. In the late nineteenth century, "revivalism cre-ated institutional linkages among Protestantism, American society, and the Republican party."[14] Revivals stressed elements of Christian theology that were isomorphic with the emerging rationality of a society increasingly shaped by the market. Revivalism, with its emphasis on the rational individ-ual freely choosing God, made sense in the context of an expanding capital-ism. This view of revival shares the understanding that a revival is not simply a religious event but also has profound cultural and social effects.

What, then, is a revival? "The essential characteristic of a revival," ac-cording to two church historians, "is that it assumes some sort of decline, whether real or imagined, out of which the faithful are called to new heights of spiritual ardor and commitment."[15] The valley of decline is the necessary prelude to the revival's journey to the mountaintop. I will discuss in the next chapter how recent changes in the American religious landscape have prompted a sense of decline or crisis among many evangelicals. For now, the essential point is that a revival calls not only individuals but churches to renew their spiritual ardor—to become, in Willow Creek's term, "fully de-voted followers of Christ."

Because the focus of this book is cultural and institutional, rather than ethnographic, I will not focus on the personal dimensions of spiritual ardor that underlie individuals' conversions. Instead, I will focus on the cultural significance of revivals. Noted church historian William McLoughlin makes an important distinction between revivals and "awakenings." Awakenings, according to McLoughlin, are "periods of cultural revitalization that begin in a general crisis of beliefs and values and extend over a generation or so, during which a profound reorientation in beliefs and values takes place. Re-vivals alter the lives of individuals; awakenings alter the world view of a whole people or culture."[16] The distinction may only be conceptual, since most awakenings are undergirded or sparked by some type of revival, but the distinction is nevertheless a helpful one as it focuses our attention on the cultural and institutional significance of religious revitalization.

What then are we to make of the seeker church movement? Is it part of the second Reformation that Don Miller claims new paradigm churches are ushering in for the new millennium? The answer, or course, depends on what one means by reformation. The Protestant Reformation of the sixteenth century had a profound impact on the theological, political, and social organization not just of religion but also of states and societies. Although I think the seeker church movement is an important and influential movement, it is far too early to claim that the innovations occurring with American evangelicalism today are anywhere as near as significant as the changes wrought by Luther, Calvin, and others. Thus, if by reformation one means an epochal event or shift in (at least) Western Christianity that parallels the impact of the first Reformation, then I do not think that seeker churches are ushering in a second Reformation.

However, if by reformation one means that the strength and significance of seeker churches and other new paradigm churches is their new form and method for organizing the church (or for delivering religious products) then, yes, the seeker churches are contributing to a *re-formation* of evangelicalism. The re-formation is clearly a major renewal movement within evangelicalism; perhaps it might even constitute a revival of sorts. But, to use McLoughlin's distinction, I do not think that seeker churches are on the verge of sparking an awakening through many sectors of American society.

Some might suggest that evangelicals already seem to be in the midst of a revival, given the emergence of the Religious Right and prominent evangelical leaders such as Pat Robertson, Gary Bauer, and others. Political engagement, however, is not the same as religious expansion. Some recent research indicates that evangelicalism is not growing quickly enough to be anywhere near a large-scale revival. While many conservative churches have increased in absolute number (unlike most Mainline churches), the overall average growth rate of conservative Protestant denominations has declined fairly steadily since the 1940s. Evangelicalism is growing, but not at a rate any faster than the rate of population growth. For example, one study found that "the growth rate of conservative Protestantism has been moving downward since at least 1950, and in the late 1980s it actually dropped below the growth rate of the U.S. population. The latter is significant because it means that the continuing slowdown in conservative Protestant growth has now reached the point of decreasing national market share."[17] This clearly does not support the notion of a major evangelical revival.

Although evangelical churches are faring comparatively better than their Mainline Protestant counterparts, they are both adversely affected by the changing patterns of religious affiliation in the United States. Since the 1950s, in fact, major mainline and conservative denominations "share virtually identical patterns of membership change"—patterns characterized by dropping rates of membership growth that parallel the decline in birthrate and population growth.[18] In sum, the fact that conservative churches have increased in absolute number may be an indication of their relative strength compared to liberal churches, but it should not be considered a measure of their absolute strength. The declining growth rates of many Protestant churches is evidence of the profound challenges posed by the contemporary religious environment.

Two

Increasing numbers of baby boomers who left the fold years ago are turning religious again, but many are traveling from church to church or faith to faith, sampling creeds, shopping for a custom-made God.[1]

Traditional Religion in a Spiritual Age

Seeker churches are re-forming church life by incorporating changing cultural understandings and pastoral entrepreneurship into their institutional arrangements (i.e., the form). Traditional, formal church services have outlived their usefulness, say seeker church leaders. Although these services may still meet the needs of some attenders, most seeker church pastors are convinced that only by abandoning outdated forms and embracing innovative models can the church reach seekers who distrust institutional, organized religion. This presents both an opportunity and a challenge to religious leaders. The spiritual searching of many baby boomers provides pastors with an opportunity to read the signs of the times and create new forms of churches that offer a better fit with contemporary culture.[2] The fact that most Americans still hold the Bible and Christianity in high regard further aids seeker churches. The challenge for these churches is not only to attract but also hold on to new customers whose interest in spirituality may not translate into an interest in a Christian church, especially a conservative evangelical one. Thus, in a religious environment characterized by expanding religious choice and eclectic spirituality, selling seekers on the evangelical message requires creativity and powerful persuasion, especially finding ways to present a message that is culturally appealing yet also faithful to the "hard" elements of evangelical theology (e.g., sin and damnation) that run contrary to cultural sensibilities.

So how do seeker church leaders respond to these challenges? Like leaders in other fields, these pastors must assess the environment in which they operate, the resources available to them, and the core values that guide their organizations. Religion is a highly competitive, dynamic, and large sector of our society. Religion is an industry—and a major one, given that it takes in over $57 billion annually.[3] This American religion industry includes denominations, churches, and seminaries as well as affiliated institutions such as schools and colleges, special-purpose groups (ranging from humanitarian agencies such as World Vision to political organizations such as the Christian Coalition), entertainment organizations that produce books, television, and music, and relatively new participants such as self-help movements, personal growth seminars, and a dizzying array of spirituality options.

Although it is a major industry given its size and scope, religion is not strictly a business. Many of the benefits (or goods) of religion cannot be ordered over the Internet. The value of worship services and close-knit community is precisely that they are not easily commodified but instead are collectively produced. You cannot come to a service once and expect the same benefit or experience as a long-time member of a congregation. Religion is thus a special kind of industry because many of its goods are collectively produced.[4] When we view religion as collectively produced, we take into account both the cultural and social significance of religion (the collective) in addition to the practical matter that prophets, priests, and pastors must produce specific things (texts, services, dogmas, prayers, buildings) in order for a religion to exist in any public way. The term "collective" in relation to religion, of course, draws on Durkheim's insights regarding the sacred—how the sacred is the *conscience collective* of the group.[5] Another distinguishing characteristic of religion is that normative commitments are at the heart of any religious or moral community. This normative dimension provides religion with a distinctive social value. It also poses a challenge for religious leaders as they seek to contextualize their religious truths (e.g., the Gospel) into a particular social context.

Nevertheless, religion is an industry. Drawing upon the sociology of cultural production, I will focus on the production, selection, and institutionalization of new cultural products. More specifically, I examine what prompted seeker churches to offer new products, in what context these producers must "sell" their products, and why certain innovations become institutions or new movements. Before discussing the catalysts for innovation (the production phase), I will examine the context in which seeker churches, sellers of a particular type of cultural product, operate. Put simply, how has the American religious environment changed since the 1960s? And why are seeker churches succeeding in this context? In brief, the success of these innovative producers is based on the fit between the cultural environment, described by one scholar as the "new voluntarism," and the products that the churches offer, such as user-friendly, low barrier-to-entry services, relevant, topical messages, and other products designed to meet the felt needs of religious consumers.

The New Voluntarism in American Religion

What is it that baby boomers are looking for in religion and how does this affect their participation in religious life? In brief, the baby-boomer generation's willingness to explore a variety of religious options (including none at all), its lack of denominational loyalty, and its disinclination to make a commitment to one particular religious institution have made it harder for religious organizations to retain and recruit members. Many unchurched Americans find traditional methods of religious recruitment, such as crusades, either irrelevant or offensive. As a result, the religious environment is characterized by high task uncertainty and goal ambiguity, a situation that, according to the sociology of organizations, is likely to spark innovation. For seeker church pastors, many of these changes have created a sense of crisis that in turn has spurred their innovations.

The changes in this religious environment are so significant that they amount, according to Robert Wuthnow, to "the restructuring of American religion."[6] Some of the most significant changes include weak institutional loyalty and the declining significance of denominationalism. According to Wuthnow, religious attendance and affiliation in the United States were originally based on a system of denominational loyalties that many people retained for a lifetime and that formed a significant part of a person's religious identity. In particular, the distinctions between Protestants, Catholics, and Jews, as well as between Baptists, Episcopalians, and Methodists, formed clear social and religious boundaries.[7] The strength of these denominational boundaries, however, has declined dramatically in the last generation. One implication of this restructuring of American religion is that people are no longer likely to attend the church of their childhood. Someone who was raised in the Presbyterian Church is today just as likely to attend a nondenominational church, a Baptist church, or no church as to have remained within the Presbyterian fold. The increased willingness of Americans to change their religious loyalties or to renounce their religious affiliation altogether poses great challenges for churches and denominations.

Another major change in American society with implications for religion is the suburbanization of the population. A plurality of Americans, as any political consultant will tell you, live in the suburbs. It was during the 1970s that the suburbs first became home to a plurality of the population, with 37.1 percent compared to 31.5 percent in urban areas. By 1990, with the rapid growth of "exurbs," or edge cities, the population in suburbia had grown to 46 percent, compared to 40 percent in urban areas. Suburbs offer many conveniences, especially that of choice. People choose to move to the suburbs and, once there, make many other choices about schools, shopping, activities, and even religion. In the city, one might attend the local neighborhood church, but in the suburbs there is less social pressure to do so, in part because residential communities are not as tightly knit in the suburbs. In short, suburban Americans who are used to choosing from a wide range of options extend this principle to their religious lives. Because suburbanites are used to driving, a church with great services or programs that is twenty minutes away or more could attract a large following. Another advantage a church might have in the suburbs is a lack of competition. Seeker churches often target new developments that do not have many existing churches nearby.

Coupled with the declining significance of denominations and the growth of the suburbs is a major cultural shift in American religion since the 1960s. Wade Clark Roof, in *A Generation of Seekers,* finds that across the religious spectrum today there is "a popular, do-it-yourself mentality, reflecting a voluntaristic religious climate where people of almost all persuasions increasingly choose their own private forms of religion rather than rely on the authority of a tradition or a religious community."[8] Elsewhere, Roof argues the common basis of that many new religious movements in

American society is "experientialism." "All of them privilege experience over belief, exploration over certitude, affirm the body as a feeling, sensing self, and hold to a Jamesian-like pragmatism emphasizing the insights and emotions garnered in emotional encounters."[9] Similarly, Philip Hammond's study of American religion found that "[g]reater numbers of persons now look upon their parish involvement as their choice, to be made according to their standards. That involvement is now calculated as rewarding or not by [an] individually derived equation."[10]

These and other analysts have found that religion has become one choice among many in the ever-expanding cultural cafeteria of lifestyle options. For example, one study found that contemporary Americans' relationship to the church is "fundamentally different from that of previous generations." It is "more 'voluntaristic,' consumer-oriented, and captive to the subjective, expressive dimension of cultural individualism."[11] This change is reflected in a Gallup survey on the motivations for church attendance. In the period between 1978 and 1988, Penny Long Marler and David A. Roozen find that "church consumerism replaced traditional religiosity as the strongest predictor of church attendance."[12] Another way of describing the shift from toward a more voluntaristic, consumerist approach to religion is that "[t]he subjective aspects of faith have expanded as ascriptive and communal attachments have declined."[13]

One implication of expanded choice in the religious marketplace is that more people are choosing not to have any kind of religious affiliation at all. Roof found that one of the noticeable characteristics of the current religious environment is that there is a higher dropout rate among church members than in years past. Two-thirds of baby boomers (67 percent) left the church at some time in their adult lives.[14] Many of those who left (42 percent of the total) have remained religious dropouts. However, one quarter-of all baby boomers who left the church at one point have since returned. It would not be accurate to conclude that baby boomers, even those who have not returned to institutional religion, are irreligious. The weakening influence of existing churches does not preclude other sources of religious or spiritual formation. Even among those baby boomers who do not participate in any organized religious activity, only 4 percent are avowedly atheistic or agnostic. What is far more common, according to Roof, is for individuals to hold highly secularized and individualistic beliefs, while also affirming "in one way or another a divine power or presence, even if they admit to uncertainty in their belief."[15] Undoubtedly, the expansion of these more individualistic meaning systems has contributed to the success of spiritual writers such as M. Scott Peck, Deepak Chopra, and Stephen Covey (to name only a few), and countless spiritual groups and movements.[16] In sum, the nature of church involvement among those baby boomers who have returned to church is different from that of previous generations. Roof describes this as a "new voluntarism" in which "church is a matter of choice, less a socially ascribed or cultural expectation."[17]

The expansion of religious choices—and the related decrease in social pressure to remain in the religious group in which one was raised—presents seekers with the challenge of finding which group, if any, best suits their interests. While this may be a daunting task, it seems likely that most Americans welcome at least the possibility of "shopping around" for a church that fits their preferences. The type of religious product that these shoppers are most likely to buy, or rather buy into, is one that stresses the direct experience of the sacred rather than accepting inherited rituals and dogmas as the path toward God. What draws religious dropouts and seekers is the possibility of direct contact with God, an unmediated experience that does not require learning liturgical formulas or doctrinal nuances in order to worship. Churches that can offer an exciting, vital experience of the sacred can win the loyalty of seekers.

Although the expansion of religious choosing indicates that there is a large market of unchurched customers, from an institutional point of view this expansion, especially the choice *not* to participate, raises challenges of a different kind: How do churches attract visitors? And how do they keep them once they have come? The high religious dropout rates of baby boomers suggest that they have relatively little loyalty to any particular religious institution.

So how do seeker churches address the challenges of declining denominational loyalty? One advantage for seeker churches is that they are often nondenominational, or at least do not make their denominational affiliation a central aspect of the church. These churches do not try to appeal to potential customers on the basis of a denominational attachment. Instead, they find other ways to attract seekers, particularly by focusing on the felt needs of the target audience.

While research on church growth and decline differs in its emphases, there is a general consensus that the crucial issue facing Mainline Protestantism today is the increasing disaffiliation and disaffection of the younger generation. In *Understanding Church Growth and Decline,* one of the first systematic efforts to assess the causes and realities of church growth and decline, Hoge and Roozen note that "most of the decline in church attendance and membership since 1960 has been among persons 39 years old or less."[18] This finding corroborates the theory that one of the main factors influencing the growth or decline of a denomination is the denomination's ability to attract and retain young members. Indeed, McKinney and Hoge argue in a subsequent study that "the ability to attract and hold young adults is a major factor in congregational growth or decline."[19] Similarly, church consultant Mike Regele concludes that "across all denominations, there is a failure [by churches] to reach the youngest generation."[20]

But why have young adults forsaken the churches, particularly Mainline Protestant churches? (Mainline Protestant churches are key because seeker churches specifically target their strategies at those who were raised in a Mainline Protestant or Catholic church.) One study of the Presbyterian Church (U.S.A.) offers a comprehensive evaluation of the decline of one denomination. Focusing on the reasons that the younger generation has left the Presbyterian church, the authors found little evidence to support the theories that baby boomers have abandoned the church because of their high levels of education, their disaffection with the leftward slant of denominations or their concern regarding church indifference toward the poor and oppressed. On the contrary, according to this study, younger people left the church primarily "because religion itself had become low on their list of priorities."[21] For these former churchgoers, religion had become just one more item on an ever-growing list of lifestyle options.

In sum, there has been a major shift in the American religious environment toward the importance of choice, experience, and personal authenticity, and away from duty, doctrine, and conformity, and this shift is contributing to a profound re-formation of religious institutions. One might describe the dominant characteristic of this cultural ethos as consumerism. People today, especially middle-class baby boomers, expect, even demand, choice in their workplace, home, shopping options, *and* their religious commitments.

The seeker church movement is an institutional response to the emergence of consumerism in the religious realm. Whether one focuses on consumerism, the new voluntarism, or the importance of experience, these changes in the religious environment provide an opportunity for innovative churches to offer seekers a religious experience and community that meets their needs, thereby contributing to the growth of the church. Although many baby boomers are dropping out of institutional religion and are exploring other forms of spiritual quests, most Americans still continue to hold Christianity and the Bible in high regard, which provides yet another opportunity for seeker churches.

The Cultural Environment for Religion

There is a great deal of evidence to suggest that most Americans are still very sympathetic to fairly conservative understandings of Christianity and the Bible. Drawing upon data from the *1996 Survey of American Political Culture*, I will document the powerful resonance that traditional religious symbols still have for most Americans—clearly good news for church leaders.[22] This resonance of traditional religious symbols, however, is not the whole story. There have been profound changes in the ways religious symbols and practices are understood or appropriated by many Americans.

Most Americans have a high regard for the role of religion and for the contributions of churches in public life. Almost two out of three Americans (65 percent) say they have either "a great deal" or "quite a lot" of confidence in organized religion. To place this data in context, organized religion is the only institution—from a list that includes the federal government, state government, economy, presidency, and Congress—in which a majority of Americans has "a great deal" or "quite of lot" of confidence.[23] Furthermore, a majority of Americans (54 percent) is either "pleased" or "content" with our nation's churches. The level of satisfaction with the role of churches increases when people are asked about the churches in their neighborhoods. Two out of three Americans (66 percent) are "pleased" or "content" with *local* churches. Not only are Americans pleased with the contributions that churches are making, they clearly think that the country would be better off if churches played a greater role in the lives of their fellow citizens. More than three out of four Americans (77 percent) think it would help either "a lot" or "somewhat" if "more people went regularly to church or religious services."

Americans' support for the contributions of religion is not simply a utilitarian assessment that churches provide valuable services. Instead, the *Survey of American Political Culture* found that most Americans strongly affirm basic religious tenets. The overwhelming majority of Americans (85 percent) believe there is a God, while a distinct minority (13 percent) believe there is a "Spirit or Life Force." This strong endorsement of the supernatural is not simply an intellectual acknowledgment: most Americans (86 percent) claim to have a "personal relationship with God." The correlation between belief and behavior is strong, although not absolute. Most Americans (56 percent) report that they attend church at least several times a month.[24] An even higher proportion of Americans (69 percent) report that they pray several times a week or daily. When asked to identify themselves on a religious spectrum, two out of five Americans (41 percent) place themselves on the more traditional end of a continuum between traditional and progressive, and three out of ten Americans (31 percent) place themselves in the middle of this continuum.[25] Clearly, religious symbols and practice are an important part of the daily (or weekly) rituals of Americans. While the support for religion is broad, the question of how deep it is remains.

Paradoxically, Americans embrace traditional notions of morality and divine justice along with highly relativist and individualist understandings of moral authority and truth. Three out four Americans (75 percent) agree that "We would all be better off if we could live by the same basic moral guidelines."[26] A similar majority (70 percent) agrees that "Those who violate God's rules will be punished." While Americans support the importance of a shared and consequentialist moral framework, they are less optimistic that such a framework is viable today. Most Americans (71 percent) believe that we lived "more moral and ethical lives 50 year ago." Despite their negative assessment of their current moral and ethical state, Americans have not abandoned the notion that moral suasion is important. A majority (56 percent) agreed that "it is my responsibility to help others lead more moral lives."

This apparent moral consensus breaks down when one tries to specify the content and foundation of morality. Americans are remarkably relativist in their views on morality. The vast majority of the public (91 percent) agree that "What is true for me is not necessarily true for others." In response to a similar statement—"All views of what is good are equally valid"—almost three out of every five Americans (59 percent) agreed.[27] Perhaps most surprisingly, demographic factors such as age, gender, class, and religion do not make a significant difference in the results. Based on this data, we can surmise that there are several sources for the public's relativist views. The first is individualism. Most Americans (85 percent) agree with the statement "values are something that each of us must decide without being influenced by others." While it is doubtful that most respondents have Emerson's or Thoreau's writings in mind, it is clear that individualism is a powerful cultural ethos that shapes our understandings of morality and obligation.[28] Another source of relativism is the sense of rapid social and cultural change. While I noted in the previous paragraph that most Americans believe that our moral and ethical standards were higher 50 years ago, few people suggest that we can somehow preserve or restore them. When asked whether "most things that are important today will probably be seen as unimportant in 25 to 30 years," a majority of Americans (59 percent) agree.

Despite the sense of rapid cultural change suggested by the response to that question, what Americans deem most important today is at least a preliminary indication of what will be important in twenty-five to thirty years. Consider the following: What is the greatest moral virtue? Traditional moral systems offer answers such as faith, hope, and love—or perhaps duty and honor. For most Americans today, the answer seems to be what Willow Creek calls *authenticity*. Four out of five Americans (82 percent) agree that "the greatest moral virtue is to be honest about your feelings and desires."

One reason for the success of seeker churches is that they have tapped into many Americans' resonances with both traditional religious language and therapeutic understandings. Although some might argue that traditional religious language and therapeutic rationales involve very different, even contradictory, forms of moral discourse,[29] what matters to most people is not so much whether their beliefs are somehow logically consistent but whether they are coherent in a personally meaningful way.[30] For many Americans, this mix of traditional belief and contemporary tolerance fits the bill. Americans, in short, are "tolerant traditionalists."[31]

The emergence of this form of tolerance, at times bordering on relativism, has many sources. For the purposes of this discussion, I want to focus on only one key trend that has particularly influenced the strategy and message of seeker churches, namely the emergence of a therapeutic ethos in American and other Western societies. The "triumph of the therapeutic," Philip Rieff's term for a broad and profound change in Western society, involves the rejection of cultural and religious codes based on social controls, personal restrictions, and moral demands and the embrace of personal autonomy and intensive exploration of one's psyche. This development is reflected in the high levels of agreement to the survey statement that "The greatest moral virtue is to be honest about your feelings and desires." Rieff argues that this therapeutic ethos has become institutionalized to the point that "[b]oth East and West are now committed, culturally as well as economically, to the gospel of self-fulfillment.[32] Other observers agree with Rieff that there have been profound cultural changes in Western societies. Ronald Inglehart argues in *Culture Shift* that "[t]hroughout advanced industrial society, there is evidence of a long-term shift away from traditional religious and cultural norms." This "culture shift" is characterized by "post-materialist values." According to Inglehart, what modern consumers of Western society value most is not the sheer quantity of goods available for purchase (materialism) but the *choice* of goods and lifestyles available.[33] Another scholar sympathetic to these arguments writes, "All of the evidence indicates the existence of a 'master trend,' a 'silent revolution,' a fundamental 'culture shift' away from an ethic of self-denial toward an ethic of self-actualization. The values and activities of the baby boom generation in particular reveal a reversal in moral priorities, in which the self and its prerogatives outweigh the importance of society and its conventions and norms."[34]

While these studies discuss the impact of cultural changes in broad strokes, the key issue to be explored is whether and how the emergence of therapeutic self-understanding has influenced American religion.[35] Clearly, seeker churches incorporate the experiential emphasis and therapeutic language that have grown in prominence in American culture. Incorporating these changes into a new model of church, however, did not happen without a push to convince pastors that old ways of doing things no longer were effective. That push is the sense of crisis that the changes in the American religious environment created for many religious leaders.

The Reasons for Innovation

Leaders of the seeker church movement recognize that there have been major changes in the American religious environment. According to these pastors, these changes have created a religious environment profoundly different from the one in which they were raised. Pastors and other church leaders describe this situation as a "crisis." The Leadership Network, a consulting organization influential in the seeker church movement, explains, "We are living in an era of unprecedented change . . . the 'in-between' times as human history [moves] from one age to another. . . . The 21st century will be more like the first century than any of the 2,000 intervening years and the thinking that brought us to the present will not take us into the future."[36] Church consultant William Easum agrees: "[N]othing in our past has prepared us for the present. We live in a time unlike any other time that any living person has known."[37]

This sense of crisis is well documented in the SCP survey by the responses of seeker church pastors to questions on the current influence of religion in the United States, the trends in religion, and the effectiveness of evangelical churches in the current environment. The vast majority of seeker church pastors (97 percent) believe that the influence of religion in the United States is "too low." Almost two out of three pastors (62 percent) believe that the influence of religion in the United States is either declining or staying about the same.[38] These pastors are somewhat less pessimistic about the influence of evangelicalism in the United States. While a majority believe that the influence of evangelicalism is either decreasing or remaining about the same, the most common single response (46 percent) was that evangelicalism's influence is increasing in the United States today. Despite this more optimistic assessment of evangelicalism's influence, pastors are not at all convinced that the evangelical church is well prepared to influence American society. Almost all pastors (91 percent) indicated that they do not think that churches are adequately concerned with evangelism. When asked whether traditional churches must fundamentally revise their strategies in order to grow, nine out of ten pastors (90 percent) agreed. In sum, these pastors overwhelmingly agreed that in order to increase the influence of evangelical churches, major changes are needed in the church's strategies. For most of these pastors, the most promising change is the seeker church. Ninety-five percent of the pastors agree that the influence of seeker churches is increasing in American society. The seeker church movement thus represents for many pastors the best hope to reverse the troubling trends in church influence in the United States.

How can pastors respond to this crisis and prepare the church for the twenty-first century? By adopting bold, conceptually innovative changes that amount to a paradigm shift in the church's strategies. The term "paradigm shift" is deliberately evocative of Thomas Kuhn's influential work in the sociology of science, *The Structure of Scientific Revolutions*.[39] By claiming that the church must change its paradigms, seeker church proponents argue that nothing less than a complete re-formation of the church will do.[40] Without such a change, the future of the church itself is at risk. The old predictable path shaped by tradition, habit, and bureaucratic inertia is, to put it bluntly, outdated. To take one example, Pastor Walt Kallestad approvingly cites the nostrum "When a paradigm shifts, then everything goes back to zero."[41]

My purpose is not to assess the accuracy of these dire predictions but to note their effect upon the strategies pursued by religious institutions. Research in the sociology of organizations documents the tendency amongst organizations toward constancy of form, stability, and inertia. Organizations do not like to change. Rather than pursue innovation, institutions prefer the status quo. In fact, they are characterized by a great homogeneity of form.[42] They are more likely to mimic other institutions than to undertake risky, new endeavors in search of even more efficient forms. In sum, the sociology of organizations demonstrates that institutional change does not happen without provocation. This is probably even more the case for religious institutions, where form is more closely associated with identity than it is among business institutions.

So why do organizations change their form? The answer, in brief, is that a perceived sense of crisis breeds innovation. In his study of the structural transformations of American industry, Neil Fligstein documents how the largest one hundred U.S. firms shifted their operations from a single product focus and became diversified corporations within the course of sixty years. The impetus behind this diversification and the development of new organizational forms was a sense of crisis prevalent in American industry. Crisis is the "push" that ends the presumptive superiority of the status quo and forces leaders and innovators to search for new solutions.[43]

I do not intend to imply by the term "crisis" that religious actors are merely passive respondents to cultural change. A crisis is simply the catalyst for *organizational* change; it may provide the motivation or legitimation for new religious movements. The claim of crisis is the answer to the question "Why should we change what we've always done?" Yet another understanding of the sociological significance of a crisis is that innovators use the notion of crisis as a critique of the status quo. If there is a crisis, according to this logic, then the existing strategies and institutions are ill equipped to develop adequate solutions that will take into account the changing context. The charge of crisis is a charge of incompetence—or at least unpreparedness—levied against the institutions and leaders that define the status quo. The implication of crisis is that new institutions and new leaders (or radical changes in old ones) are best equipped to lead an organization or movement into the future. Thus, crisis may be the legitimation that the new generation uses to push ahead of—or push aside—the old guard.

The Results of Innovation

Once innovation starts—once new products emerge—why do some succeed and others fail? I have argued that a sense of crisis, fostered by major shifts in the American religious environment, sparked innovation by pastors. Yet the mere fact that a religious leader or institution offers a new product is certainly no guarantee of future success. This brings us to the second phase of cultural production: selection. A key factor in the selection or success of a particular religious offering is its fit with the cultural and organizational resources of the environment. Religion both shapes and is shaped by its environment. George Thomas stresses that religious leaders and institutions are not passive in the face of these changes; they are active agents. New religious movements emerge, some of which "adapt the religion to the changing cultural environment to regain relevance," while others may try to discredit cultural changes or insulate themselves from these changes.[44] The critical question, according to Thomas, is how "religious symbols, practices, and organizations articulate with culturally constituted identity and action."[45]

Another way of considering this process of selection is to say that the environment favors some forms over others. The first part of this chapter focused on some aspects of the culture with which seeker churches fit extremely well, particularly the stress on choice, relevance, and therapeutic categories in the culture. The term "fit" might suggest an effortless process, such as a hand sliding smoothly into a glove. This would be misleading, for organizations compete against each other for resources in their environments. Churches compete not only with other churches for members but, as the preceding discussion about the changes in American society makes clear, also with other providers of identity (codependency, New Age, and men's movements), leisure (country clubs, athletic leagues, televised sports), and entertainment (shopping malls, movies, television).[46] The cultural environment, however, can only support a limited number of organizations. One town cannot support an unlimited number of churches. Some organizations are more successful than others in extracting resources such as members, money, or prestige from their environment.[47] This winnowing process is referred to as selective adaptation. A historical example of selective adaptation is that the Baptist and Methodist Churches in the nineteenth century grew because they developed a message and a structure that fit the individualistic and democratic environment of the American frontier. In contrast, the more traditional and class-based denominations, such as the Episcopal Church, did not fare as well. This does not mean that organizations should simply offer people whatever they want. The normative commitments of churches (i.e., theology) constrain what they are willing to offer, but churches have some leverage, as well, because they can control access to their benefits, such as membership, community, or even social status.

In sum, organizations whose cultural emphases fit the environment have a competitive advantage. A church that uses popular music and user-friendly formats makes it easier for a visitor to sample its services, while a church with ornate rituals, unfamiliar music, and unwelcoming formality poses significant barriers for first-time visitors. Thus, a lack of fit with environment contributes to the decreased plausibility of a religious movement or institution, as was the case with Calvinism in the context of the expanding market and rational action in the nineteenth century. Thomas generalizes about the conditions under which an organization—particularly a religious one—is likely to fail: "When the propositions of Christianity and its cultural environment conflict, Christianity loses legitimacy relative to the assumed cultural myth. Social movements and long-term trends 'within

Christianity' are often grounded in the rhetoric of the 'external' culture; they legitimate proposed change by linking it to the external structure."[48]

John Rice, in *A Disease of One's Own*, argues that two factors influence whether a particular idea, discourse, or organization is likely to be selected in a competitive environment. The first is the ability to reach an audience. Only those organizations with an effective means of communication will be able to reach a wide audience. The second factor, according to Rice, is "a confluence between the historical *context* and the *content* of the discourse."[49] When might such a confluence occur? A new movement will be most successful in mobilizing populations "where its claims make the most sense— where they are most isomorphic with the organization of everyday life and the corresponding cultural order."[50]

How do seeker churches successfully mobilize or attract seekers? One advantage seeker churches have in reaching their audience is that they are not invested in buildings and facilities in older urban and suburban areas with stable or declining populations. By starting off in local buildings such as schools and theaters in fast-growing suburban areas, many seeker churches, by virtue of their location, have a competitive advantage in their effort to reach their target audience. More important than location is the intentional similarity seeker churches cultivate between everyday suburban life and the church's own environment. Seeker churches have deliberately patterned their architecture, rituals, messages, activities, and forms of association to mirror the organization of everyday life. They offer user-friendly rituals that allow visitors to come anonymously: no one is asked to stand and introduce him- or herself to the rest of the congregation. These rituals feature a relaxed informality and casualness that contrasts with the formality and even reserve of traditional churches. Seeker church messages are designed for those without much knowledge of the Bible or theology. These messages apply Christianity to everyday issues so they have immediate relevance to visitors. The activities of the church, ranging from small groups arranged by demographic background to social activities, athletic leagues and other "back doors," are designed to meet the felt needs of seekers. In addition, by downplaying denominational identity, seeker churches do not impose any additional costs or burdens on visitors, such as learning the particularities of Presbyterian order or supporting the financial needs of a supervisory organization. This innovative synthesis of evangelical theology with contemporary culture has contributed to the success of not just one innovative church but a growing and influential movement of like-minded churches It is a major reason why seeker churches are being selected by religious seekers—which leads to the institutionalization of the model.

From Innovation to Institution

While an institutional field is developing, there may be a great diversity of new forms. Environmental conditions, such as a booming population and the absence of well-embedded rival institutions may promote rapid growth in a field.[51] However, once a model shows itself to be particularly successful, other institutions tend to pattern themselves after this model. As Willow Creek, Saddleback Church, and the Crystal Cathedral established successful seeker church models, other pastors followed their lead. This pattern of imitation holds true for most industries.[52] Interestingly, bigger institutions within a field are most likely to control the direction of a field's transformation.[53]

This process of imitation—isomorphism in sociological terms—is evident in the standardization of the seeker church model and in the denominational functions that the Willow Creek Association is performing. One result of isomorphism—of new producers or actors emulating established organizations in their field—is that institutionalization tends to reduce the variety of forms.[54] Once a church like Willow Creek or Saddleback shows that it can be successful, other churches tend to follow their example rather than continue to experiment with developing new forms of their own.

While one might think that an organization that distinguishes itself from its competitors by specializing in its services would have an advantage, it is also true that similarity fosters a sense of confidence among customers. Most rental car agencies offer generally similar products and services. Most churches hold their services on Sunday mornings and include singing and preaching in their services. Isomorphism thus helps to identify an organization as part of a system, and "it generally signals conformity with some larger norms in the institutional environments of these organizations."[55]

In relation to seeker churches, the process of isomorphism is evident both in how seeker churches have developed their new style of "liturgy" and in how many churches now emulate the most successful seeker models. In general, seeker churches have responded to the uncertainty of their environment by borrowing culturally established forms, such as contemporary music, casual attire, informational messages on topics of personal growth, secular architecture, and the popular parachurch and special purpose organizations at the expense of traditional denominations.

Meanwhile, a second process of isomorphism is occurring *within* the field of seeker churches as hundreds of churches look to Willow Creek as a primary model for re-forming their church life today. The Willow Creek Association institutionalized a visible alternative model of church, thereby fostering a high rate of emulation among churches looking for new approaches. Once a church like Willow Creek defines a new standard, institutional factors independent of its performance tend to perpetuate its influence.

One way in which other churches might challenge Willow Creek's influence is by developing expertise in areas not stressed by Willow Creek. This process of specialization contrasts with isomorphism. According to this model, organizations carve out a distinctive niche in their environment by offering special services or products. To return to the rental car example, some companies might offer express checkout while others might pick you up at your home. Similarly, some seeker churches offer one type of service; some (such as Willow Creek) offer two distinct types of services, while Community Church of Joy offers no fewer than five services, each with its own musical style. Although specialization can play an important role in the competition between organizations, the focus of this book will remain mostly on the characteristics that most seeker churches have in common, especially their rituals, messages, strategies, and forms of organization.

Three

If we in the church have the most important, the most exciting, the most revolutionary news in all history, then why don't we find the most creative, innovative, and irresistible ways to capture people's attention so that they will line up to hear, see, and experience it? If we have the gospel of Jesus Christ, the good news, the glad tidings that should go to all the earth, then why is boredom the primary reason people give for not going to church?[1]

Ritual: Modern Liturgies for Skeptical Seekers

Church, according to Dr. H. Edwin Young, senior pastor of Houston's Second Baptist Church, "ought to be fun." Dr. Young adds, "Most churches you go to are boring. It's like you're captured behind the stained glass. Our service moves. There's no dead time."[2] And, indeed, there is no dead time at Dr. Young's church—known as "Exciting Second"—where the service is as carefully crafted as a Disney presentation. This is no accident. The church has sent its staff to Disney for training on everything from arranging smooth parking flow to creating innovative multimedia services.

Pastor Walt Kallestad of Phoenix's Community Church of Joy also cites the Disney approach as a source of inspiration for what he calls "Entertainment Evangelism." Kallestad first realized that church services should be entertaining when he observed crowds lining up around the block for the premier of the movie *Batman*. He wondered how the church could utilize the power and creativity of modern entertainment to create a similar sense of excitement at church services. His answer was that church leaders need to engage in "imagineering," which means "unearthing new and innovative ways to worship."[3] He decided that his church should provide exciting, dramatic services that would attract crowds comparable to those at summer movies and popular concerts. To this end, Community Church of Joy offers five different services each weekend: contemporary country, spirited traditional, contemporary blend, new contemporary, and modern contemporary. Just as important as the variety in service styles, according to Kallestad, is the "key discovery" that "the Christian church needs to be even friendlier than Disneyland."[4]

Fun, lively, and contemporary services that provide new forms for worshiping God are at the heart of the seeker church movement. Seeker services, according to Bill Hybels, "merely apply Jesus's methods to our generation. While He told parables, we use drama. While He built upon the common knowledge of His day, we tap into current events. While He a-ddressed crowds from a mountainside or boat, we enhance our communication through twentieth-century technology."[5] All seeker services share a commitment to enthusiasm, innovation, creativity, relevance, liveliness, and informality. One observer of seeker churches described the common elements of each service this way: "No spires. No crosses. No robes. No clerical collars. No hard pews. No kneelers. No biblical gobbledygook. No prayerly rote. No fire, no brimstone. No pipe organs. No dreary eighteenth-century hymns. No forced solemnity. No Sunday finery. No collection plates. . . . Centuries of European tradition and Christian habit are deliberately being abandoned, clearing the way for new, contemporary forms of worship and belonging."[6]

Seeker church leaders design new, contemporary forms of worship to mirror the musical and cultural preferences of contemporary society. As a result, seeker services are nontraditional and nonliturgical in almost every way. They promote spontaneity and enthusiasm rather than ritual and contemplation. They change their content constantly rather than repeating a liturgy continuously. They strive to surprise and intrigue attenders rather than providing worshipers with the familiar and the confessional. Yet, while seeker services are innovative, they are, over time, beginning to develop their own particular format, which closely resembles, in function if not form, the liturgies of traditional churches. Informality, in short, is not without its own rituals.

The Sociology of Rituals

Rituals are the last thing in the world that seeker church leaders promote. Rituals suggest the dead, lifeless, external conformity of the

Protestant and Catholic churches in which many seeker church leaders and members were raised. Rituals, to put it bluntly, are not "authentic." They do not allow for the genuine expression of gratitude toward God. Furthermore, seeker church leaders might add, rituals focus on external, socially acceptable appearances, while neglecting the most important element of true Christianity—the heart. Rather than rituals, seeker church leaders strive to create exciting, innovative, unpredictable events—the opposite of rituals. Seeker churches want to surprise, to move, and eventually to captivate the hearts of their attenders. And they claim that by mirroring the forms of contemporary culture and by deemphasizing the outdated traditions of church services they have found a new way to cultivate more genuine, less ritualistic worship. Yet even the most spontaneous, surprising seeker service has a sense of timing, a sense of appropriateness and flow that can function as a type of ritual. This is especially the case in the carefully planned services of seeker churches where the time allotted for songs, announcements, and dramas is calculated down to the second.[7]

Rituals—whether they are highly ornate or calculatedly informal—reveal both an understanding of the sacred (in the case of religion) and the particular social context in which a ritual is embedded. Anthropologist Mary Douglas argues that, despite "a world-wide revolt against formalism," we misunderstand rituals if we simply consider them "a bad word signifying empty conformity."[8] Rituals are a type of symbolic communication to which careful observers of social life must pay heed. Douglas cautions that the common perception that rituals are external gestures performed without much inward enthusiasm, integrity, or authenticity may simply be the product of an antiritualist legacy, which is part of religious revivalism—a revivalism that is particularly important in American religion. For Douglas, the causes of antiritualism have less to do with reviving genuine spirituality and rejecting meaningless formalism than they do with the changing nature of group relations in society. When a social group "grips its members in tight communal bonds," Douglas argues, "the religion is ritualist; when this grip is relaxed, ritualism declines."[9] Tightly organized groups, such as the Greek Orthodox, Polish Catholics, or the Bog Irish workers in London, have ritualized religions, while more loosely bounded groups, such as American Protestants, are likely to have nonritualist religion. Thus, antiritualism is not simply a matter of liturgical taste but a sign of the changing nature of social relations.

A second point in Douglas's argument on rituals is also crucial. Douglas concludes that "with a shift in forms, a shift in doctrines appears."[10] In other words, a shift from ritualist forms to more "genuine" or expressive forms of worship will change not only the outward "package" but also the content of the message. To illustrate her point, Douglas cites David Aberle's work on the changing rituals of the Navaho. Whereas once the traditional Navaho religion was magical and required the repetition of fixed prayers in a ritual—with adverse consequences for those who did not perform the rituals properly—a sizable minority of the Navaho switched to a Protestant-like form of ritual and conscience. In this new religion, based on the ritual eating of peyote, spontaneity and an unfixed pattern become the preferred religious values. With the decline of clan cohesion, ritualism gave way to a more expressive form of religion.[11] Douglas's research into Aberle's work and resulting insight regarding ritualist forms indicates that forms are carriers of cultural values as well as the means of organizing toward a particular end. A change in ritual signifies both a change in the *context* (patterns of social organization) and in the *content* (doctrine) of religious groups.

While this book focuses on religious rituals, everyday rituals are also important from a sociological perspective. Using a car's turn signal or shaking another person's hand is just as much a ritual as is crossing oneself or kneeling to pray. As Robert Wuthnow points out, rituals are not "a *type* of social activity that can be set off from the rest of the world for special investigation." Instead, they are "a *dimension* of all social activity."[12] Rituals are a form of symbolic communication, designed to evoke and communicate meanings. A ritual such as shaking a person's hand may not have an instrumental purpose. The purpose of a handshake is not to press the skin of another person but to express a mutual respect, a common humanity with the other person. The handshake is a symbolic act—an everyday ritual.

Rituals consist of messages both intentional and unintentional. These messages (such as that of mutual respect in a handshake) help to regulate and define social relations. To follow a ritual is to conform to and to reinforce social norms. What may be considered a mere formality is part of a ritual governed by well-established rules. The advantage of these rules is that they increase the likelihood that the familiar messages of a ritual will be understood. Since everyone "knows" that shaking hands is proper and expected, everyone does it. However, many of the unwritten rules of social life are much less fixed today than they were in the past. As Alan Wolfe has put it, no one "seems to obey the rules anymore. . . . [This] is a reflection of the fact that traditional rules can no longer guide conduct."[13] As the rules of social life become less institutionalized, it is harder for rituals to convey their social meanings. Rituals are thus dependent not only on (unwritten) rules of communication but also on connection with social conditions.

This approach to ritual focuses on the connections between the observable aspects of ritual and the observable manifestations of other conditions in the society. It makes no claims about the hidden meanings or psychological functions of a particular ritual. The goal is not to find the "true" meaning of the ritual from the participants' points of view (not least because of the methodological complexities of such a goal). Instead, the focus is on "patterns among observable symbols themselves that appear to lend legitimacy to the event in the specific social context in which it occurs."[14] Under what social conditions are we more likely to find fixed formal ritual? Or spontaneous, expressive ritual? What then are the patterns linking the symbols used in seeker church rituals to the cultural context in which these rituals occur?

As discussed in chapter 2, religious seekers today value experience over tradition, they prefer direct involvement over observation, they tend to be suspicious of institutions and authority of any kind, and they look for fulfillment and meaning in this life. The rituals of seeker churches are designed to meet these needs.

Seeker Church Rituals

What do the nontraditional, informal, contemporary, highly rehearsed yet seemingly spontaneous rituals of seeker churches such as Willow Creek and the Community Church of Joy tell us about the role of religion and about the location of the sacred in contemporary American society? First, every aspect of seeker churches, from the design of their buildings to the attire at services, reflects a shift from the formal to the informal in American life. Whatever is traditional or ritualistic has been replaced by the contemporary and affective (which, church leaders claim, is effective). As one study of American religious life puts it, "The most prosperous religious organizations today are those that realize that this generation does not feel comfortable with traditional services full of rituals that are largely incomprehensible to irregular worshipers and are performed by robed clergy in august buildings."[15] Second, these rituals are evidence of a pronounced emphasis on the subjective and internal aspects of the faith and an accompanying deemphasis on the objective and external elements of Christian tradition (e.g., sacraments).

Denominational Denial

One of the most striking aspects of seeker churches is that they downplay any denominational identification and affiliation. This happens in two ways. First, many seeker churches that are members of a denomination choose not to list their denominational affiliation on their main sign. It is, in fact, possible to attend a seeker church for an extended period without having the slightest inkling of the church's denomination. Overall, more than half of all denominational seeker churches (56 percent) do not list their denominational affiliation on their church's main sign. Moreover, trends in the Seeker Church Pastor (SCP) survey data indicate that denominational seeker churches are increasingly unlikely to identify their affiliation. Four out of every five (82 percent) seeker churches that are more than ten years old list their denominational affiliation; in contrast, three out of every four (76 percent) seeker churches less than ten years old do not. This trend can only increase with the current, substantial growth of independent seeker churches, which are the fastest-growing type of seeker church. Thus, the tendency toward deemphasizing denominational identity is clear, as is the increasingly nondenominational nature of the seeker church movement

Why is this the case? Put simply, a denominational label, such as "Baptist," may have a variety of connotations, ranging from "Southern" to "fundamentalist." Some of these connotations may not be appealing to seekers. (The term "Baptist" is, of course, a designation of pride to many Christians, but the principal audience with whom seeker churches are concerned may not view the term positively.) Other denominational labels may have, to seekers, similarly undesirable connotations. Thus, in order to remove any possible obstacle to seeker attendance, many denominational seeker churches deliberately de-emphasize their denominational ties. Rather than naming a church based on its denominational identity, as in "First Baptist" or "Third Presbyterian," many seeker churches instead choose to identify themselves with the particular area or neighborhood where they are located, as is the case with the Southern Baptist–affiliated Saddleback Valley Community Church. Seeker churches may not be abandoning their denominations, but may instead be saying, in effect, "Don't be put off by our denomination."

Qualitative, as well as quantitative, evidence bolsters the argument that seeker churches are deemphasizing, and sometimes renouncing, their denominational identity. During my conversations with pastors, several pastors indicated that they had decided to remove their churches from their denomination in order to become more sensitive to seekers. The Discovery Church in Orlando, Florida, for example, had been a member of the Southern Baptist Convention but chose to become an independent church in the late 1980s. Similarly, Ridge Pointe Community Church in Holland, Michigan, had been associated with the Christian Reformed Church until 1993. Others simply downplay their denominational ties. In this fashion many seeker churches try to be more "relevant" to today's seekers. Sometimes the exception proves the rule, as in the case of the North Coast Presbyterian Church in Encinitas, California. The church's founding pastor initially did not want to include the term "Presbyterian" in the church's official name, since his desire was to reach seekers. But, sensing the wariness felt by many Southern Californians toward cults and new religious movements, he came to the conclusion that, in featuring the church's denominational affiliation, he might actually draw seekers, rather than keep them away. Ostensibly, in this case, the label "Presbyterian" is more a sign of cultural acceptability than of theological identity.

A second way in which denominational affiliation is decreasing in importance is evident in the fact that many seeker churches, such as Willow Creek, are independent, nondenominational churches. One out of four churches (26 percent), according to the SCP survey, are independent or nondenominational. More significantly, younger seeker churches are much more likely to be nondenominational than are older seeker churches. Given the size and the materials and training provided by "teaching churches" such as Willow Creek, Saddleback, and the Crystal Cathedral, many seeker churches find denominations to be either unnecessary or even hindrances to effective outreach. In addition, many churches claim that traditional church design is also a barrier to reaching seekers.

Secular Space: The Design of Seeker Churches

One of the most prominent features of Willow Creek is, ironically, most striking in its absence. Willow Creek is a church without a cross. Indeed, Willow Creek—and many of its fellow seeker churches—have made the conscious decision to exclude any and all religious symbolism or identification from their secular-style meeting spaces. This is part of a deliberate strategy to reduce any potential barriers to those who might visit the church. Moreover, Willow Creek's inoffensive church design clearly has inspired a broad following. Just over half of all seeker churches surveyed (52 percent) do not display any religious symbols at the site of their weekend meeting services. This pattern is most pronounced among nondenominational churches, three out of four of which (74 percent) do not display any religious symbols in their worship areas. The reverse is the case for Mainline Protestant churches that are members of the Willow Creek Association. Three-quarters of these Mainline churches (74.5 percent) do display religious symbols. Baptist churches reflect the ratio of the Association overall with just over half (52 percent) not displaying any religious symbols.[16] The trend toward removing religious symbols from meeting places is most pronounced among younger churches. The vast majority (87 percent) of churches less than five years old do not display any religious symbols in their weekend meeting places; in contrast, more than four out of five (82 percent) seeker churches more than twenty-five years old do display religious symbols.[17] Clearly, Willow Creek, with its untraditional appearance, has established an important design precedent for the seeker church movement.

The design of the Willow Creek auditorium reflects the church's preoccupation with creating and maintaining a safe environment for seekers, an environment that is not unlike other places in the secular world. Willow Creek looks and feels a lot like the carefully maintained and slightly antiseptic professional buildings of suburban, corporate America. It features the conveniences of a shopping mall, such as an atrium dining area and food court, as well as the "state of the art" facilities of a hotel conference center. Willow Creek describes its design strategy as follows: "Music, facilities, and the use of the arts should all reflect the culture within which we live." To this end, "[W]hen leaders of Willow Creek designed their buildings and campus, they didn't visit other churches for inspiration; they visited the sites frequented by those they hoped to reach, like corporate offices, malls, and civic centers."[18] Similarly, at Willow Creek's Church Leadership Conference, pastors are encouraged to "keep [the] auditorium clean and the atmosphere neutral, comfortable, and contemporary."[19]

Other seeker churches, intrigued by Willow Creek's secular look, follow similar design strategies; they hold services in refurbished warehouses, performing arts centers, or giant tents. Mariners Church in Newport Beach, California, features an inconspicuous design in which the sanctuary is "an understated horizontal brick pile with barely a peak in its auditorium roof, let alone anything suggesting a spire."[20] A *New York Times* article on the user-friendly appearance of churches reported that "megachurches celebrate comfort, ease, and the very idea of contemporary suburban life. This is 'I'm O.K., you're O.K.' architecture: friendly and accessible, determined to banish the sense of the mystery and otherworldliness that has long been at the very heart of the architecture of Christianity."[21] The design of seeker churches provides a window onto the movement's understanding of the nature of God and worship. Rather than convey the mystery and otherworldliness of a Holy God whose inscrutable Providence should cause us to fear for our salvation, seeker churches instead emphasize the reasonableness of God and the this-worldly benefits of knowing a God who is not far from the daily concerns of Americans. Thus, the change in the form of religious meeting places is related to a change in the message—in how God and the sacred are understood.

The user-friendly architecture exemplifies not only the "no offense" approach to church design utilized by many seeker churches but also indicates the degree to which the seeker church movement defines itself in opposition to tradition. Tradition is a broad term that can refer to the historic creeds of the church, one church's particular denominational heritage or confession of faith, a liturgy, a form of church government, or the habitual ways of organizing church life around such things as potluck suppers or the use of organs and choirs. What all these forms of tradition have in common is that they are legacies of the past.

In general, seeker churches have taken a very low view of tradition in all

of its various meanings. Tradition, according to many pastors, poses an unnecessary barrier for seekers who are trying to bridge the gap between
their relatively secular daily lives and the evangelical teachings of seeker
churches. As a Willow Creek brochure put it: "Traditional church forms
can be barriers to our communicating with unchurched people."[22] Tradition, in short, represents the old paradigm, an outdated way of doing things
that is largely ineffective in the current religious environment.

This disdain for tradition among seeker churches has many sources, including the classic Protestant insistence upon *sola Scriptura*, the rallying
cry of the Reformation. According to the SCP survey, seeker church pastors consistently placed little value on the legacy of tradition, such as historic creeds. When asked whether "long standing church doctrines are the
surest guide to religious truth," only one out of seven (14 percent) seeker
church pastors agreed. In fact, the majority (52 percent) of pastors disagreed with the statement, and one out of six pastors (17 percent) "strongly
disagreed" with the statement. The evangelical emphasis on the centrality
of the Bible contributes to a low regard for the church's historic creeds and
confessions as guides to orthodoxy. Furthermore, several seeker church
pastors mentioned when interviewed that tradition did nothing to prevent
Mainline Protestant churches from abandoning or substantially weakening
traditional Christian theology.

A low regard for tradition, however, is not simply a product of a distinctively Protestant emphasis upon *sola Scriptura*. For example, many Protestant denominations such as the Lutheran Church uphold this Reformational
credo while also managing to integrate their distinctive traditions into worship. In the case of the seeker church movement, a low regard for tradition
suggests that seeker churches are more committed to focusing on the
needs of seekers than on preserving a distinct religious or ecclesiological
tradition. When asked to evaluate the relative importance of tradition compared to the needs and interests of seekers, pastors consistently ranked tradition as less important. For example, the majority of seeker church pastors
(82 percent) agreed with the statement "Being relevant to seekers is more
important than maintaining the traditions of the church." Out of this group,
one out of three pastors (30 percent) "strongly agreed." An even stronger
consensus emerged when pastors were asked whether "Church education
should focus more on applying the Bible to daily life than on traditional

church teachings such as creeds." Half of the pastors surveyed (51 percent) "strongly agreed" with this statement, and more than nine out of ten
(93 percent) pastors agreed. According to the seeker church paradigm, the
relevance and applicability of a message or program is more important than
maintaining continuity with the past. Put simply, tradition is not market
sensitive.

A basic premise of the seeker service is to break with tradition and to
exploit secular media for the purposes of conveying religious truths. According to one seeker church pastor, the problem with traditional church
services is that they function like clubs with rules that must be followed by
all who attend. These rules—such as the unspoken expectation that all men
wear a jacket and tie, or the explicit theological commitment to communion
every week—constitute unnecessary barriers to evangelization. The
seeker service, on the other hand, is more like a concert, a fun event that
people attend without concerning themselves over any rules. Thus, seeker
churches, by offering a (soft rock) concert that visitors can relate to immediately, communicate to seekers that the Christian message is not offensive, or strange, or mysterious. Nontraditional, culturally sensitive seeker
services promise an uplifting, fun experience for those who are willing to
try church again—or for the first time.

The Seeker Church Liturgy

The increasingly prevalent seeker service "liturgy" features contemporary music, relevant preaching, entertaining drama and multimedia
presentations, and friendly encounters in a nonthreatening environment.
While Willow Creek stresses that it does not have a set formula and that it
tries to vary the content and flow of its services, it nevertheless tends to follow a standard pattern. The service opens with a prelude and a vocal selection, followed by a drama, a congregational song, and the message. As one
Willow Creek staff member put it, "We pretty much have a standard routine
that we build from."[23] Most seeker services feature at least one "vocal special."[24] These vocal specials have the look and feel of a rock or country
music song. The lead vocalist usually sways with emotion, cradles the mi-
crophone dramatically, and is often accompanied by backup singers. Ironically, some seeker church pastors have begun to refer to this typical seeker
service format as "traditional." One pastor, whose small Baptist General

Conference church in Colorado was unable to stage two distinct services each week, noted that his church did not follow the "traditional" seeker model. The pastor of a nondenominational church in California acknowledged that according to "traditional terms in use today, [we] are a seeker-friendly church."[25]

One of the most defining features of the typical seeker service liturgy is contemporary music. Willow Creek stresses that it is important for churches to "crack the musical 'code' for where [they] are to reach unchurched people."[26] Similarly, Walt Kallestad of the Community Church of Joy claims that "alternative forms of worship," particularly contemporary music, "must be a priority for a congregation if worship is to be effective."[27] The use of contemporary music in worship services is gradually becoming more common not just in seeker churches but throughout evangelicalism. Randall Balmer, author of an extensive exploration of contemporary evangelicalism, *Mine Eyes Have Seen the Glory*, "was astounded at how the media, especially television, have permeated evangelical worship. Soloists and musical ensembles gyrate to 'canned' orchestra music from cassette tapes played over elaborate sound systems."[28] Why is the style of music so important and why has contemporary music become the norm for seeker churches?

Contemporary music, usually light rock or soft jazz, is a critical component of the seeker services because rock music has played such an important role in the lives of baby boomers. Lutheran pastor Frank Senn notes that contemporary music has a nostalgic character reminiscent of the 1960s. The music is thus "as much a statement of confession and identity as the content of 'traditional worship.' "[29] One pastor of an Evangelical Free church in Maryland said that "music is what defines the seeker church in the average pew-sitter's mind." Another observer writes that "music, more than any other issue or symbol, divides congregations on the cusps of growth." The reason for this is that the music a church uses "defines what kind of people it wants. When it uses contemporary music, it's saying it wants unchurched people—particularly those of childbearing and child-rearing age."[30]

Rick Warren, pastor of the influential Saddleback Church, suggests that, in the 1990s, "the major battleground [in the churches] will be music."[31] This conflict over music, according to Warren, will center around what types of music will characterize Christian worship. Will churches play the types of music that people listen to on their own or the styles that people traditionally associate with church worship (i.e., choirs and organs)? Warren knows where he and his church are headed. Saddleback surveyed its members regarding the radio station they listened to most frequently and fashioned the church's music selection accordingly. Every seeker church I visited used upbeat, pop-style songs accompanied by guitars, drums, and keyboards as the predominant form of musical expression. The "feel" of the services was closer to *The Tonight Show* with Jay Leno than, say, a service at Jerry Falwell's Thomas Road Baptist Church in Lynchburg, Virginia. Furthermore, my research indicates that in many instances, a church may distinguish itself by the type of music it plays, just as radio stations differentiate themselves by their selection of hard rock, top forty, oldies, classical, jazz, or country music. One pastor of a Baptist General Conference seeker church in California suggested that the major difference between his church and Willow Creek was the music. According to this pastor, his church's music has "a little bit more of an edge to it." This church's decision to use more of an "edge" in its music was based on basic market research. As the pastor explains, "We really emulate the musical style of the radio stations that are most popular in [our] area." It is conceivable that in larger metropolitan areas several types of seeker churches might emerge, each distinguished by its particular musical preference.

Many seeker churches have found that new music is one key to new growth. In the SCP survey, most seeker church pastors (82 percent) indicated that their churches use contemporary music on a weekly basis, while another 12 percent play it several times per month.[32] Every pastor with whom I spoke also indicated that his or her church used contemporary music, usually played by a live band. One pastor of a nondenominational church in Pennsylvania admitted that his church often used songs by popular artists such as Mariah Carey, Whitney Houston, and especially Billy Joel, who, according to this pastor, is "somewhat of a prophet for our age. He has his hand on the pulse of modern baby boomers in terms of what their angst is." This pastor also added that the spiritual searching emphasized in a song, such as Joel's "River of Dreams," can direct seekers to a "personal relationship with Christ."

Not only do seeker churches use popular music, they also write their own. Willow Creek has produced several albums based on the music written for its services. While the limitations of print prevent a sampling of the musical style of these songs, we can at least examine their lyrics. Lutheran pastor Frank Senn writes that the music of "alternative worship services" such as seeker services "tends to focus on the personal relationship between the believer and Jesus." The music and liturgy of these services, according to Senn, "teach a private faith that deals with personal or domestic issues rather than a public and global faith that takes on the 'principalities and powers.' "[33] A sampling of Willow Creek's music supports Senn's argument.[34] The song "From Here On Out" proclaims:

> From here on out I want to trust in You Lord
> To guide my life and provide for my needs
> From here on out I want to trust you all the way.[35]

The reason one should trust in God, according to this song, is that God provides for one's needs. Implicit in this song is the idea that God is trustworthy. The stress, however, is on the personal benefits of trust. Another song discusses how we fail to meet our own standards, and it offers a solution to this dilemma:

> Though you'd never deny our God's a loving God
> You feel He turns away when you make mistakes
> But our Heavenly Father nurtures His own
> To Him you'll matter more than you ever know
> So let the Lord love you; Let His voice be heard above the
>   rest
> Hold on to what you know is true; and let the Lord love
>   you.[36]

In addition to a catchy melody and beat, this song offers seekers the assurance that God loves them. More than that, we have to allow ourselves to be loved by God.

Not every song focuses on reassuring us of God's love. Some songs have fairly explicit theological statements. The song "Only by Grace," expresses classic Protestant doctrine:

> There's nothing I could do to earn my way to heaven,
> there's no use in trying
> 'Cause it's only by grace through faith in Jesus
> It's only by grace, a gift He gave
> Only God's love could bridge the distance between us
> It's only by grace that I am saved.[37]

Another song focuses on the challenges and difficulties of upholding genuine Christian conviction today. The lyrics of "Man of God" proclaim:

> I'm not gonna compromise or apologize for what I believe.
> No matter who's looking, no matter what the cost,
> I'm gonna be a man—a man of God."[38]

A predominant theme in the majority of the songs is how God can provide comfort, peace, encouragement, joy, and purpose to the seeker.

The music at Willow Creek and at hundreds of seeker churches across the country continues a trend that the authors of *Vital Signs* argue emerged at the beginning of this century. According to these authors, there was a subtle shift in Protestant hymnody at the turn of the century. "The emphasis on human sin declines in favor of God's benevolent love for humanity." Thus, in 1852, a typical Calvinist hymn proclaimed the depths of human depravity:

> I know that I was born in sin
> I feel much evil work within
> Sins that offend my Maker's eyes
> Dwell in my heart and often rise.

By 1900, Protestants were more likely to sing the comforting words of this classic:

> What a friend we have in Jesus, all our sins and griefs to
>   bear!
> What a privilege to carry everything to God in prayer.
> O what peace we often forfeit, O what needless pain we bear,
> All because we do not carry everything to God in prayer.

Thus, the trend toward worshiping a God who loves rather than judges is not recent but neither is it abating.[39] The trend continues, albeit in a more contemporary form.

Other forms of contemporary culture are increasingly influential in many seeker churches. Popular music is often combined with drama and multimedia video presentations. In fact, more than half of all seeker churches (57 percent) use dramas at least several times per month in their weekly services, and four out of five seeker churches (80 percent) use dramas at least monthly, while very few of the churches (2 percent) never use drama. The purpose of drama, according to Willow Creek's drama director, is to "clarify the 'bad news' so pastors can bring the 'good news.' "[40] By engaging the mind and the emotions of the audience, dramas create a high degree of identification between the fictional characters and the congregation, especially since most seeker church dramas depict real-world situations such as marital conflicts or the frustrations of disciplining teenagers. In particular, dramas enable visitors to identify with the theme of each service.

This is particularly true at Willow Creek, where the quality of the dramas, both in terms of writing and acting, is highly professional. One drama portrays the humorous encounter between a couple meeting the pastor of a church for the first time. Pastor "Howitzer" is not very attentive to their concerns and is alarmingly eager to sign up his new "rccruits" for his "Army of God" church, complete with an IRS-regulation-size church "manual." Another drama—a mime presentation—portrays the disappointments of a man who never measures up to others', particularly his parents, standards. The actor even considers suicide, until he encounters Christ's forgiveness on the Cross. While many dramas focus on important real-life issues (raising children, divorce, job anxieties), Willow Creek often pokes fun at unflattering images of Christianity. One drama features a pastor experimenting with three types of messages: Sominex (puts everyone to sleep); Terminex (fire and brimstone); and feel good (preposterous psychobabble).[41] Willow Creek works hard to incorporate humor into its dramas and services because "humor is key for non-churched people. It shows that Christianity is not totally serious."[42] While Willow Creek is serious about developing professional drama as a tool to reach seekers, it is important to note that many other influential seeker churches, such as Saddleback and Community Church of Joy, do not choose to use drama in their seeker services.

In addition to drama, many churches are experimenting with video presentations. Excerpts from movies, interviews with church members, or conversations with a typical "Seeker Sally" might be projected at the front of the worship area. Given the predominance of television in our media-saturated society, the adoption by seeker churches of visual communication is not surprising. "This is the generation that grew up on television," says Hybels. "You have to present religion to them in a creative and visual way."[43] As usual, Willow Creek is extraordinarily adept at incorporating video into its services. One service used a segment from the movie *City Slickers* in which the character, whose life is falling apart, asks: How does one get a "do-over" in life? The message that followed afterward directly addressed that point. An even more extensive use of video took the theme from the movie *Dead Poet's Society*—*carpe diem* ("seize the day")—and built an entire service around it, including an original song ("Seize the Day") and message for the service.

At this point, video presentations at seeker churches are not as common as live drama. Two out of five seeker churches (40 percent) use video presentations monthly or more frequently in their services, and only 6 percent of churches use videos on a weekly basis Meanwhile, more than one out of five seeker churches (22 percent) have never used video presentations in their services. Newer churches are significantly more likely to employ videos in their services than are older churches. Almost half (46 percent) of the churches that use video at least once a month are less than five years old.

Regardless of their age, most seeker churches use the same calendar. While liturgical churches generally follow a calendar based on the religious seasons, seeker church proponents strive to minimize the distance between the world and the church by orienting much of their programming toward the major events of the secular year. In other words, seeker churches tend to follow a "Hallmark" chronology where, in addition to Christmas and Easter, Mother's Day, Valentine's Day, and Thanksgiving Day are more likely to be the subject of a thematic message than are Epiphany, Pentecost, and the Transfiguration. In sum, seeker churches often emphasize American holidays over Christian Holy Days.

The common thread uniting every seeker church innovation is a commitment to relevant, authentic Christianity. According to seeker church proponents, genuine faith is best expressed through direct devotion to God. Formal rituals and liturgies can only obstruct this devotion because they all smack of "dead" traditions. As a consequence, the "liturgical" style of seeker churches is characterized by informality. Seeker churches imply that this informality liberates seekers from the alienating rituals of the more traditional churches. Informality, however, is more than a matter of cultural style or taste; it has an important sociological dimension. Let us return again to British anthropologist Mary Douglas. She states that "the most important determinant of ritualism is the experience of closed social groups." That is, if social boundaries are strongly defined, then the development of ritual is likely. If, however, "social groups are weakly structured and their membership weak and fluctuating," Douglas expects a "low value to be set on symbolic performance."[44] This is precisely the situation facing churches today. High rates of mobility among the population in general, and increasing rates of denominational switching and disaffiliation among church attenders in particular, have attenuated social boundaries and caused an upsurge in informality with an attendant disdain for symbolic ritual.

One of the most obvious manifestations of the informality at seeker churches is the casual dress of attenders. For example, the only men I ever observed wearing ties at Willow Creek were the pastors. Dressed in sport shirts, khakis, and casual shoes, all of Willow Creek's attenders looked as if they had come straight from the mall or the country club. In some instances, the informal dress code even extends to the wardrobe of the seeker church pastor. Rick Warren, senior pastor of Saddleback Church, claims that he *always* wears Hawaiian shirts or some other casual attire.[45] A second way that seeker churches promote informality is evidenced in how attenders refer to their pastors. Seeker church pastors generally are on a first-name basis with their congregations. For instance, Willow Creek's founding pastor is referred to simply as "Bill." Such informality in address, as well as in dress, reflects both American democratic egalitarianism and the contemporary American social environment, in which little distinction is made between public roles and interpersonal friendships.

There are doctrinal as well as cultural implications for this increasing emphasis on informality in seeker churches. In her research, Douglas finds evidence that where there are "weak social boundaries and weak ritualism," there will be a "doctrinal emphasis on internal, emotional states."[46] Willow Creek's emphasis on emotional "authenticity," on healing the wounds caused by modern life, and on finding direct intimacy with God reflects this subjective doctrinal emphasis. Seeker churches attract visitors not so much by elucidating Christian doctrine (i.e., teaching about objective Christian truths) but by promising relevant application (i.e., showing the subjective benefits of Christianity). Senn notes that megachurches foster "effervescence" (a term originally used by Durkheim) in their services and that "elements of effervescence include a denunciation of 'formalism' of all kinds in favor of heart-felt emotion."[47] In other words, the form of the seeker service itself, including its informality, encourages an emphasis on genuine religious experience rather than abstract doctrine. It is not that the objective reality of God is denied, but that seeker churches suggest that the best way of understanding God is via the emotions.

Consider the practice of communion. One out of four seeker churches (24 percent) never celebrate communion in their most seeker-sensitive services. Fewer than one out of ten churches (8 percent) offer communion weekly or several times a month. Overall, most seeker churches celebrate communion either monthly (34 percent) or quarterly (29 percent). If we compare churches that have separate seeker services to those that do not, a clear pattern regarding communion emerges. Almost half (47 percent) of all churches that offer separate services do not offer communion at their seeker service. In contrast, three out of four churches (74 percent) with only one type of service offer communion either monthly or quarterly. Thus, seekers are much less likely to observe communion in a church with two distinct types of services.

Why should Christians take communion? Hybels, in one of his messages at Willow Creek, stressed to his congregants that the most important thing about the communion in which they were about to partake would be their own sense of gratitude toward God. "If you make a covenant with the Lord" to take communion, says Hybels, "I think you're going to sense smiles from Heaven; I think God's going to say 'That means a lot to me; your covenant moves me. Thanks for caring enough about me to remember me once a month.' "[48] In other words, the recipient's subjective response to communion, rather than the objective presence of God in the bread and the wine, is

what is most important. Thus, the significance of communion is that it provides the individual with an emotional encounter with the divine that should
promulgate feelings of wholeness and gratitude.[49]

By offering comfortable meeting places that mirror secular sites and are
unadorned by religious symbols, seeker "liturgies" promulgate an informal
atmosphere that allows people to remain anonymous. This "no offense"
packaging, even to the point of deemphasizing denominational identity, is
designed to make seekers comfortable as they browse through the church's
offerings. Seeker church rituals demonstrate the authenticity and genuineness of Christian faith by offering songs and dramas that relate to people's
tastes and concerns. Seeker churches are banking on the fact that seekers
will buy into Christianity once they see how faith can enrich their lives.
Given the growth of Willow Creek and hundreds of other seeker churches,
this is a winning formula. One important debate within the seeker church
movement centers on whether a service dedicated only to seekers is an essential part of this formula.

One for All?: The Debate and Data on Developing Separate Seeker Services

A key distinction within the seeker church movement is between
those churches that have created a separate service for seekers and those
churches that have adjusted their traditional worship format to be more
friendly and accessible to visitors while refraining from creating a service
specifically for seekers. Churches within the first camp, those with separate
services for seekers and for believers (i.e., Willow Creek), claim that the
needs of seekers and believers are so different that one service cannot begin to meet the requirements of both groups. According to Willow Creek,
"The needs of the seeker differ from those of a believer. . . . It is imperative
that they are ministered to on a level that they can understand."[50] Willow
Creek, however, does not insist that the only way to meet everyone's needs
is through a seeker-targeted service: Willow Creek "never says that two
services are necessary."[51]

Many seeker churches are finding that two distinct types of services are
not necessary—or at least not feasible. Only about two out of five seeker
churches (38 percent) have a weekly separate seeker service. Thus, while
Willow Creek's seeker service is of great interest to other churches, the

majority of churches (62 percent) within the WCA do not offer separate services. One disincentive for creating a separate seeker service is that staging two distinct services a week—and expecting loyal members to attend both—is a daunting proposition. Each service demands a great deal of time, energy, and effort. One pastor of a nondenominational church in Colorado said that his church wanted to offer a separate seeker service but that until the church grew to at least three hundred members, it would not be possible. The data indicate that the younger WCA churches are more likely to have separate seeker services than their older counterparts. As table 1.2 shows, slightly more than half (53 percent) of WCA churches less than five years old offer separate seeker services, while the vast majority of churches more than ten years old (62 percent) do not offer two types of services.[52]

The fact that most WCA churches only offer one type of service is reflected in the terms that pastors use to describe their services. The term most frequently used by churches to describe their services is "seeker sensitive." More than half of all respondents (52 percent) claimed that the terms "seeker sensitive" or "seeker friendly" described their church's services "very well." The vast majority of pastors (94 percent) said the terms "seeker sensitive" or "seeker friendly" described their church's services "very well" or "fairly well." The terms "seeker targeted" or "seeker driven" were noticeably less popular. Three out of ten (30 percent) pastors claimed that the term "seeker targeted" described their church's services "very well" and almost two out of three (65 percent) said that "seeker targeted" described their church's services "very well" or "fairly well." (This compared to the 94 percent listed above.) The preference for the terms "seeker sensitive" and "seeker friendly" over the terms "seeker targeted" or "seeker driven" reflects the fact that less than half of all seeker churches devote a distinct service to seekers.

While there are some important differences between churches that label themselves "seeker friendly" and those that call themselves "seeker targeted," the commitment to seekers is indeed a common bond that distinguishes WCA churches from their more traditional counterparts. The majority of pastors (82 percent) responding to the SCP survey said that the term "liturgical" described their services "not well at all." The term "traditional/confessional" did not fare much better, with 76 percent of pastors indicating that it did not describe "very well" or "well at all" the majority of their services. Similarly, most pastors (88 percent) indicated that the term "charismatic" did not describe their church's services "very well" or "well at all."

The data show that many churches are attempting to become seeker sensitive without developing two distinct services. Influential churches like Saddleback Valley Community Church, Community Church of Joy, and the Crystal Cathedral have experienced remarkable growth using only one type of service. Seekers are more interested in the overall tone and style of a church's worship than in the prospect of attending a distinct service that caters only to seekers.

The difference between a one-service model and a two-service model of outreach (seeker sensitive v. seeker targeted) is perhaps more important to those within the seeker movement than to those on the outside. For, ultimately, this debate centers around the pastoral question: How do we best encourage seekers to move beyond believing in Christianity to becoming, as Willow Creek puts it, "fully devoted followers of Christ." In classical Christian terminology, this debate has to do with the difference between evangelism and discipleship, and clearly seeker services are doing a great job of attracting visitors—making evangelism possible. Whether their discipleship is as effective as their evangelism is still an open question that begs further study. One pastor of a nondenominational church in Pennsylvania was particularly troubled by this issue. He noted:

> My impression from the inside of this [movement] is that there aren't that many [seeker-targeted] churches that are working. Name three churches, other than Willow Creek, with two different services that are reaching seekers and that have over 150 people. These churches can't survive at 150. They need to go to a 1,000 or more. . . . [One former Willow Creek staff member] said there are about a dozen seeker targeted churches that are really making it.

What all this suggests is that the cultural style, secular design, rituals, informality, authenticity, anonymity, and relevance of seeker churches contribute to their growth. By offering rituals and by developing buildings that reflect pervasive cultural assumptions (particularly baby boomers' interest in direct, unmediated religious experience), seeker churches are thriving. A critical question for the movement, however, is whether they are succeeding in turning Unchurched Harry into a committed disciple ("fully devoted follower of Christ") or whether the predominance of the single service model suggests that seeker churches appeal as much to "Churched Larrys" as they do to the unchurched. Pritchard's research on Willow Creek found that by "Churched Larrys" accounted for the majority of attenders at Willow Creek's weekend service.[53] If it is music and overall style that attracts seekers—the form of the liturgy—rather than different teaching philosophies for the two services—then this finding is not that surprising.

These modern rituals, incorporated so successfully into the seeker model, reveal American culture's tendency to privatize the sacred. By stressing the importance of experience over doctrine, these rituals (i.e., new liturgies) reflect the growth of individualism and the weakening of group or ascriptive identity in our culture. This trend raises the sociological question, Why are traditional religious objects offensive in our society? Seeker church leaders might well respond that it is not so much that they are offensive as that people do not connect with them because they are no longer authentic.[54]

How might Douglas and Wuthnow explain respond to this assertion? They most likely would argue that external, objective understandings of the sacred do not "make sense" today primarily because of social changes. That is, the cross and other symbols are offensive because they represent a different way of approaching the sacred, an approach that focuses more on formalism and the objective character of symbols rather than on the personal efficacy of those symbols.[55]

Four

Preachers who pick out texts from the Bible and then proceed to give their historic settings, their logical meanings in context, their place in the theology of the writer, with a few practical reflections appended, are grossly misusing the Bible. . . . Let [preachers] not end but start with the thinking of the auditors' vital needs, and then let the whole sermon be organized around their constructive endeavor to meet those needs. All this is good sense and good psychology. . . . Everyone else is using it from first-class teachers to first-class advertisers. Why should so many preachers continue in such a belated fashion to neglect it?[1]

Message: Believe and Be Fulfilled

The weekly sermon is central to, even preeminent in, most Protestant worship services. The sermon provides the pastor with the opportunity to impart biblical truths, to set forth church doctrine, to instruct the faithful, to proclaim the Gospel, to admonish the wayward, to encourage the downhearted, to afflict the comfortable, and to comfort the afflicted. But the traditional form of the sermon has, according to seeker church leaders, outlived its usefulness. The typical sermon, whether based on following the church calendar or biblical exposition, does not meet the needs of seekers. The "bottom line" for many seekers is whether messages offer help with the challenges of daily life. "The most effective messages for seekers," according to Willow Creek's Lee Stroebel, "are those that address their felt needs. Unchurched Harry and Mary want to know if a book that's centuries old can really give them practical assistance in the trenches of their daily lives."[2]

Giving seekers what they want is not new to Protestantism. Contemporary seeker church pastors have simply updated the strategy advocated by Protestant minister Harry Emerson Fosdick in 1928 (and cited in the epigraph to this chapter). Pastor Doug Murren advises pastors to limit messages to twenty minutes, to sprinkle the messages liberally with humor and personal anecdotes, and to browse the self-help section of local bookstores in order to design messages based on the themes of the top ten sellers.[3]

Other prominent seeker church pastors also suggest that the form of the sermon must change. "In order to become more effective at reaching out to people," writes Walt Kallestad of Community Church of Joy, "we have changed not only our music but also our preaching. . . . [I]n this entertainment age of technology and music videos, preaching must also change."[4] When Rick Warren of Saddleback Church decided to preach only those messages to which seekers could relate, he "ended up throwing out every sermon [he had] written in the previous ten years, except two."[5] Warren realized that he needed to shift from a preaching style based on a verse-by-verse exposition of biblical texts to one which would begin with the "common needs, hurts, and interests" of human beings.

Although the different form of these messages is often controversial among Christian leaders, pastors of seeker churches claim that they are simply contextualizing the Gospel, as did the apostle Paul throughout his missionary journeys and as Christians in every culture and country must do. Walt Kallestad of Community Church of Joy, for example, cites John Wesley, the founder of the Methodist movement, as an exemplar of faithful Christian contextualization. According to Kallestad, Wesley "would use everything from a barstool to a tombstone for a pulpit."[6] Similarly, Bill Hybels writes that, innovation "is not a new invention. . . . Just look at the lives of such mavericks as Luther, Calvin, Wesley, Booth, and Moody."[7] Topical seeker messages, according to this view, are simply the latest invention in a long history of Christian contextualization.

Regardless of what one calls it, the weekly sermon is the most important element of Protestant religious discourse for church members—and for social scientific, cultural, and theological observers of religion. Examining religious discourse offers a window into the role of religion in modern society and into how religious leaders communicate with their congregants. Marsha Witten's work analyzing the content of Protestant sermons demonstrates the value of such an approach.[8]

Employing ideal types from secularization theory, Witten classifies religious discourse into two main categories: accommodation and resistance. "Accommodation" refers to the ways in which religious speech, pronouncements, activities, and institutions increasingly conform to the norms and ideologies of the secular world. The three social processes that most influence the nature of religion's accommodation to the world are pluralization, privatization, and rationalization.[9] How might Witten's categories apply to seeker church messages? In response to pluralization, seeker messages demonstrate an ethic of civility and tolerance; they downplay God's judgment, focusing instead on God's paternal love. Similarly, in response to pluralization, seeker messages stress how "authentic" Christianity differs from its potentially unappealing counterparts, "inauthentic" or "authoritative" Christianity. Furthermore, seeker messages attempt to persuade seekers to "buy" into an "authentic" religious faith by offering inducements (for example, emphasizing the practical advantages of belief) rather than threats (for example, tirades about the consequences of disbelief).

In response to the processes of privatization, seeker messages stress the subjective benefits of belief. God provides guidance to all those who wish to join God's earthly family, namely the church. Seeker messages often promote God's therapeutic benefits for the self. Thus, the self, instead of obstructing efforts to follow God, is a primary means for apprehending the nature of God. Related to this concern with the private realm is a reluctance to discuss the public implications of Christian belief. Though some seeker messages do promote charitable activities, such as serving others, even these activities are depicted as a means toward self-fulfillment. Overall, seeker messages do not stress the public implications of Christianity.

Lastly, in response to the processes of rationalization, pastors evaluate seeker messages according to their "market value:" Do they work? Do they persuade "Unchurched Harry"? As a result, seeker messages affirm the objective truth of Christianity; they tend to stress the utilitarian and pragmatic benefits of faith. Thus, in response to the pressures of functional rationality, Christianity is itself evaluated by its utility. Is it useful in promoting life change? Does it get results? Furthermore, the process of coming to faith and becoming a "fully devoted follower" of Christ has been standardized in Willow Creek's seven-step strategy.

Despite these accommodations—or contextualizations—to the processes of pluralization, privatization, and rationalization, the religious discourse of seeker churches is still, at root, religious discourse. That is, seeker messages continue to affirm the existence of God and the eternal implications of each person's relationship with God. Thus, even while seeker church messages accommodate to the norms of secular society, they simultaneously proclaim traditional evangelical theology. For example, the messages describe God as Lord and Judge of the universe. They also proclaim the objective reality of sin and the necessity of repentance and conversion. They adamantly exhort seekers to complete their search for meaning by "crossing the line" into Christian faith.

While Witten concludes that there is more evidence of accommodation than resistance in Protestant sermons, another study of Protestant discourse finds comparable amounts of resistance to secularization. In their study of debates in evangelical colleges, Schmalzbauer and Wheeler argue that the "discourse in evangelical colleges reveals a reappropriation of the classic themes of Reformation Protestantism, and a repudiation of the separatistic elements of late nineteenth- and twentieth-century fundamentalism."[10] Thus, there is evidence of both secularizing and sacralizing forces at play in Protestant discourse. We cannot assume a unilinear path toward more secular or accommodating religious discourse. Witten also suggests a third possibility for religious discourse—a reframing of religious symbols and meanings in light of contemporary meanings. The process of reframing preserves traditional religious symbols (such as the Cross) but often interprets them in less traditional ways.

This combination of new and traditional elements in religious discourse is precisely what George Thomas predicts will emerge with new religious movements. Regardless of whether a movement is more secular (such as liberal humanism) or traditional (the Christian Right), a new movement, according to Thomas, "attempt[s] to build a new social order by drawing on traditional systems. . . . The Christian Right legitimates change by integrating the psychology of self-assertion and self-esteem into a nineteenth-century revivalism."[11] In other words, new movements create a culturally powerful synthesis of traditional and contemporary cultural elements. Movements and their messages, according to Thomas, are "carriers of a particular worldview or ontology. Such movements use religious symbols to construct a new social order, not in the abstract, but in their specific claims and demands." The goal of religious movements is "to institute their own vision of the cultural order."[12]

Let us now look at the synthesis of diverse cultural elements in seeker messages—messages that simultaneously contextualize Christian terms into therapeutic language of self-fulfillment and stress core evangelical doctrines such as the need for conversion and the possibility of eternal salvation.

Relevant Messages for Skeptical Seekers

What constitutes a good sermon? What constitutes an effective sermon? And are the two the same? Seeker church leaders insist that one of the most important strategies for reaching seekers is to preach relevant sermons that address practical, everyday issues. People want messages that will make a difference in their lives. An effective sermon, then, is one that people know how to apply.

Effective seeker church messages are full of paradoxes. They are traditional in theology, yet innovative in form; "hard" in their call for conversion, yet "soft" in their promotion of the this-worldly benefits of belief; traditional in their insistence that God is holy and righteous, yet modern in their willingness to focus primarily on God's love and forgiveness; committed to building the church, yet wary of the institutions and practices, such as denominations and traditional liturgies, which have defined Christianity in the past. In sum, seeker church messages resist the pressures of modernity in their theology but often accommodate themselves to the culture in their format and emphases.

The principle underlying innovative seeker messages is that the Gospel must be presented in a civil and inviting manner so that it will appeal to today's geographically mobile, well-educated seekers, who often regard institutional religion with great skepticism. Thus, seeker church pastors aim to present relevant messages every weekend. Their choice of the word "relevant" is revealing. What does it mean that the church must make its message relevant? At a basic level, it suggests that the traditional sermon is irrelevant. It might also imply that in order to meet the demand for relevance, pastors must not only contextualize the Gospel message but also adopt the predominant cultural idiom as a primary means of communication. Furthermore, the concept of relevance might also mean that the audience, and not the messenger, determines, at the very least, the topics and tone of the message. Put differently, the demand for relevant preaching suggests that the church as an institution has less authority to proclaim its story in its own language—that is to say, to use the "irrelevant" language of theology, doctrine and the Bible itself.[13] According to many pastors, people are no longer interested in the presentation of theological matters or careful Biblical exegesis. Instead, people only want to hear messages that they can apply directly to their lives. One pastor suggested to me during an interview that the common denominator among today's successful churches is that their teachings have "high user value."

Messages with high user value are popular, even among the unchurched, because of their practical, uplifting advice. In fact, church-growth consultant George Barna found that when unchurched people were asked what might draw them back to church, the most common response was better messages.[14] A "better message," according to Willow Creek's Bill Hybels, "helps people understand some things and then it prompts them to take action on something, to make a decision on something, to start a new pattern, to end an old pattern, to turn away from something bad, to receive Christ, to grow, to make a decision of some sort."[15] Willow Creek's strategy for delivering relevant messages has caught on. Almost three out of four (72 percent) seeker churches use Willow Creek–style topical messages weekly or several times per month.[16] Many pastors claim that these topical messages are the church's most popular offering. One pastor noted that "The first reason people say they usually come is because the message is so practical. . . . It's take-homeable." Another pastor commented that "the common denominator in churches that are growing is teaching that is very practical. It has high user value."

Topical messages usually provide the theme for each week's seeker service. Willow Creek's snappy or intriguing message titles not only prompt seekers to visit but also provide a glimpse of what kinds of topics seeker church pastors believe will be of interest to the non-churchgoing public. Willow Creek's *Seeds Resource Center* catalog lists every weekend message delivered at Willow Creek since 1980. (Every message has been recorded and is available for purchase.) While there is considerable variation in the topics of these messages, one can organize these messages into several general categories. The most frequent type of message (36 percent of the total) is scriptural or theological, such as a series on the Ten Commandments, aspects of God's nature ("Father, Forgiver, and Friend"), or the power of prayer. Teachings on personal growth and/or relationships (32 percent) make up the next-largest category of messages. This category includes topics such as "Do you have what it takes to grow?" (a series based on the twelve-step model of recovery), "Enriching your Relationships," "Discovering the Way God Wired You Up," "People Who Love Too Much," and a series on "Measuring How Much You Matter to God," which explores the sources of self-esteem, how one's self-esteem is scarred, and ways to rebuild self-esteem. The third-largest category of messages (10 percent of the total) concerns family issues. Family-oriented messages include topics such as "Fanning the Flames of Marriage," "Marriagewerks" [*sic*], and "Parenthood." The remaining categories of messages include cultural commentary (for example, "The Odds for Evolution"), apologetics ("Christianity's Toughest Competition"), work and career ("Keeping Your Head Up When Your Job Gets You Down"), financial matters ("Financial Freedom"), and others ("A Random Act of Senseless Kindness"). Overall, the majority of the message topics pertain to practical matters that are especially appealing to an audience of seekers.

Although the message topics range widely from discussing the nature of God to improving one's marriage, the pressures of privatization make it likely that these messages will in some way emphasize the *personal* relevance of Christianity, over any *public* theology of Christian involvement in the world. Furthermore, it is probable that these messages will emphasize the immanent, rather than the transcendent, aspects of God's nature. The love of God is likely to receive more attention than God's holiness.[17]

Who is God?

The most common way that seeker messages portray God is as father. God is our "heavenly father who sees what is done in secret" and will "reward you." God is not an angry father, eager to judge and condemn. Instead, God is an understanding, compassionate father. For example, in one message on divorce, the speaker asserts: "Mistakes are going to be made in [some] relationships that will lead to divorce. God knows that and He understands it." God is reassuring, loving, and always available. God provides us with "the assurances of [God's] presence," "loves [us] with a perfect love," and "is available to [us] all the time." To know this heavenly father is to be transformed by His love.

This image of God as Father is common in Scripture, particularly in the Sermon on the Mount, which provided the scriptural basis for many of the messages I examined. While the fatherhood of God is one of the most popular seeker message topics, Willow Creek pastors also discuss other appealing aspects of the divine. One series on "Our 3-D God" focused on three dimensions of God's character: God as Father, God as Forgiver, and God as

Friend.[18] Many other messages that I reviewed also stress the "softer" or more immanent aspects of God's nature. They describe God as an extravagant giver, a comforter who collects tears in a bottle, a gentle shepherd, a peacemaker, and "a God who loves you." This God never vacillates in his firm commitment to God's people. "God is consistent with His grace toward you, with His love, with His forgiveness, with His strength, with His power—He is utterly consistent in how he moves toward you." Above all, God is faithful. As one pastor put it, "God is absolutely committed to being there for you whenever you need Him." Similarly, seeker messages also tend to characterize Jesus Christ as one who is "devoted to you," who "protects you," and who "orchestrates the answers to [your] prayers." Jesus is the "ultimate role model" as He pursues: "peace, reconciliation, community, connectedness between us and God, and between each other." As one message succinctly put it: "Peace. That's what He's after."

In seeker messages, the Holy Spirit receives the least attention of the three Persons of the Christian Trinity. One explanation for this apparent oversight is that seeker churches are not particularly charismatic in their worship services. Another reason could well be that preaching on the Trinity is not particularly user-friendly; it is hard to imagine what immediate applications to one's personal life might stem from an extended exposition on the triune nature of the Christian God. When seeker church pastors do mention the Holy Spirit, however, they often describe the Spirit as acting as a sort of "divine conscience," guiding Christians away from selfish thoughts or actions that might harm others. For example, in one message, Hybels asserts, "When there is a broken relationship in my life, the Holy Spirit brings to my mind my part in [the broken relationship] that I have to own."[19] In addition to criticizing negative behavior, the Holy Spirit also prompts people to act in a positive manner. Thus, in another message, Hybels suggests that the Holy Spirit might be encouraging Willow Creek's regular attenders to reach out to newcomers. "Let's just say that the Spirit of God whispers to you," says Hybels. "Just shake [the newcomer's] hand and say [to him or her]: you matter to God."[20] The Spirit, in short, is close by, prompting those who are willing to hear to act with greater love and self-sacrifice.

Seeker message depictions of God are not, however, only interested in God's immanence. Seeker messages also discuss God's transcendent attributes, such as God's knowledge, power, authority, and righteousness. According to one message, God is "holy" and cares more about the state of our hearts than about our external compliance with the law. God is able to assess the state of our hearts because God is "omnipresent." Furthermore, God "is a God of truth," and because of this, Christians must speak the truth and live up to their commitments.

While seeker church pastors affirm that God is holy, they do not explore in much depth the implications of this holiness in their messages. For example, seeker church pastors do not commonly emphasize in their messages that God's presence is so awesome (as in "inspiring awe") that it would cause the prophet Isaiah to shudder: "Woe is me! For I am lost; for I am a man of unclean lips."[21] Rather than depicting God as the One who desires—or even demands—worship, seeker church pastors instead compare God to human examples of authority. In this vein, God is described as a "banker" who guards heavenly treasures. God is also a "judge who transfers the righteousness from Christ's account to the sinner's." And God is the "President of the cosmos" and the "CEO of the universe." These analogies for God, in effect, reduce God's Otherness. No one falls down and worships a banker or judge or CEO. One message even softens the image of God as a judge who must punish the guilty. According to this message, immediately after God pronounces you guilty, God will "get off the bench, walk around, embrace you, and say: Welcome home on the merits of my Son."[22] God the judge is eager to doff his robes and give you a big heavenly hug.

Seeker messages do stress that humans should have respect for God. Interestingly, however, this respect is motivated primarily by those aspects of God's character that inspire love, not fear. For example, a Willow Creek series entitled *Yea God!* celebrated fourteen different aspects of God's character. According to the message titles, God is "relational, expressive, wise, joyful, an equal opportunity employer, patient, a refuge, righteous, gracious, committed to me, generous, a guide, powerful, a servant."[23] From this list, only the terms "righteous" and "powerful" might indicate that the God whom we celebrate with a big "Yea!" is holy. Seeker messages do not prominently discuss the "awe-ful" (in the original sense of the word) aspects of a God whose "thoughts are not your thoughts" and whose "ways are not your ways."[24] Seeker church pastors de-emphasize God's inscrutability, God's mystery, and God's ultimate judgment, while they stress

God's love, mercy, and proximity. Clearly, the Bible refers to God in many different ways, including as a heavenly Father. The contention here is not that it is unbiblical for seeker churches to describe God as a Father full of love and mercy, but rather that the vast majority of seeker messages stress God's immanence, those aspects of God's character that are culturally appealing, over and above those aspects of God's character that inspire fear and are more culturally problematic.

Thus, in answer to the question "Who is God?" seeker church pastors portray a God who "loves you, is proud of you, believes in you, and will give you strength to stand up to the forces of evil in the world." The following passage from a Willow Creek sermon provides an example of these reassuring tenets: "[God] is holy and righteous, but Jesus says, you also need to know that He loves to meet needs and to provide resources and to give love to love-starved people. He loves to surprise people with His goodness and ambush them with His grace. He loves to heal and renew and restore and save people. And He does it with joy. It's not a hardship. He doesn't do it in a begrudging way. That's what He's like. He's not just approachable; He's benevolent."[25]

This portrait of a God who is always supportive, always present, and always loving is appealing. God is not removed from the world but is actively searching for ways to love it. As a result, seekers need not ponder an inscrutable and mysterious God. Instead, a joyful and empathetic God is ready and willing to meet people right where they are. Seekers will be drawn to this God because "He's the safest, most loving, tender, interested, long-suffering entity in the world."[26] One way that seekers can meet and understand this benevolent God through their emotions.

Encountering God Through One's Heart and Mind

Many Willow Creek messages indicate that each person, through his or her own psychological makeup, has a window into God's character. In other words, the human psyche provides a pathway to understanding God. In one message, for instance, the speaker declares, "God is vulnerable too." According to this reasoning, God's emotional vulnerability demonstrates God's empathy toward human vulnerabilities. To this, the speaker adds that God wants "to help you by giving you the love and the acceptance that you're looking for." Another message describes God's emotional vulnerability in more detail: "God has feelings too. You and I have the ability to impact the emotions of God by the way that we respond to Him." In other words, God is now so immanent that God is affected by our psychological states, that is, our feelings. While it may be gratifying to know that our emotions move God, this is evidence of how a therapeutic sensibility is influencing the theological discourse of seeker church pastors.

If one's emotions lead one to God, so too can one's mind. A basic tenet of seeker churches is that God is reasonable and has created a reasonable universe. Humankind, created in God's image, is also reasonable and consequently can learn a great deal about God through the application of reason. This does not mean that God is the divine watchmaker of Deism, whose character can be understood by the careful observation of nature. Instead, evangelicals believe that Scripture illuminates God's purposes and intentions. Thus, to say that Christianity is reasonable is not to say that Christians can understand God by the power of Reason alone. Instead, to say that Christianity is reasonable is to say that a rational presentation of Christian truths ultimately will provide an accurate picture of God.

Seeker church proponents believe that if they can successfully portray God as reasonable rather than mystical they will be able to attract more seekers. Examples of this thinking abound. For instance, in one message, the speaker asserts, "To [religious traditionalists] God was so holy and so exalted, so transcendent, so mysterious that He needed to be kept at a safe distance, or so they thought. So much so did they keep Him at that safe distance that He eventually became, in their own experience, unreachable, distant, and aloof ."[27]

The problem with religious traditionalists such as the Pharisees in Jesus's day is that their understanding of God is fundamentally flawed. They remove God from human experience. This excessive emphasis on God's mystery, according to seeker church pastors, is a disservice to Christians and seekers alike. For example, one speaker suggests, "Jesus urged true believers to think of themselves as brothers and sisters in a warm, loving family that was led by an approachable, benevolent, good and wise Dad. All throughout His teaching ministry, Jesus tried to help people see His Father as righteous and holy, but equally as fatherly, personal, warm, [and] eager to engage in loving community."[28]

The God whom seeker church pastors commend is, in short, a heavenly Father who desires intimacy with his family of true believers. Despite the appeal of this benevolent and reasonable image of God, today's individualistic seekers are nevertheless often reluctant to commit themselves to a church. Thus, one challenge facing seeker churches is that while seekers may be interested in spirituality in general, and God in particular, they are often skeptical about institutional religion, especially Christianity.

What is Christianity?

One explanation for seekers' skepticism toward Christianity, according to seeker church leaders, is that the values of Christianity are in conflict with those of the world. "The value system of Jesus and the value system of contemporary society," claims Hybels, "are always in conflict with each other."[29] As a result, Christians pay a price for adhering to their beliefs. Even amidst "society's background noise of deceit, deception, and dishonesty," Christians are called to be truth tellers.[30] This, however, is not easy in a "morally perverse" world that is "ravaged by sin and evil."[31] Interestingly, seeker church pastors do not emphasize the world's corruption in order to promote Christian legal reforms, political involvement, or even moral crusades. Instead, seeker church pastors accentuate the world's perversity so that they can present Christianity as a refuge from trouble. Christianity, then, offers the seeker's psyche a reprieve from the slings and arrows of modern life.

In order for seeker church pastors to persuade seekers that Christianity can provide this kind of refuge, however, they must first convince seekers that, contrary to popular stereotypes, Christianity is not legalistic and judgmental, and that church services need not be dull but can, in fact, be exciting, vital, and joyful. In order to accomplish this, seeker church pastors must work to distance themselves rhetorically from Christianity's negative reputation. Though one might expect theologically conservative churches to emphasize the difference between Christians and unbelievers, between saints and sinners, between the saved and the damned, and between the church and the world, Willow Creek's pastors choose instead to de-emphasize these distinctions while pointing out Christianity's links with common culture. Thus, while Willow Creek's pastors do preach about the eternal consequences of accepting or rejecting Jesus Christ, they manage to do so without stressing the contrast between those who are "in" the faith and those who are "out." The symbolic boundaries that seeker church pastors stress do not so much distinguish between the "world" and Christianity as they contrast "fulfilling" and "flawed" Christianity. The goal of many Willow Creek seeker messages is not to criticize seekers but to dispel seekers' prejudices against conservative Christianity. Willow Creek's pastors hope that by dispelling these negative stereotypes, they might also overcome some of the potential obstacles to belief amongst seekers.

To this end, Willow Creek pastors distinguish between "authentic" Christianity (as proclaimed by seeker churches) and "inauthentic" Christianity (as characterized by dead rituals and/or intolerant conservatism). Willow Creek seeker messages repeatedly emphasize the distinction between "authentic and hypocritical Christianity." For instance, pastors contrast "nurturing versus authoritative" Christianity, "genuine versus inauthentic" Christianity, and "seeker" Christianity versus "in-your-face" or "holier-than-thou" or "cosmetic" Christianity. According to Willow Creek's teaching, judgmentalism and intolerance characterize all of these negative versions of Christianity. For example, in one Willow Creek message, pastor Lee Stroebel admits that he "cringes" at the thought of street preachers with bullhorns screaming at people that they are going to hell. While this sort of "in-your-face" Christianity may proclaim the truth, says Stroebel, its communication strategy is fundamentally flawed. "The problem is that some kingdom citizens these days, even though they might have good intentions, are inadvertently repelling people from Christianity."[32]

"Holier-than-thou" Christianity, according to Stroebel, has the additional disadvantage of discouraging seekers by making them feel as if they could never be a part of the church. In a message entitled "What Would Jesus Say to Madonna?" Stroebel suggests that many seekers ask the same spiritual questions as Madonna (the rock star, not the mother of Jesus). Seekers and Madonna both have been alienated from "the boring, guilt-inducing, distant, ritual-demanding God." Both have been convinced that that kind of God is not for them. The good news, according to Stroebel, is that this picture of God is inaccurate. If someone would just take the time to introduce them to the "authentic" Christ, seekers, not to mention Madonna, would give Christianity a chance. Hence, Stroebel suggests that Jesus would say three things to Madonna (and, by implication, to the rest of us). First, Jesus would say, "I'm sorry that you grew up with such a distorted picture of me." Second, "I understand how living a life without me would cause you to seek fulfillment in other ways." And third, "I will help you find the fulfillment that you yourself say has eluded you despite your struggle to find it."[33] Rather than referring to Madonna as an example of the waywardness of the world or the follies of sin (a verbal foil to exemplars of Christian virtue), Stroebel refers to Madonna in order to demonstrate the value of seeking God and the fulfillment offered in Christ.

Madonna's main problem, according to Stroebel, is neither her almost sacrilegious use of religious symbols such as the Cross nor her morally objectionable behavior, but instead that she seeks fulfillment in all the wrong places. Whereas a typical fundamentalist preacher might castigate Madonna for her immoral, ungodly, indecent, worldly, and offensive behavior, seeker church pastors tend to be more sympathetic in their analysis of Madonna's misguided quest for personal fulfillment. Seeker church pastors prefer to minimize the radical disjunction between the ways of the world and the ways of the church because their aim is to convince seekers that one can test the claims of Christianity without having to renounce completely one's current lifestyle. In other words, seeker church pastors downplay Madonna's moral transgressions in order to focus instead on her legitimate spiritual quest.

Seeker church pastors, while they criticize "holier-than-thou" Christianity, likewise distance themselves from yet another unattractive manifestation of Christianity, "authoritative" Christianity. According to Willow Creek's pastors, authoritative Christianity is characterized by an excessive concern with power, rather than love, especially in personal relationships. For example, in one Willow Creek seeker message on one of the most culturally loaded topics for evangelicals, the speaker argues that the Bible does not give men permission to wield power arbitrarily over their wives and families. Instead, according to this speaker, the Bible teaches men to nurture. The following passage illustrates the conviction predominant in seeker churches that a "nurturing" Christianity is more authentic than an "authoritative" Christianity:

> God knew that some people would become self-centered and controlling and authoritative. Some men would even say, "I'm the man of this house

and the Bible says that I'm the head of this place, so you do my bidding."
That's not what the Scripture talks about when it talks about headship. It
doesn't mean power and authority and the rule of the roost. It means being a life-giver. It means being a fountainhead of love and nurture to those
in the family.[34]

A nurturing Christianity promotes an egalitarian view of gender, which emphasizes mutuality and love, rather than an authoritarian view of gender,
which emphasizes the culturally offensive ideas of headship and women's
submission.

Despite seeker church pastors' egalitarian rhetoric, the role of women in
seeker churches is somewhat ambiguous. According to my research,
women do not occupy prominent leadership positions within the seeker
church movement. Only three respondents to the SCP survey were
women.[35] The SCP survey does indicate, however, that one out of four
seeker churches (26 percent) has female members on its pastoral staff. Furthermore, of those churches who currently do not have any female pastors,
almost half (45 percent) claim that they are "very likely" or "somewhat
likely" to hire a woman for a pastoral staff position within the next two
years. Overall, three out of five seeker churches (60 percent) either have a
female member on their pastoral staff or are likely to have one in the near
future. Nevertheless, as I stated earlier, no women, to my knowledge, have
filled positions of senior leadership within the seeker movement. In fact, of
the three women that I know hold leadership positions in seeker churches,
none are senior teaching or preaching pastors; they are instead directors of
programming or of adult and children's ministries. Although these positions are not teaching and preaching positions, they are, especially at
seeker churches, positions of considerable influence and responsibility. In
addition, it appears as if Willow Creek would consider hiring a woman for a
senior teaching position. Bill Hybels writes that "[a]lthough a few isolated
texts are debated, we believe that when the Bible is interpreted correctly
and in its entirety, it teaches the full equality of men and women in status,
giftedness, and opportunities for ministry."[36]

Whether they are working hard to portray themselves as egalitarian or
simply as "reasonable," seeker church proponents are constantly distancing themselves from people's negative perceptions of organized Christian-

ity. Thus, for example, pastors make a rhetorical distinction between "healthy" and "unhealthy" churches. A healthy church is a "worshiping community," not "a wacked out, wild-eyed fringe group that would alienate people in the surrounding neighborhood." Moreover, a healthy church attracts seekers because of its civility, its lack of excessive emotion, and its integration into the community. But, according to seeker church proponents, a healthy church is not so integrated into the community that it is simply "an unchanging social club." Instead, it is "a center for life change [where] fellowship will be real and vulnerable, . . . teaching will be transformational, . . . sacraments will be spiritually building . . . the rich will take care of the poor, [and] . . . unity will be based on the use of spiritual gifts."[37]

In sum, seeker church leaders define their churches as places where Christians avoid the two most unappealing extremes of religious practice. Seeker churches are neither intolerant nor lifeless. Instead, seeker churches practice a sincere and authentic—not a formal and ritualistic—Christianity. For this reason, seeker church proponents contend that seeker church Christianity differs from the Christianity many may remember from their youth. For example, in a message on the Lord's prayer, Hybels interjects that while the formalized prayer found in prayer books can be "wonderful" and "beautiful," it has the potential to become "mechanical and meritorious." Thus, Hybels recommends that Christians rely on a conversational prayer style that lends itself to "more sincerity."[38]

Hybels's promotion of "conversational" prayer exemplifies seeker church leaders' conviction that one of the primary goals of Christianity is for people to develop sincerity and authenticity in their relationship with God and with others. Consequently, seeker church proponents often challenge seekers to join a congregation that emphasizes authenticity, honesty, intimacy, and relevance. Notably, while seeker church pastors discuss the emotional and supportive nature of healthy congregations, they rarely mention the church as an institution. The cover of Bill and Lynne Hybels's book *Rediscovering Church* offers two definitions of the word "church." The first defines "church" as "a building for public, esp. Christian worship." The second definition, supplied no doubt by Willow Creek, says, "People who demonstrate their love for God by loving and serving others."[39] According to this second definition, the church is not so much an institution as a vibrant community characterized by loving Christian service. The significance of the latter definition—the "real" definition of the church according to Willow Creek—is that it limits the church to expressive relationships within the private sphere. While this may have considerable appeal, this definition nevertheless excludes any sense of the historical, institutional, cultural, public, and even authoritative functions of the church. What is left is a church that is primarily a place for people to realize their full potential in service to others.

Although all members of the church are called to love and serve others, this does not mean that Christianity is a drudgery. Seeker church pastors stress that Christianity is an adventure—"one of the most exciting adventures" they have ever experienced. In the midst of this inspiring Christian message, however, seeker church pastors also weigh in with some sobering news—Christianity is also about sin, repentance, and the Cross.

The Hard Sell: Sin and Its Consequences

The Christian message contains both good news and bad news for seekers. The good news is that God is eager to adopt seekers into a warm, loving family. The bad news is that God places one condition on this adoption: seekers must be willing to repent, literally "turn away from" their sin and turn toward God in faith. How do seeker church pastors present this demand that seekers change their priorities? And do seeker church pastors make any effort to minimize the offensiveness of this demand?

Before we can answer these questions, let us first note that seeker church pastors are consistently evangelical in their personal theological views. Seeker church pastors hold evangelical theological positions on the Bible, the divinity of Christ, and the nature of—and the conditions for attaining—eternal life. They also hold a Reformed view on the depravity of human nature. When asked in the SCP survey whether it is in poor taste to emphasize damnation and repentance when sharing the Gospel, seven out of ten pastors (71 percent) disagreed. In other words, most seeker church pastors claim that the Christian message must include some mention of Hell.

Hell, according to seeker church pastors, is not an abstract or allegorical concept but instead is the final destination for those whose sin has not been forgiven. "Because we are sinners," explains Hybels, "[our] attendance is required [at the day of reckoning]. [We] will appear some day before God to give an account of [our lives]. The Bible teaches that from cover to cover. No Exceptions." Meanwhile, Hybels acknowledges that Christianity's claim that salvation comes exclusively through Christ alone is not popular in today's culture:

> People want to hear about a wide gate to God. They want to know that they can pick and choose from any religion, they can adopt any belief system, they can choose any lifestyle, and somehow, someway, through some celestial slight of hand at the end of time, everything is going to come out in the wash. . . . Life would be so much easier if I could just announce the wide gate deal. I'd have so much more receptivity to my ideas and messages.[40]

Despite the unpopularity of any message that is suggestive of intolerance and exclusivity, Hybels remains committed to Christian orthodoxy and is an opponent of the "wide gate" of universalism. His seeker messages consistently stress the need for personal faith in Jesus Christ. "In the final day of reckoning, our God will judge. . . . Have we repented of our sins? Have we put our faith and trust in Christ?"[41]

Sin is, in short, a barrier between each person and God—and a constant of the human condition. According to one seeker church message, "We all have a dark side, a sin nature."[42] And, as a result, we are "spiritually bankrupt" with nothing to offer God other than "a needy sin-stained heart that requires redemption."[43] Another metaphor for sin's effect upon human nature is the condition of blindness. In one message, the speaker asserts that sinners are "people who are spiritually blind [so that they] cannot see God for who He is . . . in spite of all the evidence pointing to [God's] existence." Furthermore, the spiritually blind cannot see themselves for who they are: "moral foul-ups, sinners before a Holy God."[44] Following classic evangelical teaching, seeker church pastors stress that the only solution to this spiritual blindness is Christ's atoning work on the Cross. As Bill Hybels puts it, "The only way to neutralize and overcome sin is through salvation in Christ."[45] Each individual, according to Hybels, must make a deliberate decision to follow God and repent of his or her old life. As Bill Hybels observes, "Nobody drifts into the Kingdom."

By emphasizing the reality of sin, Willow Creek's pastors clearly resist any theological softening of the Christian message of God's judgment. That is to say, Willow Creek affirms classic Christian orthodoxy and resists the temptation to exclude the offensive message of ultimate judgment from its religious discourse. Hell is not allegorical. It is not, as Robert Schuller has claimed, the result of unrealized self-esteem. It is the ultimate destination of sinners, the reason to seek God with all one's heart. For example, one United Methodist pastor, who founded a successful seeker-sensitive church in Virginia, emphasized to me during an interview that, while he pays attention to the needs and interests of the unchurched in his area, his messages are "rock-solid" doctrinally. "The substance of what we offer here is pure, basic fundamental Christianity in the United Methodist tradition. You will find that we are extremely firm about our belief in the Virgin Birth, the physical resurrection, eternal life, the forgiveness of sin, [and] the atonement."[46]

Nevertheless, while seeker church pastors do discuss the basics of Christian orthodoxy, including the seriousness of sin and the reality of judgment, they often frame this discussion in terms of how sin harms the individual, rather than how it is offensive to a holy God. Sin, in short, prevents us from realizing *our* full potential. As sinners, Hybels suggests, we break through the "moral guard rails" and "ethical fences" that God has established for our own good.[47] If people would only follow God's moral guidance, they would lead healthier, fuller lives that would culminate in eternal salvation.

The Soft Sell: Personal Fulfillment through Faith

While seeker church pastors are adamantly committed to the basics of evangelical orthodoxy, they are also eager to present this message without giving any unnecessary offense. For example, when asked whether "confrontational evangelistic programs intimidate more people than they convert," more than four out of five seeker church pastors surveyed (81 percent) agreed with the statement. In short, confrontation is uncivil—and ineffective. Thus, seeker church advocates are committed to developing a nonconfrontational way of presenting the Gospel. Instead of railing about eternal damnation, Hybels explains in one of his seeker messages the consequences of rejecting God: "You'll miss the reward your heart yearns for, which is to be affirmed from the Father who is in heaven. You don't want to miss His rewards. You don't want to miss His compensations, because they're rich. They're soul-satisfying." It is just this sort of angle on the

Christian faith that induces sociologist Stephen Warner to summarize the overall thrust of Hybels's preaching as "upbeat." "It's a salvationist message," says Warner, "but the idea is not so much being saved from the fires of hell. Rather, it's being saved from meaninglessness. It's more of a soft sell."[48]

Hybels acknowledges that the "soft sell" approach is appealing—and at times flawed. He recounts that, in the early years of the church, he provided "imbalanced teaching" by stressing God's love and by deemphasizing God's holiness.[49] Another example of this "soft sell" approach is found in a message where the speaker proclaims that God "is a God of truth." The primary focus of the message, however, is not on God but on the believer—specifically how God's truth will benefit the believer: "But [God] also wants [truth telling] for our own sake, for our own reputations, for our own character development, for our own healthy relationships, for our own self-esteem, for own peace of mind. Because there are lots of benefits that we reap, when we are people of the truth."[50] The overt lesson here is that if you are unsure whether you are truly living a Christian life, there is one way to know for sure. As one Willow Creek message put it: "Keep this test as your bottom line: Is your soul being satisfied?"[51]

To understand just what is meant by the term "soft sell"—and how this so-called soft sell might signal a marked shift in the content of Protestant preaching over the last two centuries—I contrast Willow Creek's seeker messages with the preaching of George Whitefield, the eighteenth-century Anglican circuit preacher. This comparison is especially interesting because Whitefield, like today's seeker church pastors, utilized innovative, mass marketing techniques to proclaim the Gospel to as many people as possible. He pioneered novel alternatives to Anglican worship, which included preaching in the open air and disregarding denominational boundaries. Furthermore, Whitefield incorporated dramatic presentation in his preaching to such an extent that "it was no longer clear what was church and what was theater."[52] Moreover, Whitefield's theatrical preaching style appealed as much to the emotions of his audience as to his audience's intellect. Like many seeker church pastors today, Whitefield proclaimed an "individualistic and subjective sense of piety that found its quintessential expression in the internal, highly personal experience of the 'New Birth.' "[53] One result of Whitefield's mesmerizing preaching, his stress on a personal encounter with God, and his tireless travels across the countryside was that Whitefield became the first celebrity known throughout the Colonies—our nation's first evangelical revivalist.

But, for all the similarities between Whitefield and today's seeker church pastors, there are some important differences. In contrast to seeker church pastors today, Whitefield was a firm Calvinist who believed that God had chosen the elect, and not the reverse. Furthermore, Whitefield's preaching continually reiterated the severity of God's wrath toward human sin and the ultimate judgment that awaited everyone after death. Consider, for example, Whitefield's sermon "The Method of Grace" in which he acknowledges each person's longing for a deep sense of personal peace—a topic that at first sounds much like today's seeker messages on finding "soul satisfaction." This initial resemblance, however, is misleading, for Whitefield had no compunction about emphasizing the grievous consequences of sin. Thus, before one can be at peace with God, according to Whitefield, one must be made "to weep over, made to bewail, [his/her] actual transgression against the law of God."[54] Yet those who have not repented of their sin have no peace with God: "But what shall I say to you that have got no peace with God? . . . You are just hanging over hell. What peace can you have when God is your enemy, when the wrath of God is abiding upon your poor soul?"[55] God, according to Whitefield, is not simply a loving father who rushes to save us. God is an angry and righteous judge who is utterly offended by our sin. Later in this same sermon, Whitefield asks: "Who can stand before God when He is angry?" Whitefield then proclaims those terrifying and uncivil words: "It is a dreadful thing to fall into the hands of an angry God."[56] Clearly, Whitefield did not shy away from stressing the wrath of God in order to motivate his audience to seek repentance and genuine faith.

But what in particular was the poor sinner, moved by Whitefield's persuasive preaching, to do? In answer to that question, Whitefield urged his listeners to "beg of God to break your hearts, beg of God to convince you of your actual sins, beg of God to convince you of original sin, beg of God to convince you of your self-righteousness—beg of God to give you faith, and to enable you to close with Jesus Christ."[57] The motivation behind this supplication for faith is not peace with God in the sense of finding personal fulfillment, but instead peace in the sense of avoiding God's dreadful judgment. In another message, Whitefield asks, "What will become of you if the Lord be not your righteousness? Think that Christ will spare you? No, he that formed you, will have no mercy on you. If you be not of Christ, if Christ be not your righteousness, Christ himself shall pronounce you damned."[58]

In all his preaching, Whitefield never veered from the hard message that Christ will unequivocally condemn the unrighteous. Hell awaits the unbeliever. In contrast, many seeker church pastors minimize God's agency in determining an individual's eternal destiny. Instead of stressing God's judgment, seeker church pastors focus on each individual's personal decision for or against God. One reason behind this not-so-subtle shift in focus is that in today's religious environment, Whitefield's hard sell message lacks plausibility and consumer appeal.

"Not Backing Off": Knowing God Is Fun

In sociological terms, today's cultural pluralism fosters an underemphasis on the "hard sell" of Hell while contributing to an overemphasis on the "soft sell" of personal satisfaction through Jesus Christ. In churches across America, it is increasingly uncommon to encounter a "hard core," fire and brimstone approach to religious revival. One pastor of a nondenominational church in Pennsylvania explained why this is so:

> How many people are sitting in those chairs listening to [preachers] say "I'm going to tell you about your sin and selfishness and this is really going to help you." It's not working. We're pragmatic enough in the seeker movement to say if this works and if it is not a sin to hold a seeker service, and it draws people so that we can then present the Gospel to them, then we should be doing it. The relevant question [is], is a seeker service sinful? If it is not sinful and it attracts people, then we should be doing it.

And, as I have stated earlier, what attracts so many people to seeker services across the country is the seeker service emphasis on how God makes the lives of Christians more fulfilling. For today's religious consumers, the search for meaning and fulfillment is as important as—and perhaps initially even more important than—the search for God. So how do seeker church pastors proclaim the "bad news" of the gospel (that we are sinners and deserve condemnation) to congregations predominantly interested in self-fulfillment? One pastor of an Evangelical Free church in Maryland admits that he uses the "back door" in order to introduce his congregation to the doctrines of absolute truth and divine judgment:

> [We make] the assumption that you can't go through the front door. In our culture absolute truth is considered a "pooh-pooh." It's an a priori decision that [seekers] have made. . . . I will talk about that issue but I can guarantee you that when I talk about Christianity versus other world religions, I will raise more ire than I will with most of my other messages because there is something about absolute truth that really [upsets] most people.

This pastor's "back door" strategy includes encouraging people to read the Bible, to pray, and to examine the claims of Jesus. Then, according to this pastor, he will not need to convince people that they need to believe: "I won't have to tell them that they have to ascribe to absolute truth. They'll come to that conclusion themselves."

In sum, seeker churches introduce seekers to the Christian message by presenting the exclusivist theology of evangelicalism in the friendly guise of an egalitarian, fulfillment-enhancing, fun religious encounter with God. As a result, seeker church pastors make orthodox theology less offensive and more civil for a pluralistic society. Seeker church proponents do not abandon the "Gospel truth " but repackage it in a kinder, gentler format. They maintain the evangelical emphasis on the importance of faith in Jesus Christ but subtly transform the reasons why one should pursue such a faith. Rather than warning the unrepentant about the damnation awaiting their eternal soul, they proclaim the riches of knowing Jesus now and on into eternity. The promise of this-worldly peace and fulfillment supplements, perhaps even supersedes, the eternal consequences of one's personal response to Christ. As one pastor of a nondenominational church in Georgia puts it: "[W]e're not at all hesitant to say [that] what you really need to live life to the fullest is a relationship with Jesus Christ. We don't back off of that at all, even in our Sunday morning services." "Not backing off at all" now means that seeker churches will not hesitate to proclaim that life without Jesus Christ is not fulfilling.

I had numerous encounters with this "seeker-friendly" approach to Christianity during the course of my research. In one of my visits to a seeker church, the pastor spoke at length about the importance of having a relationship with God, and how such a relationship entails bringing all our hopes and frustrations to God in prayer. "God is there and he cares," said the pastor. While he did outline three key aspects of Christianity—knowing God, loving God, and imitating God—the main emphasis of this pastor's message was simply: "Please consider God. You'll be so much better off."[59]

Although the "soft sell" may dispel a seeker's stereotypical misunderstandings of Christianity, and may even provide "soul satisfaction," the question still remains: Is Christianity true? In other words, while seekers might be attracted to the personal benefits of Christianity, they will nevertheless probably still want to know whether the claims of Christianity are credible. So Willow Creek pastor Lee Stroebel offers this "proof": "Christianity works! And the reason Christianity works is because Christianity is true. It works because it's true. . . . I was not only convinced by the historical evidence for Jesus's claim that He is God but I was convinced by the fact that his principles prove themselves in actual practice. "[60] This excerpt highlights the paradoxical nature of the religious discourse of seeker churches. On the one hand, the speaker affirms the objective truthfulness of Christianity both historically and theologically. On the other hand, the speaker asserts that the most convincing proof of Christianity is not so much the historical evidence for the life, death, and resurrection of Jesus but instead the practical and therapeutic benefits of belief. In other words, the principal evidence of Christianity's veracity is its utility—its many benefits.

Closing Reflections

Willow Creek's seeker messages are clearly religious messages as opposed to purely secular self-help talks. These seeker messages repeatedly stress the reality of God; the core evangelical beliefs, such as the divinity of Christ; and the necessity of repentance and conversion. Yet this analysis of Willow Creek's messages and of pastors' strategies for giving messages indicates that therapeutic discourse has re-formed the content of seeker church messages. Rather than reviewing the findings of this chapter, I will close with brief reflections on two implications of this development.

The first implication concerns doctrine. While seeker church messages try to persuade seekers that they should adopt certain beliefs, they do not emphasize doctrine. The difference between doctrine and belief is quite significant. Doctrine, according to Robert Wuthnow,

> connotes a body of systematic religious insight, rather than a purely eclectic assemblage of personal opinions. It also suggests (again) the importance of the church as an institution, for doctrine is generally regarded as a set of "teachings" associated with a religious community. To speak of doctrine is even to imply some standard of truth, and some obligation to abide by this truth, whereas belief is entirely relative.[61]

Seeker church pastors do not aim to convince seekers of the truthfulness of a coherent doctrine or set of doctrines, such as Reformed theology or the Westminster Confession. Rather, they wish to persuade seekers to adopt the few core beliefs of evangelical theology. While these beliefs may be tied to a particular doctrine, seeker church proponents do not insist that seekers "buy" the whole package of doctrine in order to become a member of the church. The criteria for membership are a personal conversion experience and an assent to a general statement of faith.

The shift in emphasis from doctrine to experience raises important questions about the role of the church in American society. In particular, critics of seeker churches ask, "What will the future form of faith be?" As contemporary modes of communication proliferate, as nondenominational churches abound, as links with Christian tradition—particularly Christianity's historic creeds—continue to weaken, the potential exists for contemporary churches to reshape Christian practice according to the entertainment and therapeutic tendencies of modern culture, even while pastors continue to proclaim evangelical theology from the pulpit—or Plexiglas podium. Christian theology and Christian praxis are, in the end, not easily distinguishable. How God is worshiped (i.e., praxis) may, in fact, subtly alter the worshiper's understanding of who that God is.

Consider, for example, the task of translating Christian theology into a language that makes sense to seekers. This is accomplished by addressing the seeker's felt needs through relevant messages. But such strategies may be more problematic than many pastors acknowledge. Take, for instance, the pioneering work of Robert Schuller, pastor of the Crystal Cathedral in Orange County, California and a very important early influence upon Willow Creek's leaders.[62] Schuller claims that in order to make the Christian message more relevant to seekers, pastors must translate traditional theological terms into contemporary idiom. At the heart of Schuller's translation project is the concept of self-esteem. Schuller argues in *Self-Esteem: The New Reformation* that Reformational theology—the foundation of Protestantism and the basis of evangelical faith—is "imperfect." Reformational theology has failed because it is "too heavy a theology."[63] It has placed "theocentric communication above the meeting of the deeper emotional and spiritual needs of humanity." As evidence, Schuller argues that the traditional theological definition of sin as rebellion against God "is not incorrect as much as it is shallow and insulting to the human being." And, rather than insulting people, the church should build people's self-esteem because "at the core of sin is a lack of self-esteem." The theology of self-esteem is "based on a solid central core of religious truth—the dignity of man." The ultimate dignity for humankind is to receive salvation, which means "to be permanently lifted from sin (psychological self-abuse with all of its consequences) and shame to self-esteem and its God-glorifying, human need-meeting, constructive and creative consequences." In contrast, "a person is in hell when he has lost his self-esteem."[64]

In the name of defending Christian theology, Schuller has managed to subjectivize it thoroughly, explicitly shifting its focus from God to the human craving for self-worth. In this schema, sin is not an objective condition of human nature that leads to separation from God but is instead a type of psychological deficit. Hell is not the absence of God; it is being less than your full self.

In his bold, even brazen, translation of Christian concepts into the argot of pop psychology, Schuller explicitly criticizes traditional theology for being overly pessimistic. He dismisses "negative theologians" who dwell on the humiliation of Christ in the Incarnation and suggests that pastors instead should accentuate the positive: "The Incarnation was God's glorification of the human being." Similarly, Schuller proposes that "negative-thinking theologians" persist in misinterpreting basic Christian doctrines. Repentance, for example, need not entail "self-condemnation, self-denigration, [or] self-abasement." Instead, it should be "a turning from sin, with its rejection of self-esteem, as the way to fulfillment [and] to sanctification." Repentance, in short, is "a positive, dynamic, and highly-motivated redirection of life."[65]

The glorification of the self, or at least the preoccupation with the self, is obviously appealing to the therapeutic mentality in modern America. As Philip Rieff has observed, "[The] self, improved, is the ultimate concern of modern culture."[66] Although many evangelicals criticize Schuller—even Bill Hybels insists on speaking directly about sin, in its traditional sense, at Willow Creek—Schuller's preoccupation with the therapeutic is common within the evangelical world. James Hunter has documented the extent to which evangelicalism has embraced therapeutic understandings of the self, which are based on the assumption that "the attention the self is receiving is legitimate and that the self, as the repository of human emotions and subjectivity, has intrinsic and ultimate worth and significance." Additionally, this evangelical fixation with the self amounts to "a fundamental assault" on the inner-worldly asceticism of an earlier evangelical tradition.[67] David Wells cites Schuller as the epitome of a minister "riding the stream of modernity." By banishing the word "sin" from the Crystal Cathedral, by insisting that we do not sufficiently esteem ourselves, by telling us, in effect, "don't worry, be happy," Schuller "is offering in easily digestible bites the therapeutic model of life through which the healing of the bruised self is found."[68]

The principal problem with the therapeutic model of the self, according to Wells, is that, even when draped in religious terminology, it is based on an assumption about "the perfectibility of human nature . . . [which] is anathema to the Christian gospel."[69] Similarly, Rieff argues that the modern commitment to "the gospel of self-fulfillment" represents a profound break with, rather than reformulation of, historic faiths, specifically Judaism and Christianity. "All attempts at connecting the doctrines of psychotherapy with the old faiths," warns Rieff, "are patently misconceived."[70] Thus, Schuller's insistence that developing people's self-esteem is the primary mission of the church is at odds with historic Protestant theology. By "riding the stream of modernity," Schuller demonstrates how Christian practice, if informed primarily by assumptions drawn from non-Christian sources like psychotherapy, can alter Christian theology.

Robert Schuller's "new reformation" is an extreme case of how catering messages to the needs of seekers has the potential to transform the theology undergirding the message. Schuller's example illustrates where a dismissal of traditional formulations of Christian theology can lead. And Schuller's "new reformation" does have implications for Willow Creek, as Schuller is closely associated with the seeker church movement. Schuller played an important part in Willow Creek's inception and founding. Many seeker church pastors cite him as one of their primary sources for ideas and training. During the course of my research, however, I did not find any seeker church pastor who fully endorsed Schuller's recommendation that the word "sin"—used in its traditional sense—be expunged from seeker churches. One of Willow Creek's original leaders (now working at a Presbyterian church in Maryland) did suggest that although Schuller's message is a lot like "pop psychology" and is a little "extreme," most of what he says "is what Jesus was teaching when He said, the Father loves you, and I love you, and you are important to God."

Schuller's influence is likely to grow amongst seeker churches because of the 1992 establishment of Churches Uniting in Global Mission, a network of over two hundred churches, including prominent seeker churches such as Saddleback Valley Church in Orange County, California, and Community Church of Joy near Phoenix. Though Willow Creek has resisted the impulse to reformulate Christian theology wholesale, as Schuller has, there is nothing in Willow Creek's set of ten core values that would recommend limitations be placed on Schuller's accommodations.[71] Schuller's theology of self-esteem demonstrates how a good will effort to translate the Gospel might result in a *transformation* of the Gospel. The distinction between translation and transformation (or between contextualization and capitulation) is part of an important theological debate that churches would be wise to rely on more than the needs of seekers alone to resolve.

The second implication of incorporating therapeutic discourse and categories into seeker messages concerns the nature of the symbolic boundaries maintained by seeker churches. The attitude of some seeker churches to the behavior of the pop star Madonna is one example. In another example, in a message on divorce, Hybels says that "there is not an ounce of judgment in my spirit for those of you who are going through or who are recovering from a divorce in your family. . . . You matter to God more than you realize you do."[72] Seeker churches, in short, are reluctant to create unambiguous moral boundaries for the purposes of judging people's behavior. Although seeker church pastors sometimes stress that *God* is a judge, there are almost no references to the *church* judging or singling out behavior that is unacceptable or immoral.[73] People may seek fulfillment in ways that will not ultimately satisfy, but seeker churches generally avoid judging these decisions. One reason for this tolerance on the part of seeker churches is that seeker church pastors recognize the importance to seekers of choice and autonomy. Thomas Luckmann, in *The Invisible Religion,* argues that "[i]n the modern sacred cosmos, self-expression and self-realization represent the most important expressions of the ruling topic of individual autonomy."[74] By narrowing the symbolic boundaries that define a Christian to the conversion experience and to participation in church, seeker churches attempt to reduce the possible conflicts between the claims of Christianity and the almost inviolable modern boundaries of self-expression and fulfillment. This strategy may contribute to the remarkable appeal of seeker churches, but it also testifies to the diminished authority of religious institutions—and religious speech—in the modern world.

Five

The megachurch is to the old-style chapel what the suburban shopping mall is to the small stores on Main Street—a replacement.[1]

Strategy: The Shopping Mall Church

In an age that emphasizes the search for personal fulfillment, consumer satisfaction, and self-realization, it is not surprising that many seeker church leaders are determined to learn from America's omnipresent shopping malls, which offer customers an almost unlimited variety of goods and choices, all packaged for convenience and easy consumption. What is more, customers can vary their level of involvement with a mall, from merely browsing and "window shopping" to making the mall into the center of one's social and communal life. For many seeker churches, the organizational insights gleaned from shopping malls offer a new way of structuring the church in order to reach the religiously uncommitted. As one sympathetic observer puts it, "In spontaneous imitation of that other late-century cathedral, the mall, the megachurch offers a panoply of choices under one roof—from worship styles to boutique ministries, plus plenty of parking, clean bathrooms, and the likelihood that you'll find something you want and come back again. This is what the customer considers value."[2]

Frank Bouts, pastor of the rapidly growing Emmanuel's Church in Silver Spring, Maryland, is enthusiastic about the "shopping mall church." He claims it represents one of the most important models of the church for the future. Bouts does not hesitate to compare visiting Emmanuel's Church to visiting a mall. "The shopping center makes you feel comfortable; it makes you feel at home. There are clear instructions on where to go and what to do. We want our church to be equally as customer service oriented or equally as sensitive to the needs of all the seekers, of all the first time visitors who come here. We want a visitor to say, 'That was a great experience. I want to come back again.' "[3]

The Leadership Network, a resource group for large churches that was founded in 1984 by Texas businessman Bob Buford, articulates a similar view. According to Buford, small, neighborhood churches are "like corner grocery stores," which have been eclipsed by the emergence of massive grocery and discount outlets and the omnipresent shopping mall. Just as shopping malls have replaced local stores, large churches with diverse programming are replacing the neighborhood church as the primary vendor of religious goods. "The large church," says Buford, "is like a shopping mall. It contains all the specialized ministries of parachurch groups under one roof."[4] The Leadership Network asserts that the large church, "like its cousin the shopping mall, has started to provide more and more specialized services for target populations" and as a result represents "the future of the American church." Small churches will continue to exist, "but in terms of market penetration, innovation, and leadership, to say nothing of financial muscle, large churches will increasingly dominate."[5]

Forms and Function

Why do many seeker churches consider shopping malls a source for strategic inspiration? The mall is certainly not a place of worship, although one could argue that the particularly American religion of self-expression and lifestyle finds its highest expression at the mall. In order to sell its commodities, a shopping mall provides an attractive environment that entices shoppers.[6] Every aspect of a shopping mall—from the width of store windows to the number of parking spaces—is carefully planned to maximize its appeal and convenience to shoppers. Seeker church leaders suggest that, just like shopping malls, churches should plan every aspect of their programs in order to create as attractive a setting as possible for Unchurched Harry and Mary. Following their strategy to reduce the gap between religious and everyday life, seeker churches mirror the convenience, cleanliness, and even bland uniformity of shopping malls. Willow Creek, for example, provides an attractive setting for visitors through its beautifully maintained campus, modern facilities, and information booth for directing lost visitors.

It is not just the design and aesthetics of shopping malls that seeker churches emulate but also their appeal to a particular lifestyle. The goods that shopping malls stock and promote are not just the basics, but instead are the extras advertised as a means for improving one's lifestyle. Malls not only sell goods but also "create needs and desires for commodities that we may never have thought of or desired before."[7] Seeker churches similarly aim to attract people by appealing first to people's "felt needs" with offerings such as men's basketball leagues, social opportunities, Sunday schools, child care, and even direction in one's search for meaning and purpose in life. After addressing these felt needs, seeker churches are then ready to "sell" attenders on an answer to their "real need": a relationship with God. As Kenton Beshore, the pastor of Mariners Southcoast Church in Orange County, California, puts it: "We give [seekers] what they want and we give them what they didn't know they wanted—a life change."[8] There is no single product offered by seeker churches that is *the* key to reaching Unchurched Harry. Just as malls rely on a variety of stores, restaurants, movie theaters, and other attractions to provide something for everyone, seeker churches appeal to their various target markets with a variety of services and programming options.

Undergirding the shopping mall's climate-controlled environment is a highly rationalized and systematized strategy for attracting sales. Seeker churches, not unlike past movements within evangelicalism, find rational planning a necessary component for growth. George Thomas persuasively argues that a belief in the rational unity of means and ends was characteristic of nineteenth-century revivalism. Evangelist Charles Finney was confident that his "new measures," such as calling potential converts to the "anxious bench" at the front of the meeting hall, were virtual guarantees of revival. God gives the methods, according to this view, in order to achieve the purpose of evangelism. Similarly, seeker church pastors today claim that with the right methods, churches not only can but *will* grow. For example, Rick Warren of Saddleback Church asserts that "the primary factor affecting the growth or decline of the church is the methods the church uses. . . . Change the method, change the results."[9]

Interestingly, seeker churches' highly rationalized and systematized strategies are used to sell an increasingly therapeutic array of "products" and services. For example, seeker churches tend to focus their programming efforts on the private sphere. There is a large market (that is, seeker interest in) for self-help and support groups, children's programs, and personal fitness and social opportunities but more limited demand for social justice and "prophetic" ministries. The shopping mall church thus caters almost exclusively to private needs.

The seeker church movement incorporates two culturally powerful—and seemingly paradoxical—myths.[10] The first has to do with the American preoccupation with pragmatic, effective action or rationality. The second pertains to America's prevalent therapeutic or consumerist ethos. While at first it might seem as if cold, hard rationality and warm, soft emotion are opposites, they are, in fact, two sides of the same coin. As the authors of *Habits of the Heart* argue, the languages or traditions of utilitarian individualism (rationality) and expressive individualism (the therapeutic) support and reinforce each other.[11] The cold rationality of the public realm—the Weberian "iron cage"—is softened by the expansion of a therapeutic ethos in the private realm. Thus, seeker church pastors are building their movement on the basis of a creative synthesis of traditional biblical beliefs, highly rationalized understandings of the church and the ministry, and an appreciation for people's therapeutic concerns. The shopping mall model incorporates these diverse elements into one appealing package—a package that allows for increased opportunities for church shopping.

Robert Wuthnow has raised the question, Given the pervasiveness of market forces in American religion, why is there not more church shopping than there already is?[12] Why do people still remain loyal to a congregation? What are the obstacles that discourage people from sampling new congregations? One factor is that congregations impose upon their members "costs" ranging from learning the intricacies of a liturgy to finding the bathrooms. To allow more "shopping," Wuthnow suggests that there needs to be greater franchising and standardization among churches so, for example, visitors can always follow the service and find the bathrooms. By emulating the musical and architectural forms of contemporary culture, the shopping mall church invites church shoppers in ways that most traditional churches cannot. While the specific strategies of seeker churches may vary, one constant is the recognition that they must find ways to make their product appealing to religious consumers with changing and unstable religious loyalties.

Marketing the Church?

"The church is a business," declares George Barna, a writer, public opinion pollster, church marketing expert, and a noted supporter of Willow Creek.[13] In one sense, this analogy is simply a description of any organization that takes in money, balances budgets, trains staff, and so on. In another sense, defining the church as a business is a prescription for what the church should be. A businesslike church operates efficiently, makes plans and goals, and uses modern marketing and managing techniques to fulfill its objectives. According to the Seeker Church Pastor (SCP) survey, most seeker church pastors engage in some form of intentional marketing. The majority of seeker church pastors (86 percent) indicated that the church must target its evangelism efforts rather than appeal to as many people as possible. Similarly, most pastors (70 percent) agreed with the statement "The church must develop a marketing orientation in order to reach people effectively."[14] One pastor of a nondenominational church in Pennsylvania summarized his church's approach: "We are marketers, we know when the new crowd is going to come and we're going to seek to interest them with something that does appeal to their felt needs. Then we're going to . . . hope that God changes their lives through . . . their true need, which is a relationship with God through Christ."

Seeker churches use a variety of strategies to attract newcomers, including some basic marketing practices from the business world. The vast majority of seeker churches (94 percent) have used some form of advertising, either radio, print, or television. The second-most popular marketing strategy, used by more than seven out of ten seeker churches (72 percent), is direct mail. Seeker churches may also employ other outreach strategies, including: phone contacts (48 percent), surveys of local residents (40 percent), and door to door visitation (31 percent). But is advertising and marketing really appropriate for the church?

Barna claims that marketing is not only appropriate for the church, it is necessary. He suggests that in marketing its religious "product" to potential customers, especially those unchurched Americans who are not very interested in formal religion, the church's main competition "is from organizations like ABC, CBS, Universal Studios, MGM, K-Mart, 7-11, etc."[15] Therefore, according to Barna, the church must consider itself a business in competition with people's other recreational interests. What must the church do to compete effectively in this environment? Barna argues that "developing a marketing orientation is precisely what the church needs to do."[16] Clearly, there is considerable demand for Barna's analysis and prescription; he publishes almost one book a year and offers conferences all over the country. As one pastor put it, "Barna is hot."[17]

One of the most common marketing strategies of seeker churches is to survey the interests and needs of the surrounding population. Willow Creek, following the example of Robert Schuller, conducted a survey to ascertain the reasons why local residents did not attend church.[18] Other pastors have followed similar strategies, sometimes without knowledge of Willow Creek's efforts. For example, one pastor of a Methodist church in Virginia said that he and his wife "set out to do raw market research by going to the shopping mall and inquiring of strangers whether or not they had a religious life and if they did, tell us about it, and if not, then please explain what kind of religious experience would attract you. . . . [W]e tracked our raw market research and designed our worship around that."[19]

The purpose of market research, of course, is not simply to gather information but also to develop an effective plan of action. Within seeker church circles, the most likely target of any marketing strategy is "Unchurched Harry." There are many good reasons for churches to focus their outreach efforts on Unchurched Harry. One is that men are less likely than women to participate in religious groups.[20] Another is that the profile of Harry—a thirty-five- to fifty-year-old, white, suburban male professional—represents a large and influential segment of the population. The profile of Harry is strikingly similar to the demographic characteristics of the leaders of Willow Creek. Perhaps not surprisingly, Saddleback Church has developed its own profile of its target audience, known as Saddleback Sam. Many of Saddleback Sam's characteristics are remarkably similar to Unchurched Harry's. Sam is "well educated, likes his job, likes where he lives, likes contemporary music, is skeptical of organized religion, is self-satisfied, even smug about his station in life, prefers the casual and informal over the formal, and is overextended in both time and money."[21] A pastor of a nondenominational Southern California church described his church's target as "the typical man in his thirties, [who earns] 40 to 60 thousand dollars a year, [is] an entrepreneur, and drives a Blazer."

Despite their targeting of potential customers, seeker church leaders insist that a church is not a business but a spiritual entity—a fellowship characterized by authentic relationships and loving community. These pastors maintain that the seeker church movement is not about building big churches or developing successful marketing campaigns but about creating biblically functioning communities characterized by love, commitment, authenticity, and spiritual growth. As Bill Hybels puts it, "I get uncomfortable when people mix business and spirituality because fundamentally we're not selling a product. Fundamentally we're proclaiming the message of amazing grace."[22]

Yet how churches go about proclaiming their message of amazing grace is often delineated as a series of carefully developed steps and strategies. These strategies outline a process to attract skeptical seekers and draw them into the life of the church. While there is some marketing involved, particularly in evaluating the tastes and interests of Unchurched Harry, marketing savvy alone does not explain the growth of seeker churches. Many consumers are careful shoppers, especially if they are considering "organized religion." A slick marketing program without any appealing substance behind it is unlikely to attract many of them. Second, religion is not a product in the same way that cars or clothes are. Religion is a collectively produced entity, more of a service than a product. Providing a service involves more than a one-time purchase; it requires an ongoing relationship. This helps explain why many seeker church leaders strongly insist that marketing is not fundamental to their success. They are in the business of creating long-term relationships based not on economic gain but on collective benefit—the growth of the church community. So how do seeker churches attempt to establish relationships with their "customers?" The key is to develop a process by which church members can build bridges between their friends (ideally, Unchurched Harry and Mary) and the church. As one pastor of a Presbyterian church in California put it, "Our biggest marketing tool is word of mouth."

Formal Strategies

One reason for Willow Creek's influence in evangelical circles is that it has developed a clear strategy for establishing relationships with the unchurched. Its seven-step strategy can be summarized easily, and its appeal is considerable. Almost three out of four seeker churches (72.4 percent) claim that they have developed a strategy similar to Willow Creek's. What is Willow Creek's strategy?

1. Build a relationship [with Unchurched Harry]
2. Share a verbal witness
3. Invite [Unchurched Harry] to a seeker service
4. Become a part of New Community [believer's service]
5. Participate in a small group
6. Serve in the body of Christ
7. Steward their financial resources[23]

I have already discussed the seeker service component of this seven-step strategy.[24] If we compare Willow Creek's strategy with those of other seeker churches, we can identify common elements or principles that contribute to the seeker model. For example, Saddleback's Rick Warren has not developed a seven-step strategy per se, but he does stress that a church must define its purposes (based on biblical imperatives) and then develop an effective process for fulfilling these purposes. The "purpose-driven church process" consists of two related elements. The first is a recognition—a market assessment, if you will—of the different levels of commitment within a church. Warren suggests that there are five primary levels of commitment. Moving from lowest to highest, these are: community, crowd, congregation, committed, and core ministry. A purpose-driven church develops effective ways to move people from the community to (ideally) the core.

Saddleback offers a simple—though challenging—process for achieving this goal. New visitors are encouraged to reach "first base," which is commitment to membership, by taking Saddleback's 101 Class "Discovering Saddleback Membership." In order to reach "second base," commitment to maturity, members must take the church's 202 class, "Discovering Spiritual Maturity." To reach "third base," the required course is "Discovering my Ministry." And, finally, to reach "home" one must take the class "Discovering my Life Mission."[25] Moving people around the four bases—Membership, Maturity, Ministry, and Mission—is the core of the Saddleback strategy. The Community Church of Joy offers an identical four-step process, including: (1) commitment to membership; (2) discovering maturity; (3) discovering ministry (gifts); and (4) discovering missions.[26]

What is it about these strategies that contributes to the success of seeker churches? A recent study of religiously unaffiliated baby boomers (raised in Mainline Protestant churches) offers some clues. Inactive church members, according to the authors of *Vital Signs*, are very willing to return to church—provided the congregation can meet their basic expectations. These include meaningful worship, relevant preaching, informal music, flexible times of worship (including Saturday evenings), and a wide range of ministries to them and to their community. Those surveyed also wanted the church to contribute to society—but not through overt political involvement.[27] Seeker churches offer this array of desired services in a very appealing package. One pastor of a nondenominational church in Florida, when pressed to identify the keys to the church's success, responded that most seekers "usually just say they enjoy the environment. They don't single out one thing like the music or drama or anything else in particular." The key to the success of seeker churches is not simply the particular strategy these churches use but the general environment that they create for seekers—safe, anonymous, contemporary, relevant, and enthusiastic. The shopping mall church allows people to browse its offerings, such as large seeker services, or to develop greater commitment through small groups and other programs. Seeker churches are big tents designed to accommodate, to use Rick Warren's terminology, different levels of commitment from the crowd and community to the committed and the core.[28] (For many years, Saddleback held its services in a giant tent.)

Rather than assessing the details of seeker churches' strategies, I would like to point out those key principles undergirding the strategies. These principles provide the incentives for seekers to engage in this journey while also providing pastors with the tools to organize their churches effectively. The key principles are: meeting felt needs; offering choices; and developing leadership.

Meeting Felt Needs

How do seeker churches attract Unchurched Harrys? If there is one principle upon which the diverse networks of seeker churches, church growth consultants, and high-profile pastors agree, it is that churches must address the "felt needs" of their potential customers. One church growth consultant claims that "felt needs are God-given channels for growth."[29] Similarly, George Barna writes that a church attracts new people "because it meets their personal needs. The more successful a church is at meeting people's needs, the more it will grow."[30] In addition, Barna claims that many pastors have learned that "without a felt needs approach, creating spiritual growth in [church] membership [is] often extremely slow, if not impossible."[31] Thus, meeting felt needs is one of the most important strategies of church growth, perhaps second only to one pastor's Golden Rule: "A church will never get bigger than its parking lot."[32]

According to the SCP survey, a significant majority of pastors (84 percent) agree with the statement "In order to gain a hearing for the Gospel, churches today must meet the felt needs of seekers." In contrast, very few pastors (6 percent) disagree with this statement, and none strongly disagrees with it. Although there clearly is a strong consensus that churches must meet the needs of seekers today, the survey does indicate that pastors are evenly divided over whether such a strategy might endanger the church's mission. When asked whether "By focusing on the felt needs of seekers, churches run the risk of conforming to the secular world," 44 percent of pastors agreed with the statement and 43 percent of pastors disagreed; 13 percent were neutral on the matter.

Overall, the importance of meeting the felt needs of seekers is well established. Many of the pastors that I interviewed in the course of my research mentioned how important this emphasis on felt needs was to their churches' success. One pastor of a nondenominational church in Georgia commented, "The things that are probably appealing to people who are not already from a church background are the contemporary nature of the service, the dramas, the fact that the messages are addressing felt needs in their lives." Pastors at seeker churches are also quick to acknowledge that some people find their way into church fellowship through the "side door," that is, they may participate in a church program that meets their needs—play on a church athletic league, attend a church concert or play, or visit a self-help or recovery group—before they ever formally attend a Sunday service.

This emphasis on meeting the felt needs of potential attenders makes sense in light of Wade Clark Roof's analysis of the religious preferences of the baby-boomer generation in *A Generation of Seekers*. According to Roof, most baby boomers, regardless of their religious involvement, agree that participating in religious activities is "something you do if you feel it meets your needs," rather than a matter of "duty or obligation."[33] Almost two-thirds (63 percent) of religious conservatives agree with that statement, as do 68 percent of religious moderates. The strongest support for this statement comes, not surprisingly, from the rest of the baby-boomer population, where the overwhelming majority (82 percent) agrees.

How can seeker churches meet the felt needs of their visitors? There is no easy answer to this question, because, as church growth consultant Carl George warns, "The felt needs of customers are in a constant state of flux."[34] George suggests that just as grocery stores had to adjust to the changing needs of customers by improving their service and expanding their inventory, so too must churches add more programming and flexibility to meet the needs of their customers. New programming can include anything from seeker services to aerobics classes, from adult education electives on the Bible or managing your finances to summer camp programs for children. The bottom line, however, is that churches must offer religious customers programming that meets their needs.

One way that seeker churches have found both to meet the needs of seekers and to provide them with training for service in the church is Willow Creek's Networking course, which is a combination of spiritual gifts analysis, Myers-Briggs personality profiles, and a volunteer placement service.[35] Most seeker churches (81 percent) also have developed a curriculum, similar to Willow Creek's influential *Networking* course, to help people to identify their spiritual gifts. Saddleback's 202 Class, "Discovering My Ministry," is one example. Many pastors claim that these courses are essential to their church's success. According to Hybels, "The development of the Network materials [is] one of the most significant breakthroughs in the 15-year history of our church."[36] By helping people identify their spiritual gifts and then by placing people in ministries that draw upon their strengths, regardless of institutional need, Willow Creek has developed a strategy to encourage people to serve in the church—and to enjoy it. In fact, seekers at Willow Creek seem to like that class so much that, according to Pritchard's study of the church, more people became members through the "Networking" than through small groups.[37] This is intriguing for several reasons. First, the reality (informal structure) of how people use Willow Creek's programs and services may differ substantially from the ideal process (formal structure) delineated by the church. Second, it should not be surprising to find that seekers are selective about which church programs they are willing to commit to. After all, choice has become a sine qua non of religious participation today.

Offering Choices

Seeker church pastors are wholeheartedly embracing this trend toward choice. According to the SCP survey, a remarkably high percentage of pastors (88 percent) agree with the statement "Church services must be designed to reflect the tastes and needs of seekers today." So, whatever the seeker church is offering—a service, a relevant message, a small group, an adult class, an outreach opportunity, or a self-help option—one of the operating principles behind it will be that religious consumers demand choice. Leith Anderson, pastor of Wooddale Church, a prominent seeker church outside of Minneapolis, warns that "religion that assumes that people will come and conform no longer works. That is the approach of a monopoly." But today, choices abound. "And the church that fails to be sensitive to the needs and desires of existing and potential 'customers' will not get a hearing for its message."[38] For instance, seeker churches offer a plethora of adult education options. The selection of available courses rivals the course options found at any typical community college in terms of class variety and scheduling. In fact, the timing and location of seeker church classes vary considerably from the traditional Sunday morning schedule. Many seeker churches schedule their programs for Saturday mornings or Friday nights. Some churches even offer special accelerated classes, which might cover eight weeks of course material in one weekend. The key to successful scheduling, according to one pastor, is that classes should be "offered all over the map so people have a wider choice."

When seeker churches expand their program offerings, many of their new courses are not primarily concerned with the Bible or Christian doctrine, instead they focus on pragmatic and practical life skills. Moreover, even those classes that ostensibly teach about the Bible often are preoccupied with meeting "felt needs." One pastor of a nondenominational church in Maryland described his church's introductory class, called "Walking with God: What It Means to Have a Relationship with God," as an "adult fun experience." This pastor noted that the class strives to present the doctrines of Christianity in a "fun, picnic-like atmosphere"—an atmosphere that will attract today's selective religious consumers. A Baptist General

Conference seeker church in California provides classes on advanced spiritual warfare, advanced prayer, and advanced witnessing, along with classes
on family finances, nutrition, aerobics, and "How to take care of your body."
Thus, while seeker church pastors do not abandon evangelical theology,
they often repackage it, deemphasizing doctrinal statements about truth
while stressing relevant biblical principles for daily living. Anderson suggests that this metamorphosis is essential to the effectiveness of the church
at the end of the twentieth century:

> Effective churches in reaching baby boomers usually include: an orienta-
> tion toward experience and practical action rather than a focus on intel-
> lectual and theoretical approaches; an emphasis on inclusion; a high
> degree of tolerance; and an acceptance of diversity.[39]

Churches that insist on "dry" doctrinal presentations of Christianity represent the "old paradigm." One church consultant suggests that Christian
education should focus on "life skills/application," rather than "Bible
knowledge." In addition, this consultant recommends that churches should
shift their training from "content/doctrine/beliefs" to learning based on
"felt needs/ministry/maturity." The reason to make this shift is that the
goal of Christian education is "not knowledge transfer . . . but obedience
[and] changed behavior."[40] According to seeker church proponents, once
seekers connect with a church, they will progress from aspiring simply to
have their own "felt needs" met to participating more fully in the life of the
church, especially through small groups.

Finding a Home within the Church

Small groups are a vital component of the seeker church strategy
to build a "biblically functioning community."[41] These groups of eight to ten
individuals provide opportunities for people to study the Bible, forge meaningful friendships, and create a sense of belonging to the Christian community. For enormous churches such as Willow Creek, small groups enable
people to find a niche among the thousands of weekly attenders. One adage
popular among seeker church leaders is that the church only grows bigger
by growing smaller—by developing an extensive network of small groups.
Willow Creek's commitment to small groups is not just a matter of logistical
efficiency (that is, finding ways to assimilate hundreds of new attenders

into the life of the church). Small groups represent, according to Willow Creek, a return to the principles of the first-century church. Bill Hybels notes that when the Bible describes how three thousand people became Christians on Pentecost, we gain a clue into how the "first-century megachurch" operated. Hybels interprets the biblical verse—Christians "broke bread in their homes and ate together with glad and sincere hearts"—as an example of a small group ministry in action.[42]

Seeker church proponents view small groups as essential to motivating people to progress from being Sunday spectators to active church participants. According to the SCP survey, virtually every seeker church (99 percent) encourages attenders to commit themselves to a small group fellowship. The survey further indicates that while traditional Bible studies are most prevalent at seeker churches, a substantial number of seeker churches offer support groups and twelve-step groups of various types. The most common forms of small group are Bible studies (91 percent), youth groups (90 percent), women's groups (89 percent), and men's groups (83 percent). Other popular types of small group include support groups (42 percent), twelve-step groups (26 percent), self-help groups (29 percent), and therapy or recovery groups (20 percent).

This diverse array of small groups is proving to be exceedingly popular in today's seeker churches. According to two out of five (40 percent) seeker church pastors, "about half [of the people who currently attend] are involved in small groups." Slightly more than one out of three pastors (35 percent) report that about one-quarter of attenders are involved in small groups. One out of five seeker church pastors (19 percent) indicated in the survey that most of their current church attenders are involved in small groups, while a relatively small percentage of pastors (5 percent) suggested that "very few" current attenders are involved in small groups. Clearly, a significant percentage of seeker church attenders have discovered the benefits of small group involvement. It is perhaps worth mentioning that few of these small groups are autonomous within the larger church body. Most are under the close supervision of the church staff. According to the SCP survey, half of all seeker church pastors (50 percent) claim that all small group leaders meet regularly with a member of the church staff. Furthermore, three out of four seeker church pastors (75 percent) offer formal training for small group leaders.

Neither the variety of available seeker church small groups nor the division of people among these groups is completely arbitrary. Seeker church pastors frequently arrange people into small groups based on people's ages and demographic backgrounds. For example, one nondenominational church in Illinois offers a group for younger singles called Impact; a group called Oasis for people in their mid-thirties and up; a Homebuilders group for young married couples and singles between thirty-three and thirty-nine years old; a Fabulous Forties group for people in their forties; and Primetime, a group for people fifty and up. This church also offers people the opportunity to participate in recovery ministries such as "Free Indeed," a group for dependents, as well as specialized support groups for parents of children with attention deficit disorder, individuals coping with grief and loss, and women who have experienced miscarriages. Willow Creek has a similar range of small group options, including four types of small groups—disciple making, community, service, and seeker[43]—as well as an extensive array of self-help groups such as Alanon, Al-Akids, Adult Children of Alcoholics, Narcotics Anonymous, Emotions Anonymous, Overeaters Anonymous, Sexaholics Anonymous, and Coda for those trying to maintain healthy relationships.

Although Willow Creek did not initially stress small group development, the church now regards small groups as essential to its mission. Bill Hybels writes, "One of my biggest regrets is not improving our small-group structure earlier in order to accommodate growth and ensure that leaders . . . didn't burn out."[44] Willow Creek has even developed and written its own small group curriculum, entitled *Walking with God*. The goal of the first study guide in the series, called *Friendship with God*, is for "participants to discover the God who loves them, who sought them out, and [who] wants to be their best friend."[45]

One explanation for this burgeoning interest in small groups is that these groups provide participants with an intimate home within the church. Just as the seeker service models itself after the large, impersonal institutions of American public life, small groups represent the intimate, private sphere that is, to borrow from the title of a book by Christopher Lasch, a "haven in a heartless world." And these "havens," by virtue of their informality and intimacy, often encourage a dramatic shift in church fellowship and instruction away from doctrinally oriented study toward relationally oriented caring. As one pastor of an Evangelical Presbyterian church in Michigan put it, "The issue [for these groups] is not knowledge. The issue is application." One author who has studied this phenomenon, predicts that this shift from doctrinal instruction to emotional support means that the churches of the future "will be known primarily as caring places rather than as teaching associations. . . . They [will have] shifted their priorities from teaching to caring, from understanding to application."[46]

Small groups are not only influencing seeker churches, they are "effecting a quiet revolution in American society."[47] Paradoxically, this revolution is a sign both of the strength of American churches and of the growing influence of non-Christian spirituality in contemporary culture. First, it is a sign of church strength that people are flocking to churches, and joining small groups, in the hope of encountering God. Yet it also demonstrates the secularity of culture, in that the God whom people encounter in small groups is a domesticated God—a God who is more of an internal presence and friend than an external authority and eternal ruler. In small groups, "the sacred becomes more personal" and, as a consequence, also "becomes more manageable, more serviceable in meeting individual needs, and more a feature of group processes themselves."[48] In other words, small groups may encourage religious seekers to view God as a buddy, a reassuring Presence that heals our wounds and guides us in our daily lives.

Small groups not only can domesticate God but can also perpetuate a view of God as "eminently useful." According to this view, knowing God is the key to having a successful life. That is, by stressing God's practical guidance for everyday living, small groups encourage a pragmatic view of the sacred. In his writings on this subject, Wuthnow cautions that the spirituality of small groups all too often makes the individual—and the goal of meeting the individual's needs—the measure of all things.[49] In this sense, small groups initiate a subtle change in our perceptions of God. When viewed from a purely pragmatic standpoint, God becomes the means toward our fulfillment, rather than the end toward whom we owe total allegiance. Moreover, in the intimacy of small group discussions, "the sacred comes to be associated with the small insights that seem intuitively correct to the small group, rather than the wisdom [that has] accrued over the centuries in hermitages, seminaries, universities, congregations, and church councils."[50] Another risk of small groups, for churches at least, is that there is no reason why they have to be associated with churches. People might initially join a group through a church, but, Wuthnow cautions, "sooner or later, people will discover that they can hold these groups just as well in their living rooms, at work, or in the town hall."[51]

In sum, small groups, ironically, are both a prominent manifestation of evangelical vitality in America and a fountainhead of subtle theological adaptation. As Wuthnow sees it, "the small-group movement is currently playing a major role in *adapting* American religion to the main currents of secular culture that have surfaced at the end of the twentieth century."[52] Small groups are one important—but not the only important—component of the seeker church strategy to adapt the form and packaging of Christianity so as to increase Christianity's appeal to seekers.

Developing Leadership:
Managing the Shopping Mall Church

While programs such as small groups are important to the growth of the church, seeker church leaders suggest that perhaps the single most important factor affecting the church is the quality of its leadership. In some cases, training in effective seeker church strategies has eclipsed training in the more traditional pastoral area of theology. Seeker church pastors maintain that, while the skills required for leading churches have changed, the nature of the church has not. Corporate strategies are simply a means to the end of building Christian community. Furthermore, seeker church pastors argue that by focusing on developing the gifts of people rather than on perpetuating programs ("But, we've always done it this way!") seeker church leaders are, in effect, representing a less bureaucratized and more holistic approach to ministry.

Managing the shopping mall church often requires the skills of a corporate executive. According to the SCP survey, three out of five pastors (61 percent) agree that "Pastors increasingly need to function as chief executive officers in their churches." Pastors, of course, have multiple responsibilities in the church. The survey asked pastors to rank separately the importance of six different tasks. These tasks were: (1) casting a vision for the church; (2) communicating to today's seekers; (3) learning more about theology; (4) managing the church's programs; (5) shepherding staff and lay leaders; and (6) working for social justice. Casting a vision (99 percent), communicating to seekers (89 percent), and shepherding staff and laity (76 percent) were the responsibilities that pastors most likely considered "very important." In contrast, only 6 percent of pastors said that working for social justice was very important to their job. The responsibilities that pastors were most likely to consider "somewhat important" were managing the church's programs (68 percent), followed by learning more about theology (60 percent). About half (51 percent) of all pastors surveyed considered working for social justice "somewhat important." Clearly, working for social justice is considered the least important pastoral role on this scale of six responses, while casting a vision for the church is the most important. Although pastors may not question the importance of social justice, they do question its "effectiveness" as a ministry to seekers. Let us look more closely at the political and social stances of seeker churches.

The Apolitical Stance of Seeker Churches

Leaders of the seeker church movement generally consider political activism an obstacle to evangelistic effectiveness. As a consequence, they generally avoid railing against secular society or bemoaning the "un-Christian" state of America. Only one out of three (33 percent) seeker church pastors agreed with the statement "It is important for religious organizations to try to persuade elected officials." There was even less support for direct church involvement in political affairs. Less than one out of every seven pastors (14 percent) agreed with the statement "Churches and pastors should become more involved in politics."

There are both pragmatic and theological reasons for this reluctance to engage in political activities. On the pragmatic side, because seeker churches strive to attract as many people as possible to their services, they must minimize the reasons why seekers might avoid coming to church. For example, to insist that all Christians vote for prolife candidates would clearly alienate those visitors who are not committed to the prolife position. Willow Creek's Hybels notes, "As a church, we've been scrupulous about staying out of partisan politics, because there can be legitimate differences of opinion among Christians about how certain biblical values can best be translated into public policies in a pluralistic society."[53] Similarly, Pastor Michael Foss is convinced that "you can be a Christian on either side of [issues such as abortion and homosexuality]." Foss adds, "[T]hese are side issues. What we're about is spiritual renewal."[54] Another practical reason that seeker churches tend to eschew political activity has to do with issues of legality. As one pastor pointed out, a church's tax-exempt status prohibits its involvement in direct political activity.

The theological reason that many seeker churches are not politically active is that, for seeker churches, the essentials of the faith do not include a commitment to certain political positions. Many pastors argue in effect that they labor "for a Kingdom not of this world." Furthermore, although the Bible has political and social implications, it does not spell out clear directives on many of today's important policy issues. Bill Hybels, for example, notes that Willow Creek would only take a political stand on an issue that was clearly spelled out in the Bible. "When Scripture is silent on a matter of conscience," says Hybels, "we don't push it."[55] Hybels cites school prayer and the nuclear freeze as two contemporary controversies on which Scripture is silent.

It seems unlikely that seeker churches will ever explicitly embrace any form of political action. One pastor of a nondenominational church in Pennsylvania described his church's opposition to political involvement:

> We never take political stands. For a few years we avoided taking controversial stands on issues like abortion. We felt that our mission was to bring people to Christ and we don't want to alienate people on the basis of things they don't believe in such as being pro-life. . . . We don't take political stands because we don't want to muddy our purpose. Our purpose is to bring people into the Kingdom and to grow them up. We then encourage people on an individual basis to be involved socially and politically, to be agents of change. We encourage people to be individually involved in those things. We don't organize anti-abortion marches, although we would support someone who did.

Political activism is not the only kind of social action that might distract seeker churches from their main task. One pastor of a nondenominational church in Florida, when asked what kinds of community involvement programs the church supported, responded, "That's not us. That's one of those things we just don't have time for. We're pretty much maxed with what we're doing right now." Pressed to speculate on whether the church was likely to add such programs in the future, this pastor responded, "Absolutely not. Some churches are real community oriented, or they're real [social] action and politically oriented. That's just not us."

While this church may be more reluctant than others to engage in community programs, it is safe to say that political and social involvement are not priorities at most seeker churches. One reason is that pastors are finding it enough of a challenge to get seekers to attend church once a week, with perhaps an added small group commitment. One pastor of a Baptist General Conference church in Colorado commented that seekers "are much more demanding than typical Christians who have been members of a church for 20 years. . . . Most of them have never heard of tithing. How are you going to run your church where half the people haven't heard of tithing, much less sacrificing their already busy time to go out and help support poor people or do missions."

Seekers may not be outwardly focused, but this does not preclude the possibility that some core members of seeker churches are politically active. In fact, there is good reason to expect that many members of conservative evangelical churches might be politically active. For example, at Saddleback Valley Community Church, I noticed some prolife pamphlets on display at an information table. Yet seeker church pastors are unlikely to try to mobilize their congregations on behalf of particular social or political causes. According to Saddleback's Rick Warren, the five New Testament purposes of the church are worship, ministry, evangelism, fellowship, and discipleship.[56] Working for social justice or issuing prophetic jeremiads does not readily fit into this list of purposes. In contrast, Willow Creek lists four purposes of the church: "exaltation, edification, evangelism, and extension [social action]."[57] Willow Creek participates in various inner-city Chicago and foreign ministries, but this involvement is a relatively recent development in the church's history.

Pastors may choose to address social and moral issues in their teaching, but they do so primarily to influence the opinions of attenders not to serve as a catalyst to reform movements. Willow Creek, for example, once gave a series of messages on homosexuality, divorce, and abortion.[58] While espousing conservative positions on these matters, the Willow Creek series was not designed to mobilize the attenders into the Greater Chicago chapter of the Christian Coalition or any type of political action group. Thus, while there might be some sympathy for conservative political causes among the members of seeker churches, church leaders typically avoid direct political involvement. The typical seeker church leader concentrates on proclaiming the message of salvation, and devising and refining outreach strategies with the entrepreneurial zeal of a corporate CEO.

The Pastor As CEO

For a pastor to be a successful CEO, he or she will need training in specific business techniques geared toward improving the effectiveness of the church. Aware of this need, church growth consultants advertise training seminars for pastors; these seminars specialize in the principles that underlie church growth. For example, Pastor Rick Warren's "How to Build a Purpose-Driven Church" offers participants the opportunity to learn "an innovative, comprehensive ministry process that moves your people from conversion to maturity. . . audience to army . . . crowd to a core!"[59] The Charles E. Fuller Institute's church planting seminar promises attenders that they will learn "how to minimize [their] risk and maximize [their] potential by equipping [them] with the essentials for a successful church plant." Many of the consultants featured at such seminars are either former pastors at successful churches or management experts and survey researchers who specialize in strategies for church growth. Thus, seeker church clergy are increasingly influenced by organizational principles that have only a tenuous connection to theology.

Another way of ensuring that churches are led by effective executives is to hire former business leaders as head pastors. One seeker church did exactly that. An assistant pastor of a nondenominational church in California told me that this was the first church position for the senior pastor. Previously, he was "a businessman, very successful for many years. Then [he] started up a ministry to businessmen."

In order to carry out its growth strategy, Willow Creek has developed an organizational infrastructure that is distinctly corporate in form. For example, Willow Creek has produced an organizational chart that indicates the departments and lines of authority within the church. Pastoral, administrative, and programming responsibilities are separated into three departments. This division of labor corresponds exactly to the three revolutions in therapeutic, management, and communications techniques that John Seel suggests are part of the megachurch movement's new way of "doing church."[60] These three departments report to the senior pastor, who, like a corporate chief executive officer, reports to a board of directors. One change currently underway at Willow Creek is the separation of the teaching from the leadership functions of the senior pastor, so that those gifted with leadership skills will not bear all of the teaching and preaching responsibilities and may offer "what chief executive officers provide companies within a corporate environment."[61] At Willow Creek, Bill Hybels has begun to assume that executive role, while new pastoral staffers undertake more of the preaching and teaching responsibilities.

The administrative coordination required at Willow Creek is extensive. Sermon series are planned nine months in advance so that all departments can coordinate their focus in accord with each week's theme. Staff members are required to submit progress reports prior to weekly staff meetings; these reports list each department's progress toward fulfilling set goals. Even the laity are actively incorporated into the church's organizational structure. After participants complete the four week Networking seminar, they are urged to join a ministry within the church that will best use their skills. No wonder management expert Peter Drucker praises Willow Creek as an example of how productive an organization can be if it is driven by a clear sense of mission and a focus on results.[62] As with any successful organization, success is dependent upon the direction provided by leaders.

As seeker churches emulate the corporate world, they are developing their own forms of professionalization and certification. Positions within seeker churches are often quite specialized; this creates a market for training that is not typically provided by seminaries. For example, in addition to a senior pastor, seeker churches often have administrative pastors; directors of programming; and coordinators for small groups, adult ministries, children's programs, and more. As new seeker churches develop, they are likely to look for staff who have trained for these specialized positions at other seeker churches. Currently, Willow Creek provides the institutional mechanism for a seeker church referral network with Willow Creek's monthly publication, *The Exchange*, a job listing whose purpose is "connecting churches and prospective staff members." The positions advertised in *The Exchange* reflect the increasing specialization of the ministry. For example, one pastor advertises his seeker church experience: "Experienced associate pastor seeks seeker-targeted church to serve in areas of small group development, administration, and/or programming and worship. Seeker-targeted and SBC (Southern Baptist Convention) church staff experience."[63] Other pastors advertise their expertise in drama, discipleship, exhortation, worship leading, leadership, developing small groups based on the meta-church model, and team building. One church is seeking a director of programming who "must be very creative and sold out to the Willow Creek vision and philosophy" in order to plan weekly seeker and believer's services.

Even the terminology reflects the specialization of seeker church positions. Most senior staff members, other than the senior pastor, are called directors. In many cases, directors are not pastors at all but have been trained in the business world in their areas of expertise (for example, theater, communications, and/or music). One of the clearest examples of this changing understanding of the pastorate is found at one of the churches in my interview sample. This nondenominational church in Illinois does not ordain pastors, which is the task of denominations, but *licenses* them. "Licensing" is a term that describes the professional certification used by trade organizations; it connotes a more rationalized view of the pastor's role compared to the theological implications of ordination.

The most dramatic change in the certification of pastors at seeker churches is the number of pastors who have never attended seminary. Bill Hybels, who founded Willow Creek when he was twenty-three, is the most prominent example. The majority of senior pastors I interviewed had graduated from seminary, but several had not. Some of these pastors participated instead in a one- or two-year internship at Willow Creek. To the extent that the "licensing" of pastors and the move away from seminary training foreshadow future trends, these developments represent a major shift in the professional training of, and expectations for, ministers. According to Schaller, large churches like Willow Creek are challenging the need for seminary by developing and training staff from within.[64] At Willow Creek, for example, over 95 percent of the paid staff have been developed from within the church.[65]

Effectiveness as a Moral Category

What is the sociological significance of seeker churches' embrace of management principles and resulting clergy specialization? In his insightful critique of contemporary moral discourse, *After Virtue*, Alasdair MacIntyre suggests that the manager is the dominant figure of the contemporary scene. "The manager," according to MacIntyre, "represents in his character the obliteration of the distinction between manipulative and non-manipulative social relations. . . . The manager treats ends as [a] given, as outside his scope; his concern is with technique."[66] For the church growth manager, the ends justify the means. One church growth expert acknowledges the inherent dilemmas of just such a utilitarian approach to religious leadership, yet qualifies it by stating, "When I assert that the ends justifies the means in strategy planning, I am referring to value-neutral means only, not to immoral means."[67] This quotation demonstrates a problematic assumption implicit in all seeker church strategies that the means to achieving church growth are value-neutral. I would argue, however, that effectiveness, though not a theological concept, is nevertheless a value-laden concept. MacIntyre concurs: "There are strong grounds for rejecting the claim that effectiveness is a morally neutral value." He continues, "We are unaccustomed to think[ing] of effectiveness as a distinctly *moral* concept, to be classed with such concepts as those of rights or of utility."[68] In contrast, when understood as a morally neutral concept, effectiveness legitimates practices that produce growth. Thus, seeker church pastors who embrace the view that effectiveness is neutral ask not "are the methods true?" but "do the methods work?"

One result of the assumption that effectiveness is neutral is that "managers conceive of themselves as morally neutral characters whose skills enable them to devise the most efficient means for achieving whatever end is proposed." In the case of the seeker church movement, pastors, because they are also managers, can justify "their claims to authority, power, and money by invoking their own *competence* as scientific managers of change."[69] Thus, pastors and church growth theorists promote those methods which produce results (that is, methods that "God has blessed"). Furthermore, the pastor/manager justifies his or her position not just on the basis of technical competence and knowledge of morally "neutral" facts but also on the knowledge of "a set of factual law-like generalizations which enable the manager to predict" the results of applying specific techniques.[70]

The seeker church movement's understanding of the church as a business indicates that the moral authority of seeker churches rests not on their theological premises but on their technical expertise buttressed by social science. Prominent ministers are known not so much for their skill in communicating the doctrines of the church and the revelation of Scripture, but instead for having mastered the rational techniques of church growth. Os Guinness concurs by noting that, with the rise of professional church growth experts, "traditional authority, such as [the] clergy, have been replaced by modern authorities—denominational leaders by church growth experts."[71] Seeker church strategies are based on principles such as efficiency and cost-effectiveness. This indicates that, in an increasingly secular and pluralistic society, moral authority based upon traditional or religious roots is suspect. James Hunter's research on evangelicalism supports this assertion. He argues that in a pluralistic situation "moral authority . . . is defined by and based upon technical competence, empirical adequacy, and linguistic precision of the positions taken. Thus, moral options in human society . . . are increasingly shaped by the values implicit in technical rationality."[72] Seeker church leaders often are well regarded not for their religious or theological expertise but instead for their managerial ability to guide churches to growth.

Summation: The Shopping Mall Church as Ideology

What does the rise of the seeker church tell us about religion in American society? On the one hand, the popularity of seeker churches reveals the continuing vitality and creativity of evangelical Protestantism. Dynamic young pastors such as Bill Hybels and Rick Warren embarked on the ambitious project of creating radically new models of church. Clearly, the evangelical message of repentance and conversion is still able to motivate Christians to sacrifice themselves for a cause.

Although the seeker church movement reveals the vitality of American evangelicalism, the nature of the strategies it employs also illustrates some of the profound challenges facing traditional religious institutions. Forms such as a seeker service or shopping mall church are not only a means of organizing to achieve a particular end. They also are carriers of cultural assumptions (such as efficiency and rationality) that define what those ends are. The seeker church movement recognizes that forms make a difference—that is why the movement has developed new forms—but may underestimate other effects of changing forms. Changing the *method* can not only change your results; it can also change your *message*.

As seeker churches embrace an ethic of civility (evident in their deemphasis of religious symbols and denominational identity and studious avoidance of political activism), the form and flow of their religious services are increasingly defined by the music, style, and concerns of the secular realm. For example, even those outside the boundaries of the religious community are politely referred to simply as the "unchurched" (as opposed to the "lost" or the "damned"). To a society increasingly characterized by market segmentation and the proliferation of new "lifestyles," seeker churches offer a diverse array of religious and secular products and services.[73] Moreover, the leaders of seeker churches do not embrace the comparatively strict inner-worldly asceticism of their Protestant predecessors but instead impart an expressive, individualized faith that celebrates the exploration of the self and its needs. Meanwhile, as churches shape their ministries around the findings of demographic and market research (for example, asking "what do baby boomers want"?), pastoral responsibilities increasingly include business and management skills—and not necessarily theological training. Seeker church leaders are sought for their leadership experience, their ability to understand the culture, and their enthusiasm for outreach. These are certainly admirable skills, but they owe more to the findings and authority of the social sciences than to the theological training previously demanded of pastors.

Again, it is my contention that the seeker church practice of emulating "the shopping mall" does not delineate one fixed program for attracting seekers and achieving growth but instead represents a particular ideology of outreach that justifies an innovative, seeker strategy.[74] Ideology, as defined by Wuthnow, "consists of symbols that express or dramatize something about the moral order."[75] Thus, the ideology of the shopping mall church expresses two related notions about the moral order. First, it expresses the idea that religion has become a privatized, consumer good. People "buy" religious products, much as they would buy products at the mall. Second, the ideology of the shopping mall church not only *describes* the preferences of religious consumers but also *prescribes* how churches should respond to these preferences—churches should aim to have the best product available that conforms with the expectations fostered by today's religious environment.

The central research question concerning ideology should explain "why particular ideologies or ideological themes (patterns) exist in some situations and not in others."[76] What are the social conditions that produce certain ideologies and not others? First, according to Wuthnow, there must be some form of disturbance in the moral order that leads to the production of new ideologies. For seeker churches (and American religion in general), the source of disturbance clearly is linked to the trends documented in chapter 2 of this book, such as the decline in denominational loyalty, the rise of special-purpose groups, and the eclectic spiritual interests of "a generation of seekers." Second, there is a selection phase in which ideologies compete for scarce resources, with the eventual result that some ideological forms are "selected for" and others "selected against." Finally, ideologies undergo a phase of institutionalization (such as the development of the Willow Creek Association) that makes them less vulnerable to competition.[77]

The ideology of the shopping mall church (or seeker church) is institutionalized in the Willow Creek Association, which one could classify as a special-purpose group. Because of their carefully limited goals, special-purpose groups are particularly likely to succeed in a heterogeneous environment. (Their rapid growth in the last few decades testifies to their adaptability.) Special-purpose groups are also likely to develop "pragmatic norms of evaluation, technical competence, specialization, and proper procedure."[78] The ideology of the shopping mall church legitimates practices such as evaluating whether or not religious symbols might drive away seekers, creating exciting services that meet the needs of seekers, and systematizing strategies. While this ideology encourages certain innovative practices, it also imposes some constraints on how religious organizations can function. For example, traditional practices that are not seeker-friendly are likely to be thrown out and replaced by more customer-sensitive practices. The enthusiastic embrace of the shopping mall ideology by many pastors suggests that, while seeker churches will continue to adapt to the current environment, the crucial question of whether religion "maintains a critical role in relation to its environment or whether it compromises in serious ways" may remain unasked.[79] One pastor of a Baptist church in California summarized the tension between the church's message and the means to promote it:

I think it's very easy for this kind of church when you use business language . . . to start acting like a corporation, rather than the church of God, and depending on ourselves and our strategies rather than the Holy Spirit. . . . I see a tendency in our church . . . to adopt the latest strategy from Barna, from Willow Creek, or from somebody else and use that rather than follow God's guidance.

Another important—and quite different—question is whether seeker churches are somehow transforming their environment, particularly in the more limited context of denominations. There is a great deal of evidence to suggest that Willow Creek, Saddleback, and other successful seeker churches are creating a new form of denomination—or at least have an influence and authority among many pastors that is more significant than any denominational affiliation. How this influence, as institutionalized in the Willow Creek Association, translates into a what I call a postmodern denomination is the subject of the chapter that follows.

Six

I think that the Willow Creek Association will become [a denomination].
It's still in its formative stages.[1]

Organization: The Postmodern Denomination

The remarkable growth of the Willow Creek Association (WCA)—from two hundred members in 1992 to more than five thousand in 2000—documents Willow Creek's role as the organizational center of a movement to renew and re-form the American church. It also points to the sociological significance of the seeker church movement in an era of declining denominational attachment. While WCA is not formally a denomination—it eschews certain traditional denominational functions—it nevertheless can be considered a type of denomination because of its critical role in defining a seeker church "liturgy," creating resources for seeker church worship, providing training for staff, and organizing networks for sharing information and hiring staff. The paradoxical effect of the seeker church movement's response to the declining significance of denominationalism is to create a new type of denomination, one based on methodological contract more than on theological covenant.

In the WCA, the methodological contract (or interchurch obligation) is defined by the market: Have churches paid their membership fee? Just as religious consumers pick and choose from a cafeteria of religious choices, so too are seeker churches now choosing which suppliers of religious goods will best meet their needs. Thus, the WCA provides a type of "pay as you go" denominational assistance for churches trying to meet the felt needs of seekers. Rather than agreeing to contribute an annual fee or a tithe to a denomination, churches simply pay for the services they want from the WCA—or any other innovative church. Religious authority structures, such as denominations, will have less and less influence over what resources these churches use. Although the influence of the marketplace upon American Christianity is not new, what is new, according to Lyle Schaller, "is that marketplace is now the widely used system of evaluation used by church-goers."[2] And by seeker churches as well.

Denominational Realignment

Why has the seeker church movement emerged now and why has it become so influential within evangelicalism? In chapter 2, I suggested several answers to these questions. An environment characterized by decreasing loyalty to denominations and people's increasing willingness to change their church, denomination, or even religion poses a crisis to conventional religious organizations. High religious "dropout" rates pose profound challenges to churches—as well as great opportunities for those churches that are able to entice religious dropouts back into the pews (or comfortable, padded seats). The emergence of the seeker church is a response to the sense of crisis caused in part by people's decreasing levels of denominational commitment. This crisis has prompted innovations among religious institutions—innovations such as the seeker church movement.

One response by innovative churches to this changing religious environment has been to downplay formal theology in their messages. While theology may be important to pastors and church members, to many seekers it can seem abstract and irrelevant. The search for meaning or purpose in this life is the core spiritual concern of many contemporary seekers. To these seekers, the theology of a church is less important than the church's ability to meet their needs. Many seeker church pastors seem intuitively to understand this state of affairs. When asked whether "the theology of a seeker church is one of its most attractive elements to seekers," less than one out of three pastors (31 percent) agreed. Discovering what, if not theology, is attractive to seekers—and how to present theology in a more appealing guise—is at the heart of the seeker church movement.

One of the broadest points of agreement among many church leaders is that the old ways of organizing church ministry are no longer adequate. Church consultant Ken Blanchard articulates this view when he claims that "[t]he thinking that got you where you are today will not take you to the future."[3] Similarly, the Reverend Walter Kallestad of the seven-thousand-member Community Church of Joy outside Phoenix suggests that "[w]e can't expect to keep doing the same thing and have different results. The Christian church is in decline."[4] The authors of *Marketing for Congregations* substantiate Kallestad's assessment by arguing that "[r]eligious organizations in America are facing a crisis. The percentage of persons not connected to a church or synagogue in virtually every county of the United States is greater than ever before in the history of our country. For the first time in history there are more non-Christians than Christians in America, making ours a 'functionally atheistic' society."[5] Leith Anderson, a prominent evangelical pastor and author, argues in his book *Dying for Change* that the new realities confronting churches in a highly mobile, consumer-oriented society require dramatic changes in the organization and philosophy of church ministry. The church that is ready for the future will make these changes. Churches that do not change, according to Anderson, will eventually die.[6]

The origins of Willow Creek stem from its founders' conviction that without major organizational changes, the church will not be effective in the current religious environment. The founders of Willow Creek were motivated by a sense that the traditional church was not prepared to connect with the needs and concerns of people today. The old paradigm was not effective anymore. The innovations pioneered by Willow Creek, Community Church of Joy, Leith Anderson, and others are a response to the sense of crisis perceived by evangelicals as they sought to proclaim the Gospel to a populace decreasingly interested in or committed to Christian beliefs or institutions.

This sense of crisis within evangelicalism is well documented in the Seeker Church Pastor (SCP) survey by the responses of seeker church pastors to questions on the current influence of religion in the United States, the trends in religion, and the effectiveness of evangelical churches in the current environment. The vast majority of seeker church pastors (97 percent) believe that the influence of religion in the United States is "too low." Almost two out of three pastors (62 percent) believe that the influence of religion in the United States is either declining or staying about the same.[7] In order to increase the influence of evangelical churches, these pastors overwhelmingly agreed that major changes are needed in the church's strategies. For most of these pastors, the most promising change is the seeker church. An overwhelming majority (95 percent) agree that the influence of seeker churches is increasing in American society. For many pastors the seeker church movement represents the best hope to reverse the troubling trends in church influence in the United States.

The sense of crisis is perhaps even more acute for denominations than for churches. While individual churches may be thriving, their denominations often are not. In fact, a large, successful church is often able to retain some independence apart from its denomination precisely because of its size and success. For example, Robert Schuller's Crystal Cathedral is not generally known as a member of the Reformed Church in America. Its success gives it an identity independent of its denomination. Even smaller churches sense the limited prospects for denominations. "The bottom line is that denominationalism is dying," suggested the Reverend Jason Garcia, associate pastor of Newport-Mesa Center in Costa Mesa, California, an Assemblies of God church. "We're proud of our denomination but we're trying to open . . . [our church] up for anyone searching for the Lord."[8] Many churches are increasingly willing to try new approaches that may not have the support of their denominations. Rather than relying on their denominations for guidance, many of these innovative churches join networks such as the Willow Creek Association, the Leadership Network, and Robert Schuller's Churches Uniting in Global Mission, that provide services tailored to their particular needs. In sum, denominations have been too slow, according to many seeker churches, to adapt to the postdenominational (and even post-Christian) era. They are too invested in traditional forms of ministry that fail to connect with people today.

The Professional Association as Denomination

Willow Creek is a model—perhaps *the* model—for numerous churches looking for new ways to reach an increasingly unchurched population. The WCA, according to its informational brochure, is "an international network of churches ministering to the unchurched." Founded in 1992, the Willow Creek Association serves churches by providing conferences, seminars, regional round tables, consulting services, and resource materials. Its mission is "to help churches turn irreligious people into fully devoted followers of Christ."[9] Churches may become members of the Association by: "1) affirming their commitment to the Evangelical Christian faith; 2) demonstrating their desire to reach lost people for Christ through implementing appropriate strategies in their church; and 3) submitting the annual membership fee."[10]

What kind of denomination might the WCA be? Like the church after which it is named, the WCA leads the way as an innovative and untraditional denomination. Bishops, priests, presbyters, elders, deacons, seminaries, and other forms common to particular denominations are of course nowhere to be found in the WCA. But it fulfills many important denominational *functions*, ranging from defining a standard "liturgy," to training and teaching. One pastor of a nondenominational church in Pennsylvania commented that although the WCA claims that it does not intend to function as a denomination, "[The WCA] is a new, modern form of denomination. It doesn't require the same things that old denominational life required in terms of assent to a more specific creed. But in terms of the pragmatics of how you do things, it does say we all share the idea of doing drama and here are the resources. We all are doing contemporary music and here are some score sheets. It's a very practical way of associating people together." In other words, the WCA's form differs from traditional denominations, but many of its functions do not. The WCA is a practical, pragmatic, task- and training-oriented organization that has defined what ministry should be like in the 1990s to such an extent that it is creating a homogeneity of form and congregational culture closely resembling older types of denominational identity.

Some, however, might object to the contention that the Association is functioning like a denomination, on the grounds that many of its member churches are already affiliated with denominations. Yet numerous WCA churches are either nondenominational or maintain loose affiliations with their denominations. For example, one pastor of a Nazarene church in California said, " I rely 90 percent on other seeker churches. I wouldn't be where I am now without other seeker churches." A church's affiliation with a denomination does not necessarily indicate the relative influence of that denomination upon a specific church compared to the influence of other seeker churches upon that same church. Almost two-thirds (63 percent) of the U.S. churches listed in the 1994 Willow Creek *Church Associates Directory* do not display any denominational affiliation in their name (see table 6.1). According

_____ *Table 6.1* _____

Willow Creek Association Churches by Denominational Affiliation,
Based on Church Listing (N)

Community church	Other non-denominational	Baptist	Presbyterian	Other de-nomination	Total
32.8%	30.8%	19.1%	3.8%	13.5%	100%
(199)	(187)	(116)	(23)	(82)	(607)

Source: Church Associates Directory, Willow Creek Association, 6 July 1994.

to the SCP survey, even though most WCA member churches (75 percent) are affiliated with a denomination, the majority of seeker churches surveyed (56 percent) do not list a denomination on the church's main sign. In other words, seeker churches are more likely than not to appear to be nondenominational to visitors.

One of the most common types of church name in the WCA directory is that of a nondenominational community church such as Coast Hills Community Church, Horizons Community Church, CrossWinds Church, or Oakbrook Community Church. Many of the denominational WCA churches find that other seeker churches have more influence upon their practices than their own denomination does. For example, the Nazarene pastor mentioned earlier also said, "If it got to the point where I'd have to cut off an effective ministry to unchurched people to support the denomination, I'd have to think real hard about [leaving]." In my interview sample, nine out of the twenty-four churches were affiliated with a denomination, but only three of the nine denominational churches included the affiliation in their name. The other six churches downplayed their denominational affiliation. One church emphasized its denomination primarily in membership class as an assurance to prospective members that the church had some supervisory oversight. Denominations may provide resources to some of these churches by training ministers or providing publications, but denominations often are not closely tied to these churches.

Others might object to the argument that the WCA is functioning like a denomination by claiming that it has no intention of becoming a denomination. Bill Hybels, for example, describes himself as "adenominational," not "antidenominational." "I just don't think [denominations are] the wave of the future. I see very little loyalty to denominations anymore, especially among non-churched people."[11] Similarly, the WCA claims that it is simply a service agency, not a denomination. Jim Mellado, president of the WCA, writes that "[w]e have zero desire to be like a denomination or get involved in many of the important things that they do (school systems, hospitals, seminary training, missionary programs, authority structures, ordination, etc.)." The WCA, Mellado suggests, will focus on writing conference curricula, training pastors, and developing products that add "value directly to local churches that want our help."[12]

Furthermore, the pastors of seeker churches generally hold denominations in low regard, viewing them as too bureaucratic and tradition-bound to reach seekers effectively and creatively. Denominations, in sum, are part of the old paradigm of church ministry. The *NetFax* monthly newsletter, a one-page briefing for pastors, produced by the Leadership Network, suggests that "complex, hierarchical, and bureaucracy centered" structures are part of the "Christendom" paradigm for ministry, which is less effective today. Churches and organizations that operate in the "new apostolic paradigm" are "flexible, contextual, and local church centered" in their structure. Rather than belonging to formalized denominations, new paradigm churches collaborate instead by means of "short term, for specific purpose networks."[13] A staff member at the Leadership Network, a church consulting organization, adds, "[T]here's no question that many pastors are looking more toward Willow Creek, Saddleback, and other churches than to denominations for modeling and resources. Denominations have been very slow to respond."

Because denominations are part of the "old paradigm" of ministry, it is not surprising that many seeker church pastors hold denominations in low regard. Three out of four seeker church pastors (74 percent) in the SCP survey disagreed with the statement "Christians should remain loyal to one denomination throughout their adult lives." Half of the pastors surveyed (50 percent) agreed that "doctrinal differences are no longer clear enough to keep members from switching their membership to other denominations." According to this thinking, one reason why Christians should not feel obligated to remain loyal to one denomination is that the doctrinal differences between denominations are no longer of major significance. Doctrine is, of course, important to seeker church pastors, as their strongly evangelical views on Scripture, Jesus Christ, and the afterlife indicate (see chapter 1). But denominational boundaries are less likely to mark significant doctrinal, cultural, and social differences in American life. Denominations are losing much of their theological distinctiveness while they are, at the same time, increasingly divided between theologically liberal and theologically conservative factions.[14] As a result, Baptist, Presbyterian, Methodist, and nondenominational churches are all just as likely and just as capable of adopting a seeker church model.

Another reason that the WCA is reluctant to claim it is performing denominational functions is that many pastors are skeptical that denominations actually deliver on their promises. For example, the existence of denominational authority structures, such as bishops or presbyters, is no guarantee that orthodox theology will be maintained. As one pastor of a nondenominational church in Pennsylvania put it, "I don't think the denominational system is effective at maintaining orthodoxy." An additional reason that many seeker church pastors do not place much emphasis on denominations is that many of them serve in churches that are of a different denomination than the seminary in which they were trained—or no denomination at all. More than half of all seeker church pastors surveyed (52 percent) are serving in a church that is of a different denomination than that of the seminary in which they were trained. (This figure may slightly exaggerate the extent to which pastors serve in churches that do not belong to the denomination in which they trained, since pastors who went to nondenominational seminaries are included in the figure.) When looking only at denominational seeker churches, more than one out of three pastors (37 percent) is serving in a church that is of a denomination different from the seminary in which the pastor trained.

This pattern of crossing denominational boundaries will most likely continue and even expand among seeker churches as the efficacy of the old denominational system continues its decline. The denominational identity of a church is no longer considered crucial to a seeker church. Instead, the most important distinguishing characteristic of churches today, according to seeker church pastors, is their seeker sensitivity. The vast majority of seeker church pastors (90 percent) agreed with the statement "the seeker sensitivity of a church today is more important than its denominational affiliation." Seeker sensitivity often eclipses denominational identity as the defining characteristic of the church for many pastors.

And therein lies a great irony. While seeker church pastors express their disillusionment with denominations to the extent that many do not even display their affiliation on their church's main sign, they are also participating in the formation of a new type of denomination: one based on contractual, rather than covenantal, ties; on specific functions rather than general forms; and on networks of mutual benefit rather than hierarchies of religious authority. What is most distinctive about this new form of denomination is that it makes little effort to establish any religious authority over its members. In response to the weakness of existing denominations, the seeker church movement is jettisoning those religious authority structures that seem no longer to exercise any meaningful form of authority over its members. What remains are networks of churches united by a common vision, mutual dependence, and the contractual bonds of the WCA.

The Denominational Functions
of the Willow Creek Association

The denominational functions that the WCA performs range from defining a core of beliefs (a seeker church "creed") and a standard liturgy to providing training, conferences, resources, and networking opportunities with potential staff. Perhaps the most compelling evidence that the WCA performs denominational functions comes from the participating pastors themselves, who use the WCA's services while incorporating the seeker church model into their own congregations.

One of the defining aspects of denominational identity is a common statement of faith or form of worship, whether it is the Westminster Confession of Faith for Presbyterians or the *Book of Common Prayer* for Episcopalians. The WCA has a statement of faith that all churches must sign as a condition of membership.[15] By requiring churches that wish to join the WCA to sign its statement of faith, the WCA exercises a form of religious "quality control" over its member churches. This statement is close to other classical Christian statements of belief (affirming the authority of the "inerrant and infallible" Scriptures, the triune nature of God, the full divinity and humanity of Christ, salvation by grace, and the "one true church universal"). In addition to this statement of faith there is Willow Creek's set of ten core values; these are even more instrumental in defining the seeker church movement. They are the basis for a common identity among seeker churches. Bill Hybels says that the ten core values are "the values that distinguish us as an Association, that bind us together."[16] The WCA also claims that these values "transcend any church's size, history, stage of development, denomination, culture, or methodology, and functionally operate as the common denominator of all churches that have joined the seeker movement."[17] The language used by these writers—values that "bind," a "common denominator" that "transcends" the particulars of a church's situation—suggests a unity of purpose that might characterize a denomination.

The ten core values of the seeker movement thus suggest a type of denominational distinctiveness and identity:

1. We believe that full devotion to Christ and His cause is normal for every believer.
2. We believe that a church should operate as a unified community of servants stewarding their spiritual gifts.
3. We believe that lost people matter to God, and therefore, ought to matter to the church.
4. We believe that the church should be culturally relevant while remaining doctrinally pure.
5. We believe that anointed biblical teaching is the catalyst for transformation in individuals' lives and in the church.
6. We believe that Christ followers should manifest authenticity and yearn for continuous growth.
7. We believe that loving relationships should permeate every aspect of church life.
8. We believe that life-change happens best in small groups.
9. We believe that excellence honors God and inspires people.
10. We believe that churches should be led by those with leadership gifts.[18]

These ten values are more than just a set of practical policy suggestions for innovative churches. They are expansive statements covering what the church is, whom it should reach, how it should reach out, and why. Because each of the ten statements of belief open with the words "We believe," the format for this set of values resembles a traditional Christian confession of faith, such as the Nicene or Apostle's Creed. Although these values are not recited in seeker services on a weekly basis, as are some of the historic creeds in liturgical churches, they nevertheless shape the teaching, practice, and approach of many seeker churches. One pastor I interviewed had developed a ten-week sermon series to teach these values to his congregation. Thus, the ten core values guide the practices of seeker churches and also inspire loyalty to the movement.

The WCA also fosters loyalty to the seeker church movement by encouraging its members to build ties with other seeker churches. For example, the WCA *1993 Directory* suggests that association members use the directory to connect with other church leaders and to refer seekers to other Association member churches. Similarly, one edition of the WCA newsletter suggests that, "When people relocate to another city from your church, refer them to WCA churches. . . . WCA provides callers with WCA church names and phone numbers and also offers to send a special packet on how to find a new church home."[19] This is an excellent example of how seeker sensitivity not only has become more important than denominationalism but also has created a sense of loyalty or affection that is akin to denominational identity. Thus, when loyal seeker church attenders move to a new area, instead of searching for another Baptist, Presbyterian, or Methodist church like the one back home, they are quite likely to search for another seeker church, regardless of its denominational affiliation.

One reason a recently relocated individual or family might search for a seeker church to join is that the seeker "liturgy" is rapidly becoming familiar to many American churchgoers. While Willow Creek's seeker service format of praise music, dramas, and relevant preaching is known for its spontaneity and innovation, it is also highly standardized, much like the liturgy of Catholic or Episcopal churches. Notably, despite this standardization, Willow Creek is reluctant to admit that its services are acting as a form of liturgy, especially because Willow Creek pastors associate the word "liturgy" with a routine that lacks spontaneity and excitement, just the things that Willow Creek tries to cultivate in its services. As one Willow Creek staff member said during a conference, "We want to avoid having [a] liturgy. It gets dull and predictable." Despite these disclaimers, the seeker service format is nevertheless becoming the standard by which many churches design their services. This same Willow Creek staff member, when pressed by eager pastors for more information on planning services, did acknowledge that Willow Creek has a standard format for each service, although it varies somewhat to foster excitement and surprise.

Further evidence that the WCA is emerging as a denomination is found in the training materials and job networks upon which seeker churches increasingly rely. When pastors of seeker churches look for help in developing their ministries and hiring staff, they are more likely to use specialized WCA publications and services than denominational or seminary resources. According to the SCP survey, the most likely sources of staff for seeker churches are lay leaders (80 percent), other seeker church pastors (77 percent), and the Willow Creek's monthly employment bulletin, *The Exchange* (64 percent). In contrast, churches are less likely to look for staff from their denominations (50 percent) and seminaries (46 percent).

The influence of the WCA and other seeker churches was even more apparent when pastors were asked where they would turn for information to improve their church's ministry. The WCA was by far the most likely source for information, with two of out three pastors (66 percent) saying they used it frequently and another three out of ten (30 percent) saying they used it occasionally. Similarly, four out of five pastors (80 percent) said they frequently or occasionally looked to pastors of other seeker-friendly churches for information. In contrast, three out of four pastors (74 percent) said they rarely or never used their denomination's publications for information, and the vast majority (88 percent) responded that they rarely or never turned to their seminaries for information. In addition, the WCA, through its regional round tables, church leadership conferences, *Next Step* seminars, consultations, and other resources (such as audio tapes and published materials), provides some of the interchurch contact and programmatic support that denominations traditionally have provided. Clearly, the WCA is on the cutting edge when it comes to training churches and providing job referrals.

The most important source of training for seeker church pastors—and for fostering a sense of loyalty and commitment to the seeker church movement—is the conferences held at Willow Creek. In 1999, the WCA hosted two Church Leadership Conferences (CLC), a Leadership Summit, a Small Groups Conference, Sonlight conferences for youth ministry leaders, a conference for the arts, its first evangelism conference, and regional workshops across the country. Registration for the Leadership Summit was full four months prior to the conference, so the WCA arranged a satellite broadcast of the proceedings to eleven locations around the country. Since 1992, when the WCA was founded, over 65,000 people have attended 33 conferences on-site at Willow Creek, representing 65 countries, 150 denominations, and 8,900 churches.[20] In addition, the WCA is sponsoring sixteen international conferences and training in eight countries.[21] These conferences cover almost every aspect of running a seeker church—from planning seeker services to teaching biblical stewardship and financial responsibility.

At the three-day Church Leadership Conference, attenders learn how to implement Willow Creek's seven-step strategy in their own congregations. One day is dedicated to explicating the principles of building a church to reach the unchurched, to creating a climate of evangelism in the church by applying steps one through three of Willow Creek's strategy, and to designing services for seekers. Another day is dedicated to training pastors to teach those who come to church. This training is imparted through sessions on worship, leadership, and steps four through seven of Willow Creek's strategy. Conference participants can also attend electives on topics such as strengthening evangelism, using the arts, developing small groups, mobilizing volunteers, strengthening adult and youth ministries, and developing leadership.

In case Willow Creek's intensive three-day conference program still does not address all the issues that concern conference participants, there are also several preconference ministry workshops, which range from one to three days in length and provide more focused training. These preconference workshops cover topics such as evangelism; developing disciples; using the arts; ministries to children, youth, and baby busters; and leadership in the church. Willow Creek has also packaged some of these sessions for broader distribution. For example, Willow Creek's evangelism course, "Becoming a Contagious Christian," is available from WCA as a book, an audio cassette, and training manual (complete with leader's guide, participant's guide, overhead masters, and videotaped drama vignettes).

This packaging of Willow Creek's materials and resources means that Willow Creek's conferences mark only the beginning of its services to pastors and churches. In addition to its evangelism course, Willow Creek has produced: *The Source*, a resource guide for using creative arts in church services; a six-volume set of *Sunday Morning Live* (Willow Creek's dramas) available in either book or video format; *Walking with God*, a six-part small-group curriculum complete with leader's guides; and *Network*, "a revolutionary, biblically based program for helping people discover their passion, spiritual gifts, and personal style—and lead them into a meaningful ministry role for service in the church."[22] Willow Creek also offers a subscription tape series, *Defining Moments*, for church leaders, as well as a variety of books produced by Willow Creek staff members including *Inside the Mind of Unchurched Harry and Mary; What Would Jesus Say?; Rediscovering Church; Starting a Seeker Sensitive Service; Atheism vs. Christianity; Christianity 101; Honest To God? Becoming an Authentic Christian; Fit to Be Tied: Making Marriage Last a Lifetime;* and *Descending into Greatness*.[23] By providing pastors with continuing training, resources, and materials, the WCA creates networks of influence that function much like traditional denominational attachments.

The strongest evidence that the Willow Creek Association performs denominational functions comes from its membership. Every pastor I interviewed suggested that the Association had the potential to function like a denomination for seeker churches, even if it never formally took on that role. The following quotations illustrate this general point:

> There is absolutely no doubt about it. There's nothing theoretical about it. . . . There is a common bond among those who want to be about reaching unbelievers that just makes the denomination seem virtually irrelevant. [Nondenominational, California]

> I don't know if you'd want to call it a denomination but I think it's already happening. People are starting to rely on churches in the Association because there is a lot of similarity. [Baptist General Conference, California]

> I think it's very possible that it could become [a denomination]. . . . Because this is such a unique form of evangelism and also of church life, there's really not many other places to go and get information and encouragement. And so it's a real necessity and one that I think is very timely. We're very excited about it because of the potential it has to help other churches. Unfortunately, most other churches that are trying this are not necessarily encouraged all that much by their denominations. So we feel like [the Association] can be real, real helpful to people. [Nondenominational, California]

I think there's a tremendous need for [the Willow Creek Association] to become a denomination. Many of the member churches are independent churches like us. And we don't have the benefit of networking and accessing the resources that some denominations have. [Nondenominational, Maryland]

There's no doubt about it. The churches that are developing more of a seeker sensitivity are networking with each other and seeing what others are doing and learning from each other. [Bible church, Virginia]

I have a sense that it already is functioning like a denomination. For example, we belong to the Willow Creek Association. We pull out and fine tune a lot of ideas from Bill Hybels. Anytime there's a church in the area that wants to be seeker sensitive or contemporary, I end up working with them. Two different people have come here to ask, "What are you doing that makes so many people come like this?" [Presbyterian, California]

Seminaries of the Future

Willow Creek's denominational functions are concentrated mostly on continuing education programs for pastors and churches, which provide practical advice about church leadership, management, and vision that is often not included in traditional seminary curricula. In general, Willow Creek's resources supplement the training received by pastors in seminary and, therefore, collaboration between Willow Creek and seminaries may be a trend of the future. At least one seminary even awards credit to pastors for attending Willow Creek seminars.

Yet there is also evidence that WCA training is beginning to rival seminary training in its importance to many churches. As pastors of seeker churches place more emphasis on practical management skills to implement the seeker church strategy, the training provided by Willow Creek becomes increasingly valuable, in some cases more valuable than seminary training. Thus, it is also possible that Willow Creek's training program may not only supplement seminary training but eventually could eclipse it.

Leadership Network, a consulting organization to churches, notes that the replacement of seminary training by professional training, which takes place at large teaching churches such as Willow Creek, is a growing trend. Because seminaries train their graduates for the demands of small churches, the Leadership Network suggests that "the large church will not be inclined to turn to the seminaries to staff itself, or for help in how to grow or how to serve its constituency." Ironically, several seminaries have actually turned to successful seeker churches for direction and help. Leadership Network finds that "it is not unrealistic . . . to regard these [successful seeker] churches as the 'seminaries of the future,' for they are well on their way to becoming precisely that."[24] Similarly, church consultant Lyle Schaller claims that more than one-third of the senior ministers of megachurches do not hold seminary degrees.[25]

One ad from *The Exchange*, the WCA's monthly employment bulletin, illustrates the growing importance of practical training in lieu of seminary training. One church seeks a senior pastor with the following qualities: "Knock-em-dead platform skills, transparent persona, aggressive leadership style and grueling background investigation required. Marketplace success respected over ministry credentials."[26] Marketplace success or experience in the seeker church model are becoming the most desirable qualifications for employment in WCA churches. The most likely source for new staff then might be from within the membership of seeker churches themselves. One study found that Willow Creek hired 95 percent of its staff from within.[27] This is especially the case when filling those pastoral positions that direct the church's innovative, seeker-sensitive programming. Training in seeker-sensitive programming is simply not available in seminaries, yet it is essential for the mission of seeker churches. Thus, while Willow Creek has no desire to perform some of the more traditional functions of a denomination, such as the formal, theological training of pastors, its approach to ministry does challenge the prevailing model of seminary pastoral training. In addition, as it becomes an essential job requirement, training in the seeker church model may potentially rival seminary theological training.

As the preeminent seeker church in the United States, Willow Creek has legitimized its ministry approach in the evangelical world through its phenomenal success and the subsequent establishment of the WCA. Having established that the WCA performs many denominational responsibilities, I will now consider the significance of these responsibilities in light of recent changes in the organization of American religion. That is, given the decreasing significance of denominations in American life, what kind of

denomination might the WCA be? And, to the extent that the WCA is functioning as a denomination, what is the sociological significance of this
development?

The Various Functions of Denominations

Nancy Ammerman suggests that there are three ways to define a
denomination: as beliefs and practices; as organizations; and as cultural
identities.[28] For example, Baptists define themselves by insisting upon believer's baptism and by their more congregational form of association; Presbyterians rely upon the Westminster Confession and other Reformed
creeds to define their identity; while Episcopalians worship according to
the liturgies set forth in *The Book of Common Prayer*. Denominations thus
provide distinctive beliefs and practices that shape their churches at the
local level. In terms of organization, denominations provide both a system
of church governance (e.g., congregational, presbyterian, or episcopal) and
resources for local congregations (ranging from hymnals and Sunday
school materials to clergy pensions, hospitals, missions, and relief agencies). Just as importantly, denominations provide cultural identities to their
members. Rick Warren, pastor of Saddleback Church, remarked during a
conference that, because he comes from a long line of Baptist ministers, the
Southern Baptist Convention's cooperative program is "in his blood." Baptist programs are not simply instrumental means to achieving various ends.
Rather, participation in these programs defines what it means to be a Baptist: good Baptists support the cooperative program. The saliency of cultural identity is most apparent when someone or something threatens
that identity, as evidenced by a remark such as "What an un-Baptist [or un-
Presbyterian or un-Episcopalian] thing to do." Denominations thus serve to
define the acceptable range of religious practice.

The significance of Ammerman's typology to the argument here is that
seeker churches already perform many denominational functions. While
the Willow Creek Association's statement of faith does not define the
beliefs of its member churches in the same way that the Westminster Catechism might for Protestant churches, it nevertheless asserts the importance of basic evangelical theology. Furthermore, the WCA significantly
influences the practices of local churches as a result of defining the standard seeker "liturgy." Willow Creek provides valuable resources and train-

ing to pastors, much like a denomination. Most importantly, Willow Creek and other seeker churches are defining a "feel" for what church should be like. Rather than fondly remembering hymns such as "The Old Rugged Cross" or "Just as I Am," seekers instead connect to casual, contemporary songs and services that are both relevant and exciting. Weekly services are big events, suitable for bringing one's friends, neighbors, and relatives. What kind of cultural and denominational identity might the beliefs and practices of seeker churches be forming in their members?

The Evangelical Denomination

Unlike Mainline Protestantism, the diverse and sprawling institutional world of evangelicalism is defined in many ways not by denominations but by a variety of parachurch organizations, prominent leaders, publications, seminaries, colleges, and so on. Thus, evangelicals are more likely to associate themselves with Young Life, Campus Crusade for Christ, World Vision, Billy Graham, James Dobson, *Christianity Today,* Fuller Seminary, or Wheaton College than with any particular denomination. Evangelicalism, in short, is a diffuse movement characterized by an individual's attachment to a local church and to specialized groups devoted to evangelism, missions, relief and development, strengthening the family, and an array of political and cultural campaigns. This diversity makes it difficult to speak of a monolithic "evangelical perspective." It is instead more proper to describe evangelicalism as a mosaic that includes groups as diverse as strict separatist fundamentalists (such as those at Bob Jones University) and black Pentecostals.

George Marsden suggests that the term "evangelicalism" can describe three different, although overlapping, groups. First, evangelicalism is a conceptual category that encompasses those who hold certain doctrinal stances (e.g., the authority of Scripture) or respond to survey questions about the Bible, God, and the afterlife in theologically conservative ways. A second way of conceiving of evangelicalism is as a more organic movement that includes common traditions and experiences such as songs, styles of evangelism, prayer, Bible study, and worship. A third and more narrow understanding of evangelicalism is as a consciously "evangelical" transdenominational community with overlapping and complicated infrastructures of institutions. For this third group, evangelicalism is a community. "In this respect evangelicalism is most like a denomination. It is a religious fellowship or coalition of which people feel a part."[29] This evangelical "denomination" includes people from an assortment of denominations who are often united in pursuing a common cause—such as "winning the world for Christ."

Creating a shared religious identity is, therefore, not the exclusive province of denominations. Within evangelicalism, special-purpose groups create many of the experiences and views common to evangelicals. Robert Wuthnow has demonstrated that special-purpose groups often provide a greater sense of religious purpose, identity, and affiliation for many church-going Americans than does their church's denomination. The rise of special-purpose groups, in fact, demonstrates the fragmentation of denominational identity and the increasing importance of self-selected forms of religious involvement. Wuthnow convincingly documents that the patterns of shared identity no longer reside within denominations but more often across denominations.[30] To take one example, Methodists are less likely today to share a sense of common identity based on their denomination than in the past, but they are more likely to find common ground with either fellow liberals or fellow conservatives in other denominations. That is, they are likely to gravitate toward and forge community within special-purpose groups that reflect their personal interests, whether their interests be peace and justice issues, prolife causes, concern for the poor, or enthusiasm for evangelism and worship renewal.

Special-purpose groups have grown rapidly in the last thirty years and now rival denominations in sheer number. While at the beginning of this century, denominations outnumbered special purpose groups by two to one, by the late 1970s special-purpose groups matched denominations in absolute number, and by the 1980s such groups were growing at a faster rate than denominations.[31] These groups tend not to be associated with any one denomination but instead they work with pastors and leaders from a diverse spectrum of congregations, although they do tend to cluster around liberal or conservative theological causes. They often imitate the form and functions of secular advocacy organizations. Their specialization also gives them an adaptive edge over denominations, as does the division they make "between institutional knowledge and theological knowledge."[32] Special-purpose groups may provide expertise in a particular field—whether influencing politics or developing strategies for church growth—that transcends denominational boundaries.

In many ways, the Willow Creek Association resembles the special-purpose groups that Wuthnow describes. The WCA is interdenominational, specialized, and similar in form to secular organizations. In particular, it does not provide resources indiscriminately, but only to churches that are interested in its services. It draws its membership from across denominational lines, most likely from the conservative side of the theological spectrum. Thus, the Willow Creek Association is similar to many parachurch organizations that have proliferated within evangelicalism.

Parachurch Organizations and Evangelical Identity

The growth of special-purpose groups, such as parachurch organizations, and the declining significance of denominational identity are interrelated. Parachurch organizations often provide the common identity for evangelicals that denominations have provided for Mainline Protestants. For example, one pastor of a nondenominational seeker church in California noted that the success of evangelical parachurch organizations contributed to evangelicals' declining attachment to particular denominations. "Most of the people in the boomer generation in the ministry," according to this pastor, "were seriously affected by Young Life, Campus Life, Campus Crusade—one of those high school or college ministries. So really their loyalties were much more towards a paraministry structure and then converted back into church."

Just as Willow Creek has combined the specialized approaches of differing parachurch organizations into one church, the Willow Creek Association is combining the diverse loyalties of various seeker church pastors (belonging to a diversity of denominations, parachurch organizations, and special purpose groups) into one movement. In other words, loyalty to the seeker church model is the "glue" that unites members of the WCA in a denominational-like commonality. One reason for this is that the relative weakening of denominational loyalty, when combined with the increasing influence of special purpose groups, creates a situation in which denominations and special purpose groups increasingly resemble each other. Wuthnow, for example, notes, "Denominations have not ceased to exist but have become to a greater extent diverse federations of special purpose groups rather than monolithic, homogeneous structures."[33] If denominations are becoming more like federations of special-interest groups, then the WCA is a likely candidate for denominational-like responsibility and influence, since it already brings together diverse specialties into one organizational structure.

Another way to evaluate the WCA's expanding influence is to note the breadth of its goals. Its goals are broader than those of many special purpose groups. It does not focus on one special strategy, such as evangelism, worship, leadership training, music, teaching, children's ministries, or reaching Generation X. Instead, it offers training and service in all these areas as part of its overall goal to transform every aspect of how the church operates in American society. Thus, while the WCA is clearly an influential special-purpose group, the scope of its mission and the extent of its influence are such that the WCA may be obscuring the boundary between special purpose groups and denominations.

Another way of looking at the expansion of the WCA is to take it as an example of a new form of denominationalism. Russell Richey has documented that bureaucratic form of Mainline Protestant denominations are a relatively recent phenomenon—and suggests that the future forms of denominational affiliation may be quite different from what they have been in the past. According to Richey, the denomination is simply one form of religious organization. He proposes that a more fruitful way to study the organization of American religion is to focus on denominationalism, an approach that treats denominations collectively, as a family, and examines their patterns of interaction. Richey argues that there are five stages or ideal types of American denominationalism: ethnic voluntarism; purposive missionary association; "churchly" denominationalism; corporate or managerial organization; and postdenominational confessionalism.[34] Each is associated with a particular historical era. For example, Richey suggests that Presbyterian churches of the eighteenth century in the Middle Colonies offer a good example of ethnic voluntarism while the Methodists and Baptists in the early national period developed purposive missionary associations to pursue their ends. Both high church (Episcopal, Lutheran) and primitivist movements (Landmark Baptist, Christian) represent types of "churchly" denominationalism. Many of the Mainline Protestant denominations of the twentieth century represent the corporate or managerial type. The fifth type—postdenominational confessionalism—emerged in the 1970s. It combines several contemporary forms, such as "the franchise, the regulatory agency, the caucus, the mall, [and] the media."[35]

Richey's typology calls attention to the social origins and social uses of the various forms of religious organization. When denominations emerge, they draw upon the organizational forms available in society. The typology also "posits that denominationalism served primarily to define the relation of the religious movement to the social order."[36] In other words, patterns of denominationalism reflect a distinct vision of American society and of Protestantism's responsibility for that society. Thus, the corporate or managerial form of Mainline Protestantism suggests a commitment to transforming the world through cooperative religious effort. The expansion of denominational bureaucracies, as well as the creation of interdenominational organizations such as the National Council of Churches, reflects this commitment by Mainline Protestantism to reform American society. In contrast, postdenominational confessionalism is more inward-focused, stressing evangelism rather than social action, and effective local programs rather than cooperative regional and national agencies. It is also more diffuse, relying on various forms, such as special-purpose groups, and various control mechanisms, such as franchising, regulation, and funding of special programs.[37] While the specific configuration of postdenominational confessionalism may not yet be fully developed, Richey suggests that its very form reveals a fragmentation within Protestantism that is best served by specialized, voluntaristic, and inward-focused organizations. The ultimate example of this new type of denominationalism, according to Richey, is the megachurch movement, made up of "mall-like congregations offering both superstore and boutique religion. Some replicate the entire set of services once rendered by denominations, setting up their own publishing operations, significant television and radio ministries, community service programs, missions, and theological education programs."[38]

Richey is not alone in viewing the emergence of nondenominational megachurches as a new form of American denomination. William Swatos suggests that, while traditional denominations face tremendous difficulties, new types of denominations are emerging that perform many of the functions once fulfilled by Mainline Protestantism. These new denominations understand that localism—preserving community identity and control from

the expanding scope of corporate structures (that is, denominational bureaucracies)—is an essential feature of American religious life. Swatos argues that nondenominational churches "are basically denomination-like
structures."[39] These churches accept the dominant local culture in which
they are located. People today are more likely to develop loyalty to a local
community institution than to an abstract, distant religious bureaucracy.
Furthermore, nondenominational churches provide people with a sense of
place in the world, stressing the pursuit of individual meaning and purpose
but within the context of a distinct community. Thus, rather than breaking
with the denominational patterns and history of the United States, nondenominational churches preserve the religio-cultural heritage of America by
performing the traditional functions of denominations in a new form.
Swatos's intriguing proposal offers an important addition to any discussion
of American denominations: rather than dwelling primarily on ideal types of
denominational organization, Swatos suggests that any comprehensive
analysis of denominations and congregations must focus on the religious,
social, and cultural functions that these institutions fulfill. Thus, how the
WCA is shaping the practices of churches at the local level provides the
most important evidence for its denominational influence in the United
States today.

The Internal Secularization of Denominations

What is the sociological significance of the Willow Creek Association's denomination-like influence? Its growth signals both a continued
weakening of existing denominations and the emergence of a new form of
denominationalism. In order to discuss the impact of the WCA's expansion
on other denominations, I shall employ organizational arguments about the
dual structure of most denominations today.

One interesting application of organizational theory to denominations is
Chaves's contention that denominations are best conceived of as dual structures. Chaves, following recent developments in the sociology of organizations, argues that denominations are not unitary entities but are composed
of distinct subunits. These subunits respond to different organizational environments, are faced with different types of task uncertainty and contain
different lines of authority. Chaves identifies two parallel structures that
make up the organizational units of a denomination: a religious authority

structure and an agency structure. According to Chaves, a religious authority structure is "a social structure that attempts to enforce its order and reach its ends by controlling the access of individuals to some desired good, where the legitimation of that control includes some supernatural component, however weak."[40] Chaves draws largely from Weber's definition of a hierocratic organization as "an organization which enforces its order through psychic coercion by distributing or denying religious benefits."[41] However, Chaves leaves open the question of whether religious authority structures "claim a monopoly on the legitimate use of hierocratic coercion," a defining characteristic of churches, according to Weber.

What Chaves adds to Weber's conception of religious organizations is that denominations also contain agency structures, which are devoted to fulfilling a variety of concrete activities such as promoting missions, producing educational material, managing clergy pension funds, loaning money to congregations, and coordinating social programs. The incorporation of agency structures into denominations occurred at the end of the nineteenth century and has important implications for the functioning of denominations today. Religious authority structures and agency structures have very different modes for relating to congregations. For religious authority structures, "congregations are the *object* of control." For the agency structure, "congregations are a *resource* base." The most important distinction between these two structures is that only one, religious authority structures, is necessary for an organization to be a religious organization. In other words, "all religious organizations . . . contain a religious authority structure."[42]

According to Chaves's classification scheme, the WCA, because it lacks an explicit religious authority structure, is not a denomination. This accords with the WCA's sense of its own mission. The WCA does not consider itself a denomination but instead a special-purpose agency dedicated to helping churches implement the seeker church strategy. The WCA clearly avoids certain denominational responsibilities, such as church oversight. A number of factors explain this lack of religious authority structure: (1) many Association churches are already members of existing denominations; (2) the WCA is reluctant to seek any formal supervisory role; and, most important; (3) the WCA claims no direct authority over its member churches.

Before returning to the question of the denominational status of the

WCA, I want to expand upon one important implication of Chaves's classification scheme. Chaves suggests that a dual structure view of denominations is an important theoretical breakthrough in discussions about the internal secularization of religious organizations. Although "internal secularization" is a widely used term, the concept of internal secularization is not well theorized, and, consequently, it lacks strong empirical support. Proponents of this idea, such as Thomas Luckman and Peter Berger, have advanced arguments about the internal secularization of religious organizations, but the debates regarding this issue remain largely unresolved due in large part to a lack of consensus about how to operationalize the concept.[43] Chaves suggests a new way to conceptualize the nature of internal secularization; it is "the declining scope of religious authority's control over the organizational resources within the agency structure."[44] As agency structures within denominations develop greater autonomy from the control of the religious authority structure, they will develop structures that mimic the forms of secular professional organizations in their field, whether finance, missions, or education. The significance of Chaves's argument for the rapid growth of the WCA is that the resources that churches divert from their own denominations to the WCA contribute to the internal secularization of those denominations. That is, a denomination's religious authority over a WCA congregation decreases when a church relies on the WCA, rather than on the denomination, to provide the training, music, drama, and other resources the congregation needs to run its programs. This is internal secularization. At the very least, the growth of the WCA has contributed to the internal secularization of those denominations whose churches are WCA members.

The Postmodern Denomination

We can extend Chaves's concept of internal secularization not only to the WCA's impact upon another denomination's control over its local churches but also to the development of the Association as a denomination in itself. According to Chaves's classification scheme, the Willow Creek Association is essentially an agency structure, offering congregations its expertise and services in exchange for financial resources such as annual fees and consulting costs. Chaves argues that it is not enough for a denomination to contain an agency structure; it must also contain some form of religious authority structure. My purpose is not so much to dispute Chaves's classification scheme, which I find most helpful but, instead, to show how an "undenominational" organization like the WCA represents a new form of denomination. While Chaves's arguments are fruitful for analyzing existing (and primarily Mainline Protestant) denominations, they may not adequately address the changing nature of denominationalism. The traditional denomination may have an agency and religious authority structure, at least as far as it was part of what Richey labels "churchly denominationalism" or corporate organization. But emerging denominations—what might be called postmodern denominations—may not include both these components. The WCA is, in short, a denomination that is *purposefully* internally secularized; it has no intention of exercising any religious authority over its members. Its primary authority is only that of persuasion, enhanced by the legitimacy its success provides.

Other scholars have noted the emergence of new denomination-like forms that might also be called postmodern denominations. Nancy Ammerman suggests that the development of special-purpose groups within the Southern Baptist Convention is an a example of postmodern denomination.[45] Drawing on organizational theory, which suggests that a crisis (in this case the ousting of moderates by fundamentalists from leadership positions within the SBC) may lead to a transformation in the way organizations work, Ammerman proposes that special-purpose groups formed in opposition to the fundamentalist takeover of the SBC (such as the liberal Alliance of Baptists and the more conservative Cooperative Baptist Fellowship) might become models for new forms of denominational structures. These new forms would be characterized by highly specialized and flexible services, rather than mass-produced programs. Similarly, they would use technology and rely more on participatory democracy than on organizational hierarchy. In organizational terms, "postmodern" refers not to a profound skepticism about philosophical and epistemological foundations, but instead to forms of organization that are less centralized than a Weberian bureaucracy. Stewart Clegg, for example, suggests that postmodern organizations are characterized by "flexible specialization."[46]

The WCA is such a flexible, specialized, postmodern denomination. The WCA's role in defining a "liturgy," in preparing materials for teaching, music, and drama, and in training leaders of seeker churches provides it with an influence over many churches that is similar to the influence traditional denominations have over their local congregations. It shapes the practices and cultural identities of seeker church members much as the Presbyterian Church might define the practices of its congregations. What distinguishes the postmodern denomination from a traditional denomination is that the former replaces religious authority based on positions in a religious hierarchy with a form of managerial/market authority. The market (are churches paying their membership fees? are they growing?), not a religious hierarchy, is the primary authority structure of the WCA. In other words, the locus of authority among WCA member churches is shifting from the religious authority structure commonly found in traditional denominations to the market-based mechanisms of an agency structure. Because of this transformation, the WCA may eventually blur the distinction between an agency structure and a denomination. Because it does not exercise *direct* religious control over a local church, the WCA, by providing market incentives for churches to join the Association (for example, discounts on conference registration and products), has institutionalized an almost completely secularized version of a denomination.

Overall, Chaves's arguments about the nature of internal secularization in religious organizations offers a valuable perspective on Willow Creek's impact upon other denominations as well as on its own development as a postmodern denomination. In both cases, the scope of religious authority becomes more limited. Churches, as well as seekers, increasingly use the marketplace as the primary source of accountability. The emergence of the WCA as a postmodern denomination may portend that traditional and modern forms of religious authority structures will be historical forms with a limited, rather than eternal, existence.

The Church in the Twenty-first Century

One point of discussion earlier in this chapter was whether the term "denomination" is too broad to describe the activities and significance of the seeker church movement. Leaders of Willow Creek and its Association contend that their goals are more focused and specialized than those of a traditional denomination. The Willow Creek Association has no intention of building hospitals, credentialing ministers, providing pensions, and performing other similar denominational functions. Jim Mellado, president of the Willow Creek Association, notes that "what distinguishes [the WCA] from a denomination is found in the kind of church we serve. God has given us a ministry that appeals to the more outreach-oriented and innovative church."[47] But while the seeker church movement often defines itself in contrast to denominations, I argue that specialization and choice of services for members may no longer be "undenominational" strategies. I want to suggest another, very different, problem with describing the WCA as a denomination: it is not that the term "denomination" is too broad to encompass the goals of seeker churches but that it is not broad enough.

The WCA's primary goal is not simply to help churches implement a new program or philosophy of ministry. Instead, the WCA strives to help as many churches as possible re-form—regardless of their denomination. Jim Mellado suggests that the job of the WCA is to promote the pioneering spirit of seeker churches as much as possible. He notes that, according to "change technology" and the theory of how societies adopt change, "it takes about 16 percent of a society to commit to a cause or an innovation before a critical mass is reached to effect widespread change. [The WCA's] goal is to stay focused on serving this leading edge of churches' activity."[48] By focusing on the "leading edge" of pioneering churches, the WCA's goal is to direct a movement that transcends existing denominational distinctions by making seeker sensitivity the most important dimension of the church ministry. If successful, this could create within American Protestantism a new axis based not on denominational affiliation but on seeker sensitivity. Thus, the efforts of the WCA and other innovative churches transcend denominational particularities in a way that might be properly understood as meta-denominational.

While the meta-denomination as represented institutionally by the WCA does not dictate policy for member churches or create authority or control mechanisms, it nevertheless shapes the organization and cultural identity of individual churches and even denominations. It defines for many churches what church services should be like today and how the church should be run. Consider the following example: Mellado notes that the Christian Reformed Church (CRC) has been sending more than two hundred leaders annually to Willow Creek conferences for the last few years. The CRC selects leaders of seeker-sensitive churches to attend these conferences. While I can only speculate on the future direction of these churches, it is highly unlikely that they will continue to resemble those in which previous generations of Reformed Christians were raised (churches that included a prominent role for the Heidelberg Catechism, traditional hymns, exegetical preaching, and a unity based on ethnic or national identity, e.g., a Dutch heritage). Seeker-sensitive Christian Reformed Churches most likely will have more in common, particularly as organizations and cultural transmitters, with other seeker churches than with their more traditional Christian Reformed counterparts.[49] In short, the meta-denominational influence of the WCA will be greater than that of the Christian Reformed denomination upon many CRC churches. This profound shift in denominational influence is reflected in Bill Hybels's own religious journey. Raised in a conservative Dutch Reformed Church, Hybels has moved away from the creedal and ethnic particularities of the church of his childhood to the cultural and lifestyle commonalities of the seeker church.

Whether the meta-denominational aspects of the WCA and other seeker churches represent a new form of denomination, a type of meta-denomination, or an extremely influential special-purpose group, it seems clear that the seeker church represents one of the fastest-growing and most influential forms of the American church for the twenty-first century. As Jim Mellado puts it, the WCA is experiencing a coalescing of a vision that is "larger than any other organization I know."[50] With a membership of five thousand churches in 2000, and growing at the rate of one thousand a year, the WCA will be in a position to define the form and function of the twenty-first-century church, both in the United States and across the world. This postmodern denomination of innovative, contemporary churches may enjoy considerable success in the free market for the religious loyalty of seekers. These churches will offer the appealing goods of faith and fulfillment—but without any religious authority to compel obedience or to discipline those who have taken contextualization to an unintended result.

Seven

The challenge is this: as [seeker] churches try to attract sellout crowds, are they in danger of selling out the Gospel?[1]

Translation and Tradition

Why are seeker churches growing? What does this postmodern denomination's re-form of church life tell us about the role of religion in America? In short, what are we to make of this remarkable movement? As a result of the changes in American culture and the religious environment since the 1960s, many pastors have concluded that traditional models of church, of denominational association, and even of seminary training have become outdated and ineffective. These older forms fail to resonate with the interests of spiritual seekers, many of whom may have little or no attachment to the denominations in which they were raised. Even if seekers do have some sense of residual denominational identity, many find that traditional services—whether Roman Catholic masses or formal Protestant services—do not connect in a personally relevant way with their lives. Although these seekers have not completely rejected the possibility of Christian belief and belonging, many have not found a church or other religious institution, movement, guru, or other form of spirituality that presents its message in a compelling and plausible way. Responding to the changing spiritual interests of the baby-boom generation, innovative religious leaders are, to use the title of a book by Bill and Lynne Hybels, "rediscovering" church.

This rediscovery takes as its starting point the "new voluntarism" of the religious environment in which church and other forms of spiritual seeking

163

have become a matter of choice, part of each individual's journey rather than an ascribed characteristic or closely held (and sanctioned) social custom. This new voluntarism stresses a subjectivist and therapeutic understanding of religious participation that is based less on duty or obligation and more on whether it meets people's needs.[2] Three essential traits define the current religious environment. The first, already alluded to, is that religious participation is increasingly understood as a matter of individual choice. In sociological terms, religion today is less of an ascribed (that is, inherited) status and more of an achieved status. The implication of what one might call the consumerist approach to religion is that religious identity is much more likely to change over time. People are more likely to switch their religious affiliation, including dropping out of religion altogether. Of course, the fact that religious participation is now based on consumer choice might also mean that people are more committed than ever to the religious identity that they have freely chosen and not simply inherited.[3]

The second trait that defines the current religious environment is the expansion of a therapeutic ethos in religion. The subjectivist and psychological orientation of many seekers reflects the therapeutic ethos of contemporary society. The therapeutic legitimates an individual's quest to enhance one's self and self-esteem. The days of Puritan self-denial and inner-worldly asceticism, even in evangelical circles, are long gone. Finally, the third trait that defines today's religious environment is people's strong anti-institutional bias and suspicion of authority. This bias leads many baby boomers to distrust established institutions, particularly those institutions that are hierarchical in nature. Current interest in spirituality, in contrast to organized religion, reflects this anti-institutional sentiment.

How have seeker churches responded to the challenges posed by today's cultural environment? Seeker churches have developed culturally innovative strategies for attracting baby boomers while preserving evangelical distinctiveness regarding the authority of Scripture, the need for salvation, and the existence of an afterlife. The programs and services that seeker churches provide address today's consumerist, therapeutic, and anti-institutional cultural ethos by offering seekers choices, meeting their personal needs, and pioneering informal and culturally contemporary forms of worship. Seeker churches are addressing people's desire for friendship, community, and family through carefully designed ministries—

and by offering the freedom to investigate the church's offerings anonymously. Interestingly, seeker churches have managed to address these felt needs while still stressing that every sinner must make a Christian conversion. It is this synthesis of therapeutic language along with the traditional evangelical stress on conversion and ongoing commitment that is at the heart of the seeker church movement's success.

When innovative churches are successful, they quickly become the model for others. This process of isomorphism explains how Willow Creek and other pioneers such as Saddleback Church have become such influential congregations. Once pastors were convinced that Willow Creek offered a successful model of how to "do church" in today's religious environment, they emulated its approach. Success, in short, breeds success. This does not mean that all seeker churches are clones of Willow Creek. Many adapt the principles of the seeker church movement to their own congregations. These principles are reflected in terms such as "authenticity," "informality," "relevance," "fulfillment," and "choice," which are prevalent in seeker church literature. These terms sum up the seeker church's appeal to Unchurched Harry.

Why Does Unchurched Harry Come to Church?

Seekers come to seeker churches because they are invited. Church members feel comfortable inviting friends and acquaintances because their churches make every effort to nurture a comfortable, creative, and exciting—yet safe—atmosphere for visitors. Seeker churches offer low barriers to entry by providing for anonymity at services, state-of-the-art sound systems, Christian contemporary music, a relaxed informal atmosphere, a plethora of small groups, and topically focused practical messages. Visiting a seeker church is a nonthreatening experience. This is the first component of Willow Creek's outreach strategy. The second part of the strategy—convincing seekers who visit to return—includes an emphasis on relevant messages and on the need for Christian conversion and commitment, as well as opportunities to make friends and participate in small groups . Undergirding all of the seeker church's innovative programming is a theologically conservative understanding of human nature, sin, God, and conversion.

The key to the success of the seeker church movement is not simply good programming but the principles behind the programming, principles that incorporate key elements of contemporary culture as well as core components of evangelical theology. The most important principle is that of "authenticity." Willow Creek uses this term constantly in its material. An authentic church is one whose leaders are open, honest, even transparent about their faith, their struggles, and their commitments. Authenticity requires that you are true to your convictions not because your parents believed, or because you have always thought a certain way, but because you have actively appropriated the convictions as your own; it is not enough to accept a belief because of a tradition, habit, or inertia. The criterion for authentic belief is individual engagement.

What this boils down to in practical terms is that church services are designed to stimulate personal commitment. Longtime church practices may not necessarily meet this criterion. Old hymns, responsive readings of the Psalms, organ music, robed ministers and choirs, readings from the Old and New Testaments, and other practices common to more traditional Protestant and Catholic services will be discarded if they do not meet the test of authenticity—that is, if they do not help each seeker directly encounter the sacred. Instead of these traditional practices, seeker churches offer an environment that eschews tradition. There are no crosses, religious symbols, or reminders of unfamiliar architecture from centuries past. Everything is user-friendly and familiar, including comfortable seats and modern sound systems. Contemporary music plays constantly during the service—silence is apt to make seekers uncomfortable. Real-life dramas, the use of the arts, and practical, topical messages are carefully crafted to stir an emotional response in the seeker. All external trappings of religion are removed in order to promote genuine religious experience, the direct, emotional response of an individual to the sacred. These innovations in technique and presentation are incorporated into an evangelical setting that is, to paraphrase the Oldsmobile commercial, most definitely "not your father's evangelicalism."

Although seeker churches are fairly strict in their theology, they are flexible in how they express their theology socially, culturally, and in their services. Their mainstream, middle-class, suburban target niche need not forswear drinking, dancing, smoking, cardplaying, or moviegoing—as previous generations of evangelicals once did. Authentic religious experience is not dependent upon obedience to rigid behavioral strictures on social issues. In addition, visitors need not learn the intricacies of a prayer book or liturgy, or even familiarize themselves with the "God-talk" that is prevalent in many churches. They are not required to "sit and stand and kneel and pray, kiss [their] neighbor, pass the plate and listen," as one wag has humorously described the typical Episcopal church service.[4] Instead, the seeker service strives to convey how one can relate to the divine in terms and categories that are immediately accessible to everyone precisely because those terms and categories are drawn from daily life.[5]

Closely related to this notion of authenticity is the principle that a seeker church must be relevant to the felt needs of its audience. In today's buyers' market, religious seekers have little or no brand loyalty. They are not likely to attend any one church or denomination faithfully years or even months at a time. They evaluate the worth of participation up front. Are the teaching messages topical, practical, applicable, and entertaining? Seeker churches answer this question by offering message series that cover a particular topic, usually in a few weeks in order to provide a convenient trial period for seekers. The packaging of these messages is also important. While seeker churches are ultimately concerned with the seeker's "real need" for conversion, they also emphasize how Christianity can be relevant to the this-worldly desire to find fulfillment, meaning, and community in a confusing world. By stressing the therapeutic benefits of faith—the bottom line that Christianity is helpful in this life, as well as the next—seeker churches have found a hook that catches the attention of seekers across the country. But once seekers come, why do they stay?

Why Does Unchurched Harry Stay?

The growth of seeker churches suggests that seekers not only find their way to the service but that many like it enough to stay and eventually make a commitment to the church. Most successful seeker churches work hard at incorporating occasional attenders into the more regular activities of the church. In order to accomplish this, seeker churches provide a wide range of programming options for attenders of all ages, including small groups, and age-targeted classes and social opportunities.[6] Willow Creek's Networking seminar helps attenders assess their spiritual gifts and connects them with a particular ministry or service opportunities. Rather than relying on professional clergy to develop programs (which many endowed Mainline Protestant churches have done), seeker churches use a bottom-up strategy of developing programs that depend upon lay involvement and initiative. This democratization of church programming serves to energize and inspire the laity.

A second strategy for keeping attenders plugged into the church is based on the principle that the church must grow smaller even as it grows larger. This is accomplished by placing people into small groups. The formal purpose of these groups includes bible study, singles groups, service ministry, hospitality and so on, but they all share the goal of providing a home within the larger church for attenders. This cell-based strategy, which Willow Creek embraced relatively recently, is central to the success of seeker churches—and many other churches in the country today. What these small groups provide in the increasingly isolating landscape of suburbia is a form of new community not based on geography or ethnicity but on shared affinities and religious identity.

Seeker churches have also developed innovative ways for connecting congregations to each other. Early leaders of seeker churches did not find that their own denominations were much interested in their seeker-friendly innovations (in part because denominations felt threatened by the changes). Furthermore, denominations often embodied the very traditionalism to which seeker church leaders attributed membership losses. As a result, seeker churches have turned away from existing denominations and have extended the evangelical parachurch model of localized, decentralized, and independent church organizations. Denominations require extra work, such as learning a liturgy or gaining official credentials through a seminary, and, perhaps more importantly, extra money to support an often distant bureaucratic structure. These are costs that many seeker church leaders are unwilling to bear, primarily because they see little if any benefit from a denominational affiliation. The Willow Creek Association thus serves as a type of postmodern denomination—flexible, decentralized, and dynamic. The nature of the connection between churches within this association is primarily voluntary contractual, rather than covenantal.

With all their innovations, seeker churches have created a new model of human community uniquely suited to a largely suburban population with few ties to local neighborhoods and a greater willingness to commute long distances to find a church that speaks to its needs. By making the sacred accessible through contemporary rituals, informal services, and an emphasis on the practical applications of Christian teaching rather than abstract doctrine or creeds, seeker churches have developed a remarkably successful approach to growing local congregations.

What does this success tell us about religion in contemporary America? Institutionally, it tells us that at least some sectors of American religion are vital. New organizations now meet the needs of one large segment of the public that was not being served by many traditional churches. Culturally, the success of seeker churches tells us that evangelicalism that is culture-affirming while theologically traditional, individualistic while concerned with creating fellowship, therapeutic while serious about personal sin, and program oriented while reticent about politics can thrive in present-day America. This movement, like previous revival movements in American history, is built on the selective acceptance of the cultural currents, not their outright rejection.[7] Seeker churches are successful precisely because they do not condemn the "world" of modern culture, as some fundamentalists have done. Instead, they have synthesized a therapeutic concern for self-fulfillment with evangelical understandings of Christ salvation, and the Bible. These churches embody, at times paradoxically, the new and the old, the innovative and the traditional, in a way that complements the consumerist, therapeutic, and anti-institutional cultural presuppositions of today's American society.

The "New Paradigm" in Religion

There is always a tendency to romanticize the past, perhaps especially in the case of religion. For some, there was an (often undefined) Golden Age when people knew their neighbors, were ready to help others in their community, went to church, and generally upheld fairly admirable standards of personal piety and morality. What recent research has revealed, or at least has clarified, is that early Americans were not as faithful in church attendance as we might assume. In fact, Finke and Starke's *The Churching of America* reports that rates of religious participation were actually lower in colonial America than today. As a result of a series of revivals, such as the Second Great Awakening in the early nineteenth century, and other innovations, rates of church adherence increased from only 17 percent in 1776 to 45 percent in 1890, and up to 62 percent in 1980.[8] This is surprising not only in light of the widely held notion that Americans are not as religious as they used to be but also given scholars' understanding of traditional notions of secularization that predicted, if not religion's demise, its substantial decline.

What explains the increasing rate of church attendance among Americans over the last two centuries? Many scholars of American religion have found a remarkable vibrancy and entrepreneurial spirit in American religion that has contributed to the comparatively high rates of religious adherence in this country. Furthermore, this vitality is not a recent development. Nathan Hatch's *The Democratization of American Christianity* argues that the populist and democratic spirit of the early republic also influenced American religion in the early nineteenth century. According to Hatch, populism sparked a reaction against the established (both socially and de facto in many states) churches whose clergy were well educated and whose preaching demonstrated philosophical and theological refinement but did not speak to the needs of the masses. "Increasingly assertive common people wanted their leaders unpretentious, their doctrines self-evident and down to earth, their music lively and singable, and their churches in local hands."[9] Rather than abandoning Christianity, however, the masses found innovative new suppliers who were offering religious messages, and especially music, that appealed to their tastes. The religious populism of the early nineteenth century influenced not just preaching and hymns and patterns of denominational growth (the Methodists and Baptists prospered while the Episcopalians and Congregationalists declined), but also people's understandings of religious authority. Instead of depending upon the clergy to interpret religious doctrines and mediate access to the sacred, the people demanded religious experiences that offered direct encounters with God. By democratizing access to the sacred, the innovative churches offered the laity significant congregational roles, which in turn reinforced the civic republican ideology of the day.

Although Hatch writes about the period known as the Second Great Awakening, new paradigm theorists of religion contend that the development of successful new churches and movements is not limited to the past. Just as the Baptists and Methodists supplanted the Episcopalians and Congregationalists in the nineteenth century, the Assemblies of God, the Vineyard, and seeker churches today are supplanting more established churches and denominations. This pattern of institutional vitality, flexibility, and renewal persists throughout American history and forms the basis for the new paradigm in the sociology of religion. The basic insight of the new paradigm approach to religion is that churches and other religious institutions in the United States compete in an open religious market. Rather than weakening religion by undermining the social consensus behind a particular denomination or by tearing the "sacred canopy" that binds together a particular society, the open religious market strengthens religion.[10] Because the United States lacks an established church, provides for the legal separation of church and state, and is home to a remarkable religious, ethnic, and cultural diversity, institutional religion is inherently pluralistic. Furthermore, American religious institutions have emulated the example of the American economy by exhibiting a high degree of structural flexibility (that is, innovation) over time. According to Steven Warner, one of the clearest articulators of the new paradigm, "In contrast to the 'old paradigm' view that religion is most viable under conditions of monolithic consensus and unquestioned stability, the 'new paradigm' draws on American history to argue that religion can flourish under conditions of social diversity and change."[11] The congregational form of American religion in particular is well adapted to this open market, allowing an almost infinite variety of subcultural groups to create their religious communities. One of the keys to this new paradigm approach is its stress on the supply side of the religious equation. Rather than positing that there is a universal or constant demand for religion, this approach emphasizes the role that innovative religious suppliers play in promoting religious vitality by providing products that meet the needs of specific segments of the religious economy.

A considerable amount of recent research applies this new paradigm model of religion to the religious situation in United States. Donald Miller's *Reinventing American Protestantism* is most relevant here because there are strong similarities in methods, cultural style, and theology between what Miller calls "new paradigm" churches and seeker churches. Miller argues that new paradigm churches, much like the nineteenth-century revivalists that Hatch studies, promote unmediated communication between an individual and God. Renewal movements, according to Miller, "attract people outside the religious fold, and they intensify the faith of those who are members by promoting encounters with the sacred that go far beyond ordinary religious experience."[12] People are thus attracted to these churches because they offer a religion of the heart that is based on primal religious experience (particularly in the more charismatic of these churches), not formal theology, complex ethical systems, or abstract exhortations to love one's neighbor. For the middle-class and blue-collar people who attend these churches, it is the simplicity and expressiveness of the ritual, the genuineness and lack of formality (such as titles or robes) of the ministers, and the generally charismatic and nonroutinized nature of both the service and the church itself that are appealing.

Miller attributes the success of new paradigm churches to several factors. The first is that these churches offer a countercultural religion that has purged itself of all forms of establishment. This is appealing to the antiinstitutional impulses of baby boomers. Second, these churches develop programming that appeal to the needs of their attenders. Third, the style of the service and messages is in the vernacular, that is, the language and forms of popular culture. Perhaps most importantly, these churches appropriate elements of contemporary culture such as popular music and casual dress while still making moral and spiritual demands upon their members.[13] Colloquially speaking, new paradigm churches are "hip," but they are not "loose."

There are clearly many similarities between new paradigm churches and seeker churches. Although seeker churches are generally less charismatic and more middle class than the new paradigm churches that Miller studied, both share the same entrepreneurial innovation, contemporary cultural style, empowerment of the laity, and antiestablishment or antidenomination sentiment. Both also testify to the dynamic religious sector in American life. They are both clearly part of a major re-form movement in American religion, although I am not convinced that their growth amounts to a Second Reformation. Instead, they represent a major re-formation or reorganization of the church, but the extent of their cultural and social influence in the long-term is very much an open question.

Other contemporary studies support the general proposition that open religious markets lead to vitality. For example, in her study of congregations across America, Nancy Ammerman concludes that religious pluralism—a result of the religious free market—is not bad for religion. Pluralism allows religious suppliers to provide goods that meet people's needs. Using ecological analogies, Ammerman stresses that new religious forms emerge as a result of the changing environment. While this does mean that some established churches will die out (as some in the Protestant Mainline are doing), it also means that the religious sector overall is thriving. As the institutional environment in which religious institutions find themselves changes, new patterns of congregation and organization will emerge.[14] The new paradigm model in Miller's and Ammerman's work helps to account for the remarkable vitality and innovation that seems to be a constant in American religious life.

Another work on evangelicalism that draws on the new paradigm model offers a more nuanced assessment of the sources of evangelical success. In *American Evangelicalism: Embattled and Thriving,* Christian Smith and colleagues employ subcultural identity theory to argue that "religions can survive and thrive in pluralistic modern society by situating themselves in subcultures that offer morally orienting collective identities which provide their adherents meaning and belonging."[15] In other words, evangelicals are successful because they create strong religious communities that have clearly defined boundaries in relation to the larger culture. The fact of pluralism also contributes to the success of evangelicalism because it both creates a context against which evangelicals can unite and prevents evangelicals from becoming a ruling majority. This argument certainly has relevance for seeker churches. These churches create strong religious communities that are defined by their commitment to the values of relevance, seeking, and Christian truth but also define themselves in opposition both to staid churches that have little passion for the "lost" and to generic spirituality that is cut off from the Christian faith. Thus, the winners in American religion are groups that are innovative and entrepreneurial, yet also serious about meaning and commitment from a distinctively religious point of view. Seeker churches clearly follow this pattern of innovation and commitment in American religious history.

While the new paradigm is an important development in the sociology of religion, it is by no means an exhaustive approach to analyzing the role of religion in society. For example, Warner has written that he suspects that the dynamics of the new paradigm operate particularly within the "distinctive institutional parameters of the U.S. religious system."[16] Important questions about the social role and cultural influence of religion lead to assessments of religion other than the one the new paradigm approach offers. Consider the differences between the revivalist movements of the late nineteenth century (discussed by George Thomas in *Revivalism and Cultural Change*) and the contemporary seeker church movement. Thomas found a great deal of entrepreneurial innovation and energy among these revivalists. What was distinctive about nineteenth-century revivalism was that it drew upon a cultural understanding of the individual as a citizen and of the church as an agent of social change. As a result, revivalism sparked important social reform movements and had strong links to the Republican Party.

In contrast, the seeker church movement does not conceive of itself as an agent of social reform. Despite the political activism of the Religious Right today, social reform is not on the agenda of the seeker church movement. Willow Creek has recently begun to stress the importance of serving the poor in inner-city Chicago, the Dominican Republic, and other impoverished communities. But these valuable efforts nevertheless differ from the social activism of previous evangelical generations. One difference is that the evangelical call to "Christianize" America no longer has the appeal, and particularly the plausibility, it once had. Furthermore, because seeker churches stress the importance of giving to others in part as a means toward self-fulfillment, the social involvement of these churches is unlikely to display the crusading zeal for the social order that characterized previous Protestant activism. In general, seeker churches are more likely to stress the need for reform of the self than of the social order.[17]

New paradigm scholars who focus on the institutional dimensions of religion see a vital and renewing sector of American society. According to this argument, there is in the religious economy—as in the market economy—an ongoing cycle of revitalization, stagnation, and replacement. In sociological terms, dynamic, world-denying sects gain adherents with their strong message. With each successive generation, however, the passion of the founders becomes routinized. The sect, in short, becomes a church. However, the success of various innovative religious movements still leaves open the question of what kind of religion prospers under particular social conditions. Here is where neosecularization theory offers some valuable insights.

Neosecularization Theory

Given the relative vitality of the American religious sector that new paradigm scholars have documented, it might seem incongruous even to raise the question of whether secularization is a factor in American religion and society. Scholars who find that religion is surviving and even thriving in contemporary America could claim that secularization theory has been definitively disproved, yet other scholars who are sympathetic to secularization theory argue that the case against secularization has been overstated. They contend that, even with the growth in the American religious sector, there have been important transformations in religion's cultural and social role. Thus critical questions for neosecularization theorists include, How does the institutional vitality of religion relate to societal level questions about the scope and influence of religion? What difference does belief in God and the existence of religious institutions make to society?

These scholars, without denying the shifting patterns of denominational affiliation in the United States, argue that there is strong evidence of a decreasing social role for religion. Although this one study of the seeker church movement will not definitively resolve the theoretical differences between those who focus on America's religious vitality and those who stress the diminishing social influence of religion, does the seeker church movement provide evidence that American society is not secularizing but instead sacralizing?

The answer of course is in the details, particularly the devilish detail of what one means by secularization. If by secularization one means the decline of religion—the progressive disappearance of religion from society reflected primarily by lower rates of religious attendance—then this research, by demonstrating a surging interest in the sacred, refutes such a notion of secularization. Long-term trends that suggest that rates of religious participation have remained stable or, even more dramatically, are increasing, contradict this notion of secularization. This is precisely what Stark and Finke found in *The Churching of America*.[18] Yet attendance is by no means an exhaustive factor in the sociological study of religion. Nor can secularization be measured merely in terms of church attendance rates, or numbers of individuals who make personal professions of faith.

Secularization can be a remarkably slippery concept, in part because this one term is used to describe changes at three levels of analysis—the societal, institutional, and individual. Although these categories of analysis can often overlap, they are nevertheless distinct. High levels of religiosity at one level (the personal) do not necessarily mean there will also be high levels of religious influence at the societal level. It is conceivable that there could be a society that is 100 percent spiritual, in which people cultivate their connection to the sacred by participating in activities such as yoga, twelve-step groups, spiritual retreats, and channeling and yet institutions of religion have little authority or influence upon the public sphere. Theoretically, it would be possible to have a society with high degrees of religious involvement that is nonetheless highly secularized. The reverse is also conceivable. A society might exist that is strongly shaped by religious authority (for example, perhaps some modern Muslim societies) but where individual levels of religious participation remain comparatively low. Secularization, then, is not an inevitable fact or iron law of the modern world. It is, in contrast, historically contingent and, at least theoretically, reversible.

If secularization does not mean the complete disappearance of the sacred from the modern world, then what does it mean? Rather than positing the disappearance of religion, many theorists of secularization have stressed the transformation of religion. According to this view, religion may persist, even thrive, while the social significance of religious institutions, actions, language, and norms diminish. Neosecularization theory therefore posits that secularization refers to the transformation, not the decline, of religion and that the key level of analysis for secularization theory is not individual or institutional but societal.[19] Thus the primary concern in neosecularization theory is not religious attendance, one of the main variables in many new paradigm examinations of religion, but the scope and force of religious authority in a society.

Religious authority is a much trickier concept to define and measure than is rate of religious attendance. Mark Chaves offers some valuable insight into how one might sociologically approach the concept of religious authority. Chaves suggests that one sign of secularization is the degree to which nonreligious authorities increasingly define the norms and practices of religion. When studying religion, one should not only study patterns of religious attendance but also the nature and character of religious belief, practice, and institutional identity. According to Chaves,

[T]he relevant, individual level questions for secularization are not questions about belief (how many people say they believe in God?) or mere organizational affiliation (how many people are members of religious organizations?). In such a society, the relevant questions about the scope of religious authority over individuals are questions about the extent to which actions are regulated by religious authority. . . . Hence, data about religious intermarriage, religious authority's attempted control over reproductive behavior, diets, voting, etc. are much more relevant to debates about secularization than are data about belief in God or church membership.[20]

Beliefs and attendance are an essential part of any religion, but they, in and of themselves, do not exhaust the sociological significance of religion. They are only part of a complex and interrelated set of codes, behaviors, and institutions that set the boundaries of a particular religious community. The sociological task, according to Chaves, is to assess not only the extent of institutional vitality but also the nature of the religion that these institutions promote.

Neosecularization theory examines the changes in religion at the individual, institutional, and societal level. At the individual level, the shift from achievement to ascription in religion suggests that there is a move away from accepting the authority of religious institutions and toward selective appropriation of religious traditions based on individual needs. Autonomy and choice become the organizing principle of religious practice and signs of the shifting locus of religious authority toward the individual and away from religious institutions. This might also mean that levels of religious participation or involvement increase because people feel freer to develop religious practices that fit with their understanding of the world. At the institutional level, the Willow Creek Association's flexible, decentralized structure may be more effective at galvanizing a movement, but it also might signal the declining scope of institutional or denominational authority over local congregations. The shift from covenantal to contractual language suggests the increasing importance of instrumental rationality in defining the connections between congregations. At the societal level, the degree to which seeker church pastors proclaim their message in the therapeutic language and terminology suggests that religion is valued in public more for its instrumental value in meeting personal needs than for its substantive claims about truth.

Some of this research does suggest that the insights of neosecularization theory merit further consideration, particularly regarding the nature of religious authority in the postmodern denomination that is the Willow Creek Association and in the religious lives and practices of seekers. I will examine briefly two issues that highlight the relevance of neosecularization theory to this discussion of the seeker church movement: language and experience. The theme that relates these concepts is authority, specifically the authority of religious institutions to proclaim their message.

Language and Experience: The Dimensions of Belief

One of the keys to the success of seeker churches is their ability and willingness to translate theological concepts into the idiom of everyday speech. Seeker churches describe the quest for God as part of every seekers' journey for fulfillment in this life as much as it is for salvation in the next. Ancient rules such as the Ten Commandments are not outdated; rather, they provide a blueprint for living a successful life. Although God is a mighty judge, the great news is that following God is good for you. In short, the Christian faith is true—but see what benefits it brings to your life. This is the genius of seeker churches, their synthesis of traditional evangelical doctrines with contemporary therapeutic and individualistic understandings.

The issue I want to raise here is not whether this type of religious speech is effective but what kind of religious speech it is. In *Religion and Globalization*, Peter Beyer examines the possibilities for religion to be a determinative factor in the social structures of the modern world beyond the private sphere of individual practice and belief. In short, what are the possibilities for religion to have an influence beyond where it is "supposed" to be, namely the private lives of adherents? To take but one example from this theoretically rich volume, Beyer focuses on religious leaders and their communication. Arguing that the public importance of a social system rises or falls with the public influence of its professionals, Beyer notes that the non-religion sectors of social life, such as economics, the state, and science, have little need for religious professionals. This is a result (and a mostly desirable one at that) of societal differentiation, which contributes to the privatization of religion. In order to reach beyond their limited private sphere, religious leaders can make claims about the public benefits or significance of religion, as leaders of the Christian Right do when they claim that Christian morality is the basis for a sound political order. Drawing on Luhmann's analysis of the societal features of differentiation, Beyer classifies religious speech into two main categories: function and performance. Function refers to "pure" religious communication, such as worship or devotion, while performance occurs "when religion is 'applied' to problems generated in other systems but not solved there."[21] Beyer argues that religious performance rather than religious function is more common given the structural constraints of privatization.

Much of what seeker churches communicate is "applied" religion: how belief in God makes a difference to one's happiness, family, self-esteem, direction in life. By stressing the applied benefits of their products, religious professionals demonstrate the importance of religion for secular areas of life but, in the process, "non-religious concerns impinge upon pure religiousness, demonstrating the fact that other societal concerns condition the autonomy of religious action."[22] The desire of seekers for fulfillment and meaning presents an opportunity for seeker churches to meet their needs and convey the value of Christian belief and community, but the extent to which these benefits are conveyed as addressing nonreligious concerns is an example of the limits upon religious speech today. Seeker churches accept this privatization of belief, which contributes both to their numerical growth and to the declining cultural authority of specifically religious speech.

To take another example, one of the great strengths of seeker churches is their ability to provide a powerful and relevant experience of the sacred to their attenders. God is not remote and distant but close by and relevant in the carefully crafted spontaneous liturgies of these churches. In *Reinventing American Protestantism*, Don Miller argues that the ability to convey a sense of the sacred is both a primary reason for the growth of these churches and a sign of the emergence of a new epistemology that he calls "postmodern primitivism." This new way of knowing stresses that beliefs emerge out of experience, rather than follow from the intellectual apprehension of a dogma or creed. For Miller, postmodern primitivists are cultural pioneers who are reintegrating the bodily experience into religious life.[23] This also explains why leaders of new paradigm churches are doctrinal minimalists, given that they stress the importance of a personal encounter with Jesus over adherence to creeds and dogmas. Applying the lessons of new paradigm churches to the future of Mainline Protestantism, Miller suggests that theology in the twenty-first century will have to draw upon reason, tradition, and, especially, experience in order to be persuasive and compelling.[24]

There is no doubt that the stress on authentic religious experience is crucial to the success of new paradigm churches, including seeker churches. While Miller is correct to stress that tradition can be a hindrance to genuine religious experience, I want to look at some potential unintended consequences of an evangelical reliance on experience that minimizes the roles of tradition, doctrines, and creeds. An emphasis on experience does lead to vital worship, perhaps best represented by the growing charismatic movement across the world, but it is also the standard by which contemporary spiritualities such as the New Age movement discount traditional religious teachings.

Consider the role of small groups in both seeker churches and American society. Robert Wuthnow notes that many religious functions once performed by the church are now performed by special-purpose groups or by noninstitutional purveyors of spirituality.[25] Seeker churches use small groups to connect newcomers to the church—or at least to one group in the church. While they provide a "home" within a church for many of the faithful, small groups also have weaknesses that tend to reinforce the amnesia of our modern culture. Wuthnow observes how small groups stress personal insight over tradition, and church wisdom. "In simplest terms," writes Wuthnow, "the sacred comes to be associated with small insights that seem intuitively correct to the small group, rather than wisdom accrued over the centuries in hermitages, seminaries, universities, congregations, and church councils."[26] Small groups make the sacred relevant, but they also can convey a very limited conception of Christianity's tradition, history, and even obligations .

An example might be helpful here. Suppose that instead of theologically conservative yet socially moderate seeker churches we were examining the proliferation of twelve-step groups such as Alcoholics Anonymous (AA). Suppose further that AA had progressed beyond being a support group to becoming a more formal religious organization complete with services, paid staff, and its own facilities. This is not a far-fetched example. A *Time* magazine article on innovative megachurches featured, in addition to Willow Creek and other evangelical megachurches, the Unity Church in Chicago, which bases its teachings on twelve-step groups and no specific religious doctrine.[27] The Unity Church features a giant teddy bear on the main stage and an explicitly self-help or therapeutic message of personal transformation. What if the Unity Church were to become a model for another religious movement? Here would be a church that meets the felt needs of seekers through its emphasis on inner healing but without the evangelical message of the uniqueness of Christ (just the necessity of a Higher Power). In other words, nonevangelical and even non-Christian groups and organizations might be the successful innovators a generation from now eclipsing the seeker church movement.

The key issue here is whether church-based small groups, which are at the core of the seeker church model, will still be attractive to future generations or whether the next generation of seekers will find that independent small groups that focus on spirituality without any formal connection to church meet their needs. Succeeding generations, beginning with what is now known as Generation X, may be more skeptical of "institutional religion" and of seeker churches. The success of seeker churches with baby boomers may not carry over to the next generation.[28] Eclectic spirituality in which seekers define themselves by drawing from myriad religious traditions (such as a Baptist-Jewish-Hindi-Baha'i-Native American spiritualist) without a strong commitment to any one particular tradition could eclipse comparatively traditional forms of religious commitment such as seeker churches. How might seeker churches maintain their evangelical doctrines when the experience of seekers suggests that a cafeteria model of spirituality best meets their needs?

This question leads to the point that the re-form of the church is not merely an organizational adaptation that simply recasts an unchanging core of Protestant doctrine but is also a transformation of the contours of evangelical belief, thought, and doctrine. The innovative forms of the seeker church are not simply neutral containers into which the Gospel message is poured; these forms also shape the content of what is taught. In other words, how Christianity is conveyed may influence what kind of Christianity is developed. This suggests that seeker church leaders may not be aware of the paradox of unintended consequences, of how leaders cannot always control or predict where their movements will go. In the seeker church movement's creative synthesis of evangelical core beliefs coupled with a commitment to meeting the needs of seekers and translating its message into therapeutic terminology, the innovative cultural packaging might re-form the religious content. The central issue here is the perennial Christian and missiological tension between translation and transformation: How does one present the Christian message in ways that are culturally relevant yet doctrinally consistent?

Many seeker church leaders recognize that this is a central issue facing the movement. Willow Creek's Lee Stroebel says the seeker church movement must "remain focused on the fact that our mission isn't to *transform* the Gospel into something it isn't in order to soft sell it to secular people. Our mission is to *translate* the Gospel—to maintain its integrity [while] creatively presenting it in such a way that Unchurched Harrys and Marys in the 1990s can understand."[29] Similarly, the *Willow Creek Monthly* suggests, "The most difficult question that each church must wrestle with before God is, 'When does cultural relevancy undermine the biblically functioning community? In other words, at what point is the adoption of a contemporary style pushed too far, compromising the life of the church and the honor of God?'"

In general, seeker churches have basically agreed on the positive benefits incurred by using contemporary music, drama, and relevant messages. According to the *Willow Creek Monthly*, practices whose cultural relevancy might compromise the life of the church include "[p]astors who preach sanitized talk-show fodder, vocalists who play 'rock star,' or churches that stage purely sensational events with no substance or purpose other than to attract attention. [These] produce a hollow imitation of the Church that caters to the applause of men."[30] The line between *Donahue*-style messages and "relevant felt needs preaching," between inappropriate "rock star" imitations and God-honoring "vocal specials," and between sensational, purposeless proceedings and substantive, salient events is not extensively explored in seeker church literature. In part, this is because the non-negotiables are based primarily on a few basic theological doctrines; seeker churches thus far have not inquired with much diligence into what limits it might be prudent to set on cultural adaptation.

There is some uneasiness, or at least awareness, among seeker church pastors about the potential cultural consequences of the movement's translation strategy. When asked if "by focusing on the felt needs of seekers, churches run the risk of conforming to the secular world," pastors were evenly divided, with 46 percent agreeing with the statement and 43 percent disagreeing. Furthermore, several pastors who were interviewed expressed concern that an uncritical emphasis on felt needs might compromise the church's theological orthodoxy. One pastor acknowledged that "there has been a powerful tendency, even among strong evangelical churches, to become more pop psychology oriented."

The task of translating the historic truths of Christianity into a more contemporary form raises the question, "How far can one we go?" Some pastors are wrestling with this question as they design their ministries to seekers. In an interview on the ABC News television program *In the Name of God*, Pastor Dave Guerin of Ridge Pointe Community Church in Holland, Michigan, commented, "The danger is always that we will so accommodate ourselves to the culture in which we find ourselves that the message will be watered down. We'll give in to modernity. The key to avoiding that is to determine ahead of time what are the non-negotiables, what are the hills that you'll die on. Let's determine those up front. Let's do everything we can to protect and preserve those. As for the rest, that's all negotiable."[31]

Despite this awareness, no church, according to my research, had established guidelines regarding how much innovation, such as incorporating therapeutic categories into messages, is appropriate. In general, most pastors conceded that their chief criterion for determining the appropriateness of an outreach strategy was whether an action or statement conflicted with Scripture. As one pastor acknowledged, "We don't have a statement that says we'll only go this far. I think we'll do whatever it takes, as long as its biblical." "I think a commitment to Scripture and being Bible based," admitted another pastor, "is what prevents or protects us from wandering to the whims of the culture."

Where the whims of the culture may be strongest—and most challenging—for seeker churches is in the role of experience. By stressing the importance of reaching seekers emotionally, these churches have developed an effective means of communication. Focusing on the felt needs of visitors and the idiom of the culture helps make the sacred more accessible to many visitors. But the challenge for evangelical churches in stressing experience is that it is also the standard by which liberal denominations have justified theological innovations such as the ordination of women or the blessing of same-sex marriages. Experience is thus a double-edged sword for evangelical seeker churches. The stress on relevant, contemporary services and messages enhances the fit between these churches and the culture. But the therapeutic ethos of contemporary culture might unwittingly reshape the practices and beliefs (if not actual doctrine) of seeker churches.[32]

The most cautionary example for seeker churches might be Robert Schuller's "new reformation" of theology. Schuller argues that traditional theological terms should be translated into contemporary language. This translation exercise becomes more controversial when Schuller translates a central concept such as sin as the "absence of self-esteem." In a cultural environment suffused with therapeutic terminology, this translation could result in an unintended transformation of religious meaning. One resource that seeker churches could reconsider in their effort to translate the evangelical message, given the entrepreneurial character of the movement, its lack of strong denominational identity, and its relative distancing from seminaries, is tradition.

Tradition Reconsidered

How might tradition help seeker churches negotiate the tensions between translation and transformation? Seeker church leaders are likely to view tradition, as Yale's Jaroslav Pelikan has put it, as the dead faith of the living, rather than the living faith of the dead. For purposes of this discussion, I use "tradition" simply to refer to the church's concerted commitment to remember and retell the Christian story, whether through liturgy, music, teaching, preaching, storytelling, the church calendar, denominational distinctiveness, or personal identification with a religious tradition. Tradition, in short, represents a willingness to incorporate the lessons and practices of the past into the present.

What role might tradition, understood in this way, perform in the church? Robert Wuthnow suggests that tradition empowers the church to impart an identity upon its congregants—it helps people to understand themselves as

Christians. If this term "Christian" is to have any meaning, then the church must convey the significance of this identity to its members and the world at large. The church, according to Wuthnow, defines the Christian identity (and subsequently bestows this identity upon its members) in three ways. First, it identifies Christians as part of a community of memory. Then it locates them within various denominations. Lastly, it incorporates them within a supportive community.

To begin, Wuthnow asserts that, as a community of memory, "the church must . . . be backward looking; it has a special mission to preserve the past, to carry on a tradition."[33] Accordingly, tradition links people to the past and helps them forge shared identities based on these links (that is, people identify themselves in corporate terms as Presbyterian, Baptist, or even Reformed Christians, rather than simply as Christians). Tradition places an individual's personal narrative into a larger, historical framework concerning the good toward which he or she should strive. Alasdair MacIntyre argues that each person's identity is forged out of an inherited past that is informed by tradition. Contrary to the modern perception of individuals as self-creating and autonomous, MacIntyre claims that one's identity is not a hyper-subjective creation but is the concrete product of our entanglements with the past and present. "I find myself part of a history and that is generally to say, whether I like it or not, whether I recognize it or not, one of the bearers of a tradition." Thus, "the history of each of our own lives is generally and characteristically embedded in and made intelligible in terms of the larger and longer histories of a number of traditions."[34]

While MacIntyre's conception of tradition is broad—he considers utilitarianism and individualism as much as any specifically religious system of thought—his discussion nevertheless highlights tradition's formative role upon individual identity. To discount tradition completely, as most seeker churches do, is to embrace a modern conception of the self as completely autonomous. Such a view may impair the church's ability to confer the identity of Christian upon its members. Lutheran writer Marva Dawn echoes MacIntyre's analysis of the social value of tradition by arguing that "tradition serves as mode for relating to the present through contact with both the practices of the past and our collective hope for the future."[35] Thus, remembering the past is vital to the continuing vitality of a tradition and the church's subsequent designation as a community of memory.

The church not only identifies Christians as part of a community of memory, but it also locates Christians within particular denominations. Denominations preserve and reinforce tradition by reasserting specific theological statements (for example, the Westminster Confession of Faith) and enacting particular orders of worship (for example, *The Book of Common Prayer*). The gravitation of seeker churches' away from denominationalism, especially when viewed from the perspective of Wuthnow's three identity-forming functions of the church, is revealing. Granted, denominations have many functions, including some rather prosaic organizational and administrative ones. But they also are carriers of traditions that impart a sense of historical connection to Christians while providing a corrective against present ideologies and forms.

Of the three identity-forming functions described by Wuthnow, seeker churches tend to stress, often exclusively, the role of the church in creating a supportive community. The appeal of this is that it highlights the church's potential to meet the needs of individuals. Seeker churches tend to view themselves as a form of support group rather than as a community of memory or denomination, largely because this view of the church makes sense to Unchurched Harry. As the previous discussion of small groups suggests, the memory of many groups may not extend much beyond the personal experiences of the group members. Tradition may not be user-friendly, but it can be an invaluable source of time-honored wisdom to these groups and to these churches. When the church becomes another support group, it reinforces a trend toward the privatization of religious belief, a development that is consistent with neosecularization theory.

Interestingly, there is some evidence of a growing dissatisfaction within Protestant circles with evangelicalism's lack of historical perspective. Evidently, there is now a small but nevertheless visible move toward Catholic, Anglican, and Orthodox churches on the part of some prominent evangelical leaders.[36] Intrigued by this development, John Seel documents a widespread dissatisfaction among evangelical leaders with what they describe as the superficiality of evangelicalism. As one evangelical pastor put it, "Some folks like me [are] more at home in one of the old historic traditions . . . because [we] are so depressed over the state of Protestantism."[37]

Some seeker church pastors are concerned about the potential for contemporary culture to reshape the movement in the long run. One pastor, whose church left the Christian Reformed denomination, noted the devaluation of tradition within the seeker church movement. When asked whether seeker churches tend to foster distrust in the church's historic creeds, this pastor answered, "That's a terribly dangerous development—a dangerous potential that exists within the seeker movement." His concern was that, although some seeker churches are sensitive to the importance of tradition, others are not sufficiently connected to historic Christian orthodoxy and do not appreciate its importance as a bulwark against excessive accommodation to the culture.

> I would feel much better if I were confident that [seeker churches] shared an appreciation of, and commitment to, some of the traditional creeds and confessions of the church that, when we're dead and gone, will still be around. So churches can say this is biblical, this is orthodox. [That's] one of the real dangers. As is often the case, the greatest strengths lie next to the greatest weaknesses. And so the willingness to push the envelope, to break the paradigm, to stretch and grow people out of their comfort zones—that's the wonderful strength of this movement, but unfortunately it exposes our real weakness, which is that we sort of throw the lines on the dock and we're not moored to anything. So the tendency to drift is much greater. . . . I think people are beginning to drift.

A Final Word

Is the seeker church movement is not only a modern revival but also, and more importantly, a second Reformation, based not on doctrine but on form? The organizational innovations of seeker churches have resulted in dramatic growth of these congregations. These churches could also have a major cultural impact (by being "salt and light" in the world) as they pursue the evangelical strategy of changing the world by changing individuals. Thus, the impact of tens of thousands of "fully devoted followers of Christ" would have a noticeable and beneficial effect on society. Seeker churches would become, in Willow Creek's terminology, "prevailing churches." In addition, seeker churches might become in effect the new Mainline in American Protestantism, or at least the vital center. Prominent pastors such as Bill Hybels, Rick Warren, and their successors might be known not only to other innovative evangelical pastors but also to the broader public. They might become the new "Billy Grahams" of evangelicalism. Although none of the prominent seeker church pastors has as far as I know expressed any interest in such a prominent public position, it is a potential result of the ongoing growth and influence of seeker churches.

The road to this influence will also be shaped by the inevitable tensions between translation and tradition. These tensions also reveal that some of the important questions about the seeker church movement are theological, not just sociological. Sociological analysis can connect the development of seeker churches to larger changes in the American religious environment, examining under what social conditions certain types of religion or other cultural products are more likely to prosper. There is also, however, a normative dimension to most discussion of seeker churches. Pastors, scholars, and other observers ask not only "What are these churches doing?" but also "Are they doing what they *should* be doing?" Some critics caution that pursuing relevance at all costs might unintentionally influence the content of Christian teaching.[38] To guard against this, pastors may need to reconsider the ways in which tradition can moor their quest for relevance.

The question of what churches *should* be doing is fundamentally theological, although there are undoubtedly sociological aspects as well. Some of the debates regarding seeker churches resemble "high brow"/"low brow" debates in culture. Should churches play traditional music such as Bach or should they reach the masses with soft rock and smooth jazz compositions? Should pastors educate the laity on the finer points of theology or should they address the daily concerns of parishioners? And how would one assess whether various innovations are careful contextualizations or excessive accommodations to modern culture? The Archimedean vantage point from which to assess the purity of such innovations is always out of reach. However, it seems that a basic principle for evaluating these tensions might be to examine the balance between theology and technique within the seeker church movement. What role, if any, does theology play in seeker churches?[39] Although many pastors assume that the theological underpinnings of what they do are secure, will they continue to be secure after a generation of leaders is trained largely by the seeker churches themselves?

To say that the answers are elusive is not to say they are not worth pursuing. Given the emergence and potential future influence of seeker churches, an exploration of the tensions between contextualization and capitulation is worth further consideration by those inside and outside the movement, by theologians as well as by sociologists. There is not a pure model of the first-century church that one side can hold up as the final justification for what they do. There is, however, a long history of Christian engagement with the societies in which churches find themselves that might offer some useful principles for how to be "as wise as serpents and as innocent as doves." What is now clear about the seeker church movement is that it will be shaping the American religious landscape well into the twenty-first century. What is not as clear is how much the culture will be reforming these churches as well.

Appendix A

Most dynamic movements in church history have been led by people who were willing to break the mold and try ministry a new way.[1]

A Brief History of Willow Creek Community Church

On October 12, 1975, Willow Creek Community Church held its first service at the Willow Creek Theater in Palatine, Illinois. On this night, a group of young, dedicated Christians led approximately one hundred teenagers and their parents, friends, and neighbors in a rousing evening of song, drama, and teaching. The dream of the leaders "was to build a church that would speak the language of our modern culture and encourage non-believers to investigate Christianity at their own pace, free from the traditional trappings of religion that tend to chase [non-believers] away."[2] In this endeavor, the Willow Creek leaders were phenomenally successful. In just over a year, attendance at services had soared to one thousand. By the church's third year, it was at nearly three thousand.[3]

In 1977, just two years after its founding, Willow Creek purchased ninety acres of land in nearby South Barrington and started to build its own modern worship center. In February 1981, the church's spacious, modern auditorium was complete, but attendance soon eclipsed the building's capacity—a trend that continues to this day. Eventually, the church increased the auditorium's seating capacity to forty-five hundred. In 1984 it added an educational wing; in 1988 it opened a chapel. Between 1985 and 1987, attendance at Willow Creek nearly doubled from around five thousand to nine thousand.[4] By 1988, attendance had reached an unprecedented eleven thousand.[5] This rapid growth placed immense pressure on Willow

Creek's facilities. In 1992, another expansion nearly doubled the existing space, adding an atrium food court (referred to as Willow Creek's "great room"), a gymnasium with three basketball courts, conference meeting facilities, and long hallways full of classrooms and nurseries. Along with this growth in facilities came another surge in attendance. Today, fifteen thousand people navigate their way through Willow Creek's vast facilities every weekend.

Willow Creek's rising popularity is not limited to its exceedingly popular seeker services. In 1992, Willow Creek established the Willow Creek Association to help provide training and resources to pastors intrigued by Willow Creek's dramatic growth. This association reaches out to churches and pastors, both nationally and internationally, who express interest in applying Willow Creek's outreach philosophy. Today its membership roll includes more than five thousand churches.

No one could have predicted the extent of Willow Creek's phenomenal success, least of all its founders.[6] As Lynne Hybels, wife of founder Bill Hybels, admits, "[T]he unimpressive truth is that we made the whole thing up as we went along."[7] Leaders followed their instincts as they experimented with innovative changes, some successful and some not. Indeed, just as the success, and even worldwide influence, of Willow Creek could never have been predicted by its founders, neither could they have envisioned the toll that the pioneering model of church would have on their personal lives, their families, and their growing congregation. Willow Creek has blossomed in extraordinary ways, but the path to success has been marked by hardship, struggle, disillusionment, and crisis. Before we discuss what Willow Creek has dubbed the "train wreck," its darkest hour, let us take a closer look at Willow Creek's founders, whose backgrounds in business and music, respectively, shaped the church's philosophy and its future.

Willow Creek's Founding and Philosophy

Willow Creek's tremendous success as well as its shortcomings stem from origins tied closely to the friendship and creative partnership of two very different men: Bill Hybels and Dave Holmbo. Bill Hybels, the son of a successful Michigan businessman, was groomed from an early age to inherit his family's business, a wholesale vegetable company. Hybels was raised in the Christian Reformed church, "a group of about fifty tightly knit, hard-working, independent, decent people who met in a one-room school house [and taught] the high value of Scripture, the importance of family, work integrity, [and] perseverance in faith."[8] In retrospect, Hybels also learned that a tightly knit, traditional Dutch church was not a particularly welcoming place in which to investigate the claims of Christianity. Meanwhile, Hybels recalls that after two years of college, "The study of business theory nearly bored me to death." He returned to the family business prepared to follow in his father's footsteps. "I loved the adrenaline of the marketplace. I was charged up by the challenge—to do things a little more efficiently, to organize better, to maximize resources, and then to make a ton of money. I knew where I was headed and what I wanted."[9]

Despite this confidence, Hybels's ambition soon took an unprecedented turn. It all began when the director of a Christian camp where Hybels was working asked him, "What are you doing with your life that will last forever?" The question prompted a wholesale reevaluation of Hybels's priorities. He decided to leave the family business. When he announced his intentions to his father, his father accepted his decision—and demanded that his son relinquish his company credit cards and keys to the company plane, boat, and cars. Having made this sacrifice, Hybels then took a job in the shipping department of a Christian organization in the Chicago area, unsure how exactly to pursue his calling in the ministry.

In 1972, Dave Holmbo, an old camp friend of Hybels, took a job as assistant music director at South Park Church, in Park Ridge, Illinois. South Park was an independent evangelical church that, while conservative theologically, was open to innovation in its services and had started a service that featured contemporary music. As one attender described it, South Park demonstrated "an unusual degree of openness and spiritual authenticity."[10] Dave Holmbo, a gifted musician whose talents were underutilized in his parents' strictly fundamentalist church, quickly found his niche there.[11] At South Park, Holmbo founded Son Company, a Christian rock band complete with singers, guitars, saxophones, trumpets, and drums. When looking for an additional guitarist, Holmbo enlisted his old camp friend Bill Hybels, who had just started attending the church. Soon after, Hybels began to lead a Bible study for students after music rehearsals. By the spring of 1973, the group had grown to eighty students. The leaders then decided to dedicate a whole evening to reaching teenagers and their "seeking" friends. Members of the group suggested that the meeting be moved out of the church basement, that songs such as "Kumbayah" be replaced with Christian rock, that dramas be used to illustrate key themes, and that Hybels substitute thematic and practical Christian messages for his usual in-depth studies of Scriptural passages.[12] This new teen outreach was dubbed "Son City." On its first appearance in 1973, more than one hundred students attended. Within six months, there were more than three hundred attenders. Holmbo later reflected, "I think we knew after the first few Son Cities that something powerful was happening."[13]

The early success of Son City established some key principles that Willow Creek would later adopt for its own. The first was the importance of a separate service for seekers that featured contemporary music, lots of creative entertainment, and relevant messages. South Park's Son City was not a traditional church youth group by any stretch of the imagination. Not only was the music contemporary, but the whole meeting had a playful, even ir-reverent, edge. One year, Son City held a "Hallowed Queen" contest in which the men dressed in drag. After the Halloween event, South Park's senior pastor confronted Hybels and Holmbo, "Why are there bright polka dots painted on the baptismal walls?" The motto of Son City could well have been "Anything bigger, better, and more bizarre."[14] Son City's zaniness re-flected the personalities of its leaders, as well as the influence of such para-church organizations as Young Life and Campus Life. The second key principle was the need for an additional weekly meeting geared toward practicing Christians, hence the establishment of Son Village. This dual structure of services for seekers and for believers undergirds Willow Creek's approach today.

Leaders of Son City emphasized other principles in addition to the prior-ity placed on having fun. Responsibilities, ranging from teaching to manag-ing the sound and lighting technical equipment, were doled out to leaders based on their gifts and interests. Leaders expected high levels of commit-ment from core group members. And the concept of promoting leaders from within the group was established as well. All of Son City's distinctive characteristics—a separate seeker service, gift-based ministry, the use of the creative arts, hiring from within—later would become hallmarks of Wil-low Creek's strategy of ministry.

By the summer of 1974, attendance at Son City surpassed five hundred and, by the next year, had doubled to more than one thousand.[15] The businessman-turned-teacher and the Christian rock musician made a good team. Hybels provided the teaching while Holmbo developed the music, drama, and programming. What these two men shared, according to Lynne Hybels, was "a mutual frustration with how (the church) had been done in their past; and a mutual yearning to do it another way."[16] As Son City grew, the interest in presenting Christianity in an attractive, contemporary, and at times irreverent way continued to mount. Hybels, at the age of twenty-three, now began to think about starting a church. As successful as Son City was, it was not having much of an impact on anyone over the age of eighteen. Hybels recalls, "I just felt that if we were ever going to reach a city or a state or a country or a world, as Jesus asked us to, then we were going to do it through whole families, not just youth."[17]

The vision to establish a church was catching on at the same time with some of the other Son City leaders. One of these leaders believed that starting a church was "just a natural response to what was going on at Son City."[18] Logistical pressures were also fueling change. By 1975, twice as many students were attending Son City as there were adults attending South Park Church. Additionally, the leaders' vision for a new kind of church was significantly influenced by two of Hybels's mentors: Gilbert Bilezikian, one of Hybels's college professors, and Robert Schuller, the founder of the Crystal Cathedral.

Gilbert Bilezikian was a professor of Biblical Studies at Trinity College in Deerfield, Illinois. While a student there, Hybels took several classes with him. Hybels recounts in one of his later sermons that Bilezikian's great strength was that "he was a fantastic vision caster and vision clarifier of the Bible and the church." Bilezikian taught that God's "A priority" was "the establishment and development of biblically functioning communities." This enthusiasm slowly ignited Hybels's interest:

It took me a long time to understand what it was he was trying to describe, many, many months. But when he talked about these biblically functioning communities that God wanted to establish and build in the world, he reminded me of . . . Martin Luther King on the steps of the Lincoln Memorial when he said "I have a dream!" That's the kind of energy that Dr. B. brought to this passage.[19]

These communities, according to Bilezikian, would be "different from every other group and organism in society. They will be supernatural communities where the awesome will become commonplace, where God's activity will be palpable, where lives will change, where the unwelcome will feel welcome, and racial lines will be blurred, and the rich and poor will come together." The appeal of this vision persisted to grow on Hybels until he was ready to commit himself to the establishment and development of such a community. Hybels recalls:

> At a point along the way, I was a goner. I could not imagine going to my grave without at least trying one time to see if what happened in the first century in that biblically functioning community could happen in the twentieth century in the United States. I could not give my life at that point to a lesser dream, not until I had first tried to do the big one. And so for the last twenty-two years, . . . this passage [Acts 2:42-47] has been the magnetic beacon for my life, and it's not getting weaker.[20]

Over the last twenty years, Bilezikian has continued to play an important role in the development of Willow Creek, and one of Hybels's books is dedicated to him.[21] The *Willow Creek Monthly* magazine claims that Dr. Bilezikian's influence upon the church was so critical that "we trace the beginning of our congregation back to a French-born professor [Bilezikian]."[22] But while the professor helped to spark the vision for the new church, Hybels and the other Son City leaders needed to find some existing models of churches that were attracting the unchurched. They found such a model at Robert Schuller's Garden Grove Community Church.

The church, subsequently renamed the Crystal Cathedral, was an inspiration to many of Willow Creek's early members. Schuller's first influence on the development of Willow Creek was through his book *Your Church Has Real Possibilities*. One early member recalls that all the Son City leaders read it and "it just turned us on. This guy really [understood] the kinds of things that we're trying to do and he's doing it and doing it in this positive, incredibly exciting way."[23] In 1975, Bill Hybels attended Schuller's Institute for Church Leadership and, a year later, approximately twenty-five key staff and lay leaders of Willow Creek attended. At one point during the conference, the Willow Creek contingent found itself in Schuller's office in the Tower of Prayer. Hybels asked Schuller if he could give them any advice regarding their plans to buy land for a future building. Schuller replied, "If God chooses to do a miracle, you'd better be ready for it. Don't buy a thimbleful of land. Buy a fifty-gallon drum."[24] In 1977, Schuller spoke at Willow Creek's fund-raising banquet to help the new church raise the money to "buy a fifty-gallon drum." Although the initial effort fell short of the mark, Willow Creek was eventually able to purchase the land upon which Willow Creek's extraordinary facilities are now located.

Leaders at Willow Creek tend to downplay Schuller's influence in part because many evangelicals have reservations about Schuller's approach.[25] Nevertheless, one pastor of a nondenominational church in California said, "Willow Creek is an updated version of Schuller. He was the forerunner." Another pastor of a nondenominational church in Pennsylvania concurred. Remarking that on his first visit to Willow Creek he was reminded him of Schuller's Crystal Cathedral: "You don't hear [Hybels] talk about [Schuller's influence] much but I think he mainstreamed the concept that Schuller had done and turned a lot of people off. I got to know Hybels's ministry quite well and read some of Schuller's stuff and thought, well, this is just a mainstreaming of the Schuller concept." "Mainstreaming" involves convincing evangelical Christians that a seeker-oriented approach does not necessarily water down the Gospel. According to this pastor, Hybels, unlike Schuller, has "been able to package [the seeker approach] in a way that appeals to evangelicals rather than alienates them. . . . Hybels has been able to let [evangelicals] know that he is passionately interested in the same things that they are. I don't think Schuller was as good at that. Schuller could reach seekers but Hybels could do both."

For example, evangelicals have criticized Schuller's translation of biblical concepts into contemporary language, particularly the language of psychology. One of Schuller's main works, *Self-Esteem: The New Reformation*, is particularly troubling to many evangelicals because in it Schuller argues that the church must abandon theocentric language and focus instead on communicating the truth to seekers in terms they will understand, terms that draw largely on the vocabulary of pop psychology. While Willow Creek does use terminology that is more explicitly Christian than Schuller's "positive" updating of Christian concepts, his influence was nonetheless significant in the formative stages of Willow Creek's model development.

Even with the inspiration of Dr. Bilezikian and the practical example provided by Schuller, the initial reaction to Hybels's proposal to found a new church was unfavorable. Holmbo wanted to stay with Son City. Bilezikian doubted that the Son City approach would work with adults. Still, by the summer of 1975, both Hybels and Holmbo had quit their jobs at South Park. One of their first steps, inspired by Schuller's own church-planting efforts, was to conduct a door-to-door survey of local residents, asking them if they attended church and, if not, what their reasons were for not attending.[26] The survey yielded five insights: (1)nonattenders think that the church is always asking for money; (2) the church's music is off-putting; (3) the message is irrelevant; (4) the services are predictable and boring; and (5) the church makes newcomers feel guilty. This survey confirmed much of the Son City approach to ministry. Later that fall, Willow Creek Community Church began.

The demands of creating a seeker church were formidable. The church's accelerated growth and the ensuing need for larger facilities placed tremendous pressure on the young staff. An initial effort to raise six hundred thousand dollars to buy property for a church building fell short of its goal. Long hours, low accountability, and high levels of burnout started to take their toll. In early 1978, Hybels gathered the staff and suggested that someone needed to take charge. Hybels volunteered himself for the "senior pastor" position, and a new era in Willow Creek's brief history began.

The first thing Hybels did at the helm was to form a three-member board of elders to deal with the financial, administrative, and moral crises of the church. Holmbo, cofounder of the church, resigned largely because of "critical errors" regarding his "personal moral life and integrity."[27] A few months later, Hybels asked another staff member to leave because of personal indiscretions. From 1979 to 1981, Willow Creek endured its darkest hour. "We were always one New Community [mid-week believers' service] away from extinction," admits Hybels.[28] Many of the church's staff and leaders left during this period, and attendance dropped by about two hundred (from a high of eighteen hundred). Despite this turmoil—referred to by Willow Creek as "the train wreck"—the church began construction on its new building in June of 1979. On February 15, 1981, when Willow Creek held its first service in its new building, there was a sense that the church had indeed survived its darkest hour.

Consequences of the "Train Wreck"

The "train wreck" was a transformative episode in the history of Willow Creek. The content of the preaching, the management of the church, and the tone of the services were all affected. Hybels admits that it was a struggle "to keep a biblical balance between God's holiness and His love" in his preaching and his relations with church members. Lynne Hybels recalls that those coming to the seeker services "too seldom heard the truth of God's love . . . against the backdrop of God's justice and holiness. Without the proper balance in teaching, Willow Creek became a breeding ground for spiritual carelessness."[29] A special edition of *Willow Creek* magazine noted that the word "sin" was "almost never heard in the early days of the church."[30] In addition to imbalanced teaching, Lynne Hybels suggests that the insane pace of life, financial stress, and reliance upon immature leaders contributed to the implosion at Willow Creek in 1979.

In order to correct some of these imbalances, Hybels embarked on a teaching program that strongly emphasized the holiness of God and exhorted the members of New Community to "pursue purity" more deliberately. This remained a regular theme of teaching for the next few years. In 1982, Hybels studied at R. C. Sproul's Ligonier Valley Study Center. Sproul's teaching on "the holiness of God was pivotal in Bill's spiritual development, both theologically and experientially."[31]

The "train wreck" also demonstrated that Willow Creek needed to place a much stronger emphasis on accountability.[32] Hybels vowed to put more effort into leading his staff and to develop a more formal reporting structure. The writings of management expert Peter Drucker, particularly *The Effective Executive*, began to circulate among the staff. Kenneth Blanchard's *Leadership and the One Minute Manager* was also popular. Structurally, the overall leadership of the church passed from the staff to the board of elders; Hybels, too, came under the authority of the board. With the continuing growth of the church, the board transferred leadership responsibilities to an executive pastor so that Hybels could focus on teaching. Church elders also took on more responsibility. They interviewed potential staff and new members, instituted checks and balances on the handling of finances, and oversaw the general direction of the teaching. One important result of this response to the earlier difficulties was that "the church became a spiritual business and adopted the techniques of management."[33]

While the Willow Creek staff adjusted to the major changes, it discovered in the mid-1980s that its ministry was once again beginning to grow. When Hybels launched a series on the Ten Commandments in 1983, Sunday attendance increased from forty-one hundred to forty-six hundred. And the church's weekend services grew steadily throughout the decade. With growth came increasing respectability in evangelical circles. According to Lynne Hybels, it was only during the late 1980s that Willow Creek "finally seemed to have shed its image as the black sheep of the Christian community."[34] Hybels was invited to speak at conferences across the country, and attendance at Willow Creek's church leadership conferences began to grow rapidly. Evangelical pastors and the national media had discovered Willow Creek.

As more people came to Willow Creek, the church needed to expand its facilities again. The church began a $23 million building program in 1989. To cope with the extraordinary demands upon Hybels's time, Willow Creek hired another pastor, Jim Dethmer, to "team teach" with Hybels in 1990. Growth continued at Willow Creek in the early 1990s, placing even greater strains on the staff and the church's various ministries. Willow Creek also adopted church consultant Carl George's metachurch model of small-group ministry in order to help the church integrate the explosion of new attenders into the church and to involve more of the church's laity in positions of leadership. The goal of this adaptation was to incorporate newcomers into the church while, at the same time, making Willow Creek "smaller." This was done by emphasizing the development of small groups in every church department. Initially, many staff members were demoralized by this transition from "doing ministry" to "utilizing volunteers." Lynne Hybels suggests, however, that the changes inherent in building a small-group ministry were well worth it because the development of a churchwide small-group ministry enabled Willow Creek to do a better job of discipleship, which had been "a tough challenge."[35]

During all these changes, Willow Creek opened its new building addition in 1992, launched the New Community Institute to provide more teaching opportunities for church members, and later that year created the Willow Creek Association to respond to the international demand for information and training on seeker-oriented ministry. Additionally, Willow Creek has turned its focus more deliberately to outreach, an area in which the church had been hindered by "the nearly overwhelming challenge of responding to the extraordinary work of God through the evangelistic 'mission' of our seeker services."[36] In November 1994, the church announced that it would dramatically expand the scope of its international ministries. Today, Willow Creek works in partnership with Christian service organizations such as World Vision, Prison Fellowship, and Habitat for Humanity. It especially focuses its efforts on Chicago and the Dominican Republic and also operates its own food bank and creates service-oriented small groups that minister to the community in many capacities.

One of the remarkable aspects of Lynne Hybels's account of Willow Creek's history is the amount of pain, loneliness, and isolation church leaders have undergone: "In December 1989 Bill crashed in an explosion of tears in his office on a Saturday afternoon, and in December the following year, I was overwhelmed by the depression that had tormented me for years. For the past five years our personal life has been in turmoil as we have tripped over one another's pain and stumbled over one difficult lesson after the next."[37]

Success has come at a high personal price to Willow Creek's leaders. One response to these personal crises has been the church's emphasis on "emotional authenticity and healing." For example, the church regularly offers teaching series on personal healing; "Hunger for Healing," for example, was based on the twelve steps of the recovery movement. In fact, insights from the recovery movement have clearly influenced Hybels, along with the entire Willow Creek staff. Hybels even argued that the concept of "codependency" was the fundamental idea of the 1980s.[38]

This brief history of Willow Creek illustrates some of the strengths and weaknesses of the seeker church movement in general. Clearly, evangelism, creativity, and relevant communication are the movement's strengths. Discipleship, teaching on the holiness and transcendence of God, not just God's love, and a dedication to service are some areas of weakness in the seeker church model. One of the greatest challenges to the seeker church movement is its incorporation of psychological themes in its "relevant" messages. When does emphasizing the this-worldly fulfillment of the Christian life become enmeshed in a psychological worldview that tends to undercut classical Christian understandings of sin, holiness, and the call to self-sacrifice? Twenty years after its founding, Willow Creek is taking significant steps to address its areas of weakness—and to help other churches learn from its experiences through the various services provided by the Willow Creek Association.

While many churches and writers are contributing to the rising tide of seeker-friendly ministries, Willow Creek is clearly one of the most influential. The rapid growth of the Willow Creek Association testifies to the church's influence in evangelical Protestantism. For example, George Barna, in *Marketing the Church,* acknowledges his debt to Bill Hybels and the vision of Willow Creek. Writing that he first understood "the meaning of evangelism and church growth" when visiting Willow Creek, Barna hopes that "one day [there] would be 100,000 Willow Creek churches in this country."[39]

Appendix B

Methodology and Survey Information

In order to document the growth of the seeker church movement and the influence of Willow Creek among seeker churches, I conducted the Seeker Church Pastor (SCP) survey of the membership of the Willow Creek Association. This survey, conducted with the assistance of the University of Virginia's Center for Survey Research, provides an original data set for my analysis of the seeker church movement.[1] In order to determine the survey sample, I first obtained the U.S. membership list of the Willow Creek Association. This list consisted of 700 entries. I eliminated those entries which did not appear to have any clear connection with a church (for example, the address lacked a reference to a church or excluded either the title of "pastor" or "minister"). This reduced the sample size to approximately 650. Because of financial limitations, I needed to reduce the sample size to 600 entries. I did this by removing every fourteenth address.

In planning the SCP survey, I relied extensively on Dillman's "total design method" for writing the questions, arranging the layout, selecting the size and length of the instrument, and every other aspect of the survey process.[2] Dillman's guidelines convinced me to use a mail survey and helped me ensure that the survey questions were precise, fair, accurate, and not overly demanding for the respondent. Furthermore, Dillman's careful elaboration of the mechanics and timing of the survey mailing—including topics such as how to write a cover letter and when to send a follow-up reminder—helped me achieve high response rates to a survey that some respondents said took between thirty and forty minutes to complete. Professor Thomas M. Guterbock, director of the University of Virginia's Center for Survey Research, offered his considerable expertise in developing and refining the survey instrument. Several local pastors graciously agreed to participate in an informal pretest of the survey instrument. The survey, cover letter, and prepaid business return envelope were first mailed on 12 March 1995. Ten days later, a reminder postcard was sent to the entire sample. On 4 April 1995, a second letter (this time from Professor Guterbock), a second copy of the questionnaire, and a return envelope were mailed to those pastors who had not yet returned the initial survey. Out of six hundred total contacts, only eight were ineligible for inclusion in the final count, either because of a lack of forwarding address or the respondent's self-description as ineligible. Of the remaining 592 contacts, 462 returned a completed survey, resulting in an overall response rate of 78.0 percent. Only three surveys (0.5 percent) were either refused or returned blank. The staff of the Center for Survey Research performed the data entry and reliability checks with professionalism and remarkable efficiency.[3]

Content Analysis of Messages

I analyzed more than one year's worth of transcribed Willow Creek seeker church messages for my content analysis. In preparing my sermon sample, I narrowed this set of sermons to a one-year span and then eliminated any messages that were delivered by guest speakers. Because the vast majority of Willow Creek messages are part of various topical series, such as "Dealing with Anger," "The Greatest Sermon in the World," or "Facing the Family Challenge," I selected for my sample only messages that were part of a series. That narrowed the set of messages for my content analysis to approximately forty. In order to conduct my analysis, I relied on the methodology suggested by Williamson.[4] After an initial reading through a subsample of the messages, I derived the categories that would direct the coding of the messages. In the Willow Creek seeker messages, I was especially interested to see how God is presented: Do seeker church messages stress God's love more than divine judgment? Do the messages focus more on God's immanence more than on God's transcendence? Is God mysterious and inscrutable or friendly and accessible? In addition, I examined how the sermons presented sin, how they attempted to convince seekers that should consider Christianity's truth claims, and the reasons they gave for belief. Marsha Witten's substantive work also proved to be invaluable as a guide toward understanding the richness and subtlety of religious discourse.[5]

Conferences and Critics

In order to learn more about the broader seeker church movement, I attended three conferences offered by some of the most influential leaders in the field. The conferences were organized by Willow Creek, Saddleback Valley Community Church, and church consultant George Barna.[6] Popular media accounts of prominent churches, including Willow Creek and Houston's "Exciting Second," were another important source of information on the seeker church movement. I have included the most helpful of the popular accounts in the bibliography.

Not all Christians are enamored of the seeker church movement. Many traditional churches are disturbed by the contemporary style of seeker churches. Moreover, some denominational leaders recognize the challenge that the seeker church movement poses to their institutions. In order to represent correctly the views of seeker church opponents, I read many recent books that are critical of the movement.[7]

Interviews and Site Visits

In order to develop a greater understanding of the seeker church movement, I interviewed two dozen seeker church pastors from across the country, six each from the East, Midwest, South, and West. To preserve the confidentiality of my interviewees' identity, I refer to them only by the denominational affiliation and regional location of the church. All of the pastors that I interviewed were remarkably cooperative and generous with their time, and I am most grateful for their assistance.

The interviews that I completed before designing the survey helped me identify those areas of interest that the survey needed to address. One area of particular interest was raised by numerous pastors, all of whom emphasized how the Willow Creek Association was far more influential to their work than was the denomination of their church.

In addition to my interview work, I visited ten seeker churches, including Willow Creek, which I visited three times. Three churches, including Saddleback Valley Community Church, were in Southern California, and six were within driving distance of Charlottesville.[8] A list of the churches I visited follows.

Willow Creek Community Church, South Barrington, Illinois

Immanuel's Church, Silver Spring, Maryland

Seneca Creek Community Church, Germantown, Maryland

Cedar Run Community Church, Chantilly, Virginia

Blue Ridge Community Church, Lynchburg, Virginia

Discovery United Methodist Church, Richmond, Virginia

Glen Forest Baptist Church, Richmond, Virginia

Sea Breeze Community Church, Tustin, California

Saddleback Community Church, Mission Viejo, California

South Coast Community Church, Irvine, California

Notes

Introduction, Throwing out Tradition

1. A sign in the office of Willow Creek Community Church's founding pastor, Bill Hybels. Robert Wuthnow mentions this sign in "The Religion Industry: Further Thoughts on the Production of the Sacred" (plenary address, Society for the Scientific Study of Religion, Nashville, Tennessee, 11 November 1996).
2. The name of the church and the pastor have been changed to ensure confidentiality.
3. Nicholas Wolterstorff, "The Grace the Shaped My Life," in *Finding God at Harvard*, ed. Kelly K. Monroe (Grand Rapids, Mich.: Zondervan, 1996), 150–151.
4. Rick Warren, "The Purpose-Driven Church" (seminar, Atlanta, Georgia, 31 January 1995). Warren recently published a book summarizing his church's innovative strategy. The subtitle of the book reads "growth without compromising your message and mission." See Rick Warren, *The Purpose Driven Church* (Grand Rapids, Mich.: Zondervan, 1995), 4.
5. Interview with Linda Wertheimer, "All Things Considered," National Public Radio, 9 November 1995.
6. Gustav Niebuhr, "Mighty Fortresses: Megachurches Strive to Be All Things to All Parishioners," *Wall Street Journal*, 13 May 1991, A1.
7. Kenneth L. Woodward, "A Time To Seek," *Newsweek*, 17 December 1990, 53–54.
8. Gustav Niebuhr, "Where Shopping-Mall Culture Gets a Big Dose of Religion," *New York Times*, 16 April 1995, A14.
9. "Do You Think Church Just Isn't Worth the Time?" (brochure published by Shiloh Crossing Community Church, Indianapolis, Indiana, n.d.)
10. Os Guinness, "Sounding Out the Idols of the Church Growth Movement," in *No God but God*, ed. Os Guiness and John Seel (Chicago: Moody Press, 1992), 152. While the term "church growth movement" can refer to a specific school of evan-

gelism associated with the Charles E. Fuller Institute of Evangelism and Church Growth and the teachings of Donald McGavran and C. Peter Wagner, Guinness uses the term more widely to refer to the types of churches discussed here.

11. Lyle Schaller, *The Seven-Day-a-Week Church* (Nashville, Tenn.: Abingdon, 1992), 44.
12. George Barna, *Evangelism that Works* (Ventura, Calif.: Regal Books, 1997), cited in *Willow Creek Monthly*, August 1995, 4.
13. Cited in Russell Chandler, " 'Customer' Poll Shapes a Church," *Los Angeles Times*, 11 December 1989, A28.
14. Mary Beth Sammons, "Full Service Church," *Chicago Tribune*, 3 April 1994, sec. 6, p. 18.
15. "Clinton Sought Guidance from Man of God Monthly," *Washington Times*, 21 January 1997, A7.
16. "Preview 1996, The Conferences at Willow Creek," Willow Creek Conference brochure, n.d.
17. Wade Clark Roof, "God is in the Details: Reflections on Religion's Public Presence in the United States in the Mid-1990s," *Sociology of Religion* 57 (Summer 1996): 157.
18. Interestingly, the Willow Creek Association gained its first Catholic member church in 1996. Jim Mellado, president, Willow Creek Association, interview by author, South Barrington, Illinois, 19 January 1996.

One   A New Reformation?

1. Staff member of the Leadership Network, interview by author, tape recording, Tyler, Texas.
2. David L. Olsson, "Defining A Movement," *WCA Monthly*, June 1994, 2.
3. Thomas A. Stewart, "Turning Around the Lord's Business," *Fortune*, 25 September 1989, 117.
4. Seven pastors chose the statement "Different religions are the different ways in which people approach God and they should be treated with equal respect." One pastor selected all three possible responses. While the responses in general follow a conservative evangelical line, there is some preliminary evidence that grappling with the religion (or lack of religion) of suburban professionals is leading to a more nuanced understanding of the relationship between Christianity and other faiths.
5. The *Yearbook of American and Canadian Churches 1997* lists 170 religious bodies in the United States, with 23 (13.5 percent) of them having more than three thousand member churches. With three thousand U.S. member churches in 2000, the WCA ranks near the top 10 percent of religious bodies in the United States. Kenneth B. Bedell, ed., *Yearbook of American and Canadian Churches 1997* (Nashville, Tenn.: Abingdon, 1995), 252–258.
6. Two out of five (40 percent) churches six to ten years old grew between 1993 and 1995, while only 29 percent of the churches more than ten years old grew in this

period. This relationship is statistically significant at the p = .00001 level and is somewhat strong (gamma = -.36773).

7. The usefulness of the 1992 NES data was suggested to me by Lyman Kellstedt of Wheaton College. For more on how the 1992 NES data contains improved measurements of evangelicals, see Lyman A. Kellstedt and John C. Green, "Knowing God's Many People: Denominational Preference and Political Behavior," in *Rediscovering the Religious Factor in American Politics,* ed. David C. Leege and Lyman A. Kellstedt (Armonk, N.Y.: M. E. Sharpe, 1993), 53–71.

8. Paul Braoudakis, ed., *Church Leader's Handbook*, 3rd ed. (South Barrington, Ill.: Willow Creek Association, 1996), 35. The distribution of other denominations in the WCA data was consistent with the SCP survey findings. No other denominational family (e.g., Methodist, Lutheran) accounted for more than 10 percent of the WCA membership.

9. Reginald W. Bibby and Merlin B. Brinkerhoff, "The Circulation of the Saints," *Journal for the Scientific Study of Religion* 12 (September 1973): 273–282.

10. Robert J. McClory, "Why Did the Catholic Cross the Road?" *U.S. Catholic*, January 1991, 7.

11. Donald Miller argues that "we are witnessing a second reformation that is transforming the way Christianity will be experienced in the new millennium." Donald Miller, *Reinventing American Protestantism* (Berkeley and Los Angeles: University of California Press, 1997), 11.

12. Robert Schuller, *Self-Esteem: The New Reformation* (New York: Jove, 1982).

13. See Christian Smith et al., *American Evangelicalism: Embattled and Thriving* (Chicago: University of Chicago Press, 1998), 187–203, for a discussion of evangelicals' personal influence strategy.

14. George Thomas, *Revivalism and Cultural Change* (Chicago: University of Chicago Press, 1989), 4.

15. Edith Blumhofer and Randall Balmer, "Introduction," in *Modern Christian Revivals* (Champaign, Ill.: University of Illinois Press, 1993), xii.

16. William G. McLoughlin, *Revivals, Awakenings, and Reform: An Essay on Social Change in America, 1607–1977* (Chicago: University of Chicago Press, 1978).

17. David A. Roozen, "Denominations Grow and Individuals Join Congregations," in *Church and Denominational Growth*, ed. David A. Roozen and C. Kirk Hadaway (Nashville, Tenn.: Abingdon, 1993), 24.

18. C. Kirk Hadaway and David Roozen, "Denominational Growth and Decline," in *Church and Denominational Growth*, 39. The one major exception to this trend is charismatic and Pentecostal churches, which have grown rapidly.

Two   Traditional Religion in a Spiritual Age

1. Richard N. Ostling, "The Church Search," *Time*, 5 April 1993, 45.

2. See Wade Clark Roof, *A Generation of Seekers* (New York: HarperCollins, 1993).

3. Robert Wuthnow, "The Religion Industry: Further Thoughts on the Production

of the Sacred" (plenary address, Society for the Scientific Study of Religion, annual meeting, Nashville, Tennessee, 9 November 1996).

4. I will explore how the discussion of religion as industry relates to theoretical issues in the sociology of religion in chapter 7.

5. Emile Durkheim, *The Elementary Forms of Religious Life* (1915; reprint, New York: Free Press, 1965).

6. Robert Wuthnow, *The Restructuring of American Religion* (Princeton, N.J.: Princeton University Press, 1988).

7. For an example of the saliency of religious identity in American life, see Will Herberg, *Protestant, Catholic, Jew* (New York: Anchor Books, 1960).

8. Roof, *A Generation of Seekers*, 131.

9. Wade Clark Roof , "God is in the Details: Reflections on Religion's Public Presence in the United States in the Mid-1990s," *Sociology of Religion* 57 (Summer 1996): 152.

10. Philip Hammond, *Religion and Personal Autonomy* (Greenville: University of South Carolina Press, 1992), 169.

11. David A. Roozen and C. Kirk Hadaway, "Individuals and The Church Choice," in *Church and Denominational Growth*, ed. David A. Roozen and C. Kirk Hadaway (Nashville, Tenn.: Abingdon, 1993), 243.

12. Penny Long Marler and David A. Roozen, "From Church Tradition to Consumer Choice: The Gallup Surveys of Unchurched Americans," in Roozen and Hadaway, *Church and Denominational Growth*, 264.

13. Wade Clark Roof and William McKinney, *American Mainline Religion* (New Brunswick, N.J.: Rutgers University Press, 1987), 67.

14. Roof, *A Generation of Seekers*, 155.

15. Ibid., 126.

16. It seems that many of these new spiritual advisors have their own PBS special these days.

17. Roof, *A Generation of Seekers*, 110.

18. Dean R. Hoge and David A. Roozen, "Some Sociological Conclusions about Church Trends," in *Understanding Church Growth and Decline: 1950–1978*, ed. Hoge and Roozen (New York: The Pilgrim Press, 1979), 322.

19. William McKinney and Dean R. Hoge, "Community and Congregational Factors in the Growth and Decline of Protestant Churches," *Journal for the Scientific Study of Religion* 22 (March 1983): 65.

20. Mike Regele, *Death of The Church* (Grand Rapids, Mich.: Zondervan, 1995), 107.

21. Benton Johnson, Dean Hoge, and Donald Luidens, "Mainline Churches: The Real Reason for Decline," *First Things*, March 1993, 15.

22. The project director for the *1996 Survey of American Political Culture* was James Davison Hunter at the University of Virginia, and the director of survey research was Carl Bowman of Bridgewater College. The fieldwork was conducted in the first quarter of 1996 by the Gallup Organization. The data are based on more than two thousand face-to-face interviews with a representative sample of Americans. I served as a research associate on the survey design team. The source for data in

this chapter is: *The State of Disunion: 1996 Survey of American Political Culture*, vol. 2: Summary Tables, James Davison Hunter, Project Director, and Carl Bowman, Director of Survey Research (Ivy, Va.: In Media Res Educational Foundation, 1996).

23. The actual percentage of Americans placing either "a great deal" or "quite a lot" of confidence in these major institutions are as follows: organized religion, 65 percent; the Presidency, 39 percent; state government, 39 percent; federal government, 32 percent; economy, 32 percent; and Congress, 26 percent.

24. Only 16 percent of Americans report that they "never" attend church or temple, while almost one out of three Americans (28 percent) report that they attend "once a month or less." There is, however, some evidence that reports of church attendance are inflated. See C. Kirk Hadaway, Penny Long Marler, and Mark Chaves, "What the Polls Don't Show: A Closer Look at U.S. Church Attendance," *American Sociological Review* 58 (1993): 741–752.

25. Another way of putting this is that 72 percent of Americans identify themselves in a way that suggests they might be receptive to the message of seeker churches.

26. The data in this paragraph are based upon table 74 A-L in *The State of Disunion*.

27. This is a consistent pattern. Sixty-four percent of the public agreed with a similar statement—"Everything is beautiful—it's all a matter of how you look at it."

28. For an extended discussion on how individualism may be weakening other moral traditions in American life, see Robert Bellah et al., *Habits of the Heart* (Berkeley and Los Angeles: University of California Press, 1985).

29. See David Wells, *No Place for Truth* (Grand Rapids, Mich.: Eerdmans, 1993), and Wells, *God in the Wasteland* (Grand Rapids, Mich.: Eerdmans, 1994), for such an assessment by an evangelical theologian.

30. See Robert Wuthnow, *Meaning and Moral Order* (Berkeley and Los Angeles: University of California Press, 1987), for more on the importance of coherence, rather than logical consistency, in beliefs.

31. See Alan Wolfe, *One Nation, After All* (New York: Viking, 1998), for a discussion of the comfortable contradictions of the American middle class.

32. Philip Rieff, *The Triumph of the Therapeutic: Uses of Faith after Freud* (New York: Harper and Row, 1966), 252. Rieff soberly warns on page 255 that "all attempts at connecting the doctrines of psychotherapy with the old faiths are patently misconceived."

33. Ronald Inglehart, *Culture Shift in Advanced Industrial Societies* (Princeton, N.J.: Princeton University Press, 1990), 205.

34. John Steadman Rice, *A Disease of One's Own* (New Brunswick, N.J.: Transaction, 1996), 207. Rice cites the following works: Cheryl Russell, *The Master Trend: How the Baby Boom Generation is Remaking America* (New York: Plenum, 1993); Ronald Inglehart, *The Silent Revolution: Changing Values and Political Styles among Western Publics* (Princeton, N.J.: Princeton University Press, 1977); and Inglehart, *Culture Shift in Advanced Industrial Society* (Princeton, N.J.: Princeton University Press, 1990). If this notion of a "silent revolution" has any validity, we would expect to observe institutional as well as attitudinal changes. As evidence of this trend, Rice points out that, in the last three decades, the number of Ameri-

cans consulting mental health professionals has tripled. Furthermore, there has been a dramatic increase in the number of clinical psychologists, clinical social workers, psychiatric hospitals, and "paraprofessional" counselors. See Rice, *A Disease of One's Own*, 27–28.

35. For an examination of the therapeutic ethos as a master trend in civil and criminal law, welfare, education, and other areas of public life, see James Lawry Nolan, *The Therapeutic State* (New York: New York University Press, 1998).

36. "Living in an Age of Whitewater," *NetFax*, Leadership Network, Tyler, Texas, 20 March 1995.

37. William Easum, "Sacred Cows Make Gourmet Burgers," *Next,* Leadership Network, Tyler, Texas, October 1995, 1.

38. Actual figures are that 46.4 percent say the influence of religion is decreasing, 37.7 percent say it is increasing, and 15.9 percent say it is about the same.

39. Thomas S. Kuhn, *The Structure of Scientific Revolutions*, 2nd ed. (Chicago: University of Chicago Press, 1970).

40. Paradigm also has important connotations in the sociology of religion. Don Miller refers to innovative churches such as the Vineyard, Calvary Chapel and Willow Creek as "new paradigm" churches. In the sociology of religion, proponents of the new paradigm in religion argue that pluralism, rather than harming religion by rendering the "sacred canopy" under which belief and institutions were protected, instead has contributed to the vibrancy of religion, especially in the United States. The debate over the new paradigm will be discussed in chapter 7. For an overview, see Stephen R. Warner, "Work in Progress toward a New Paradigm in the Sociology of Religion," *American Journal of Sociology*, 98 (March 1993): 1044-1093.

41. Walt Kallestad, *Entertainment Evangelism* (Nashville, Tenn.: Abingdon, 1995), 24.

42. Paul DiMaggio and Walter W. Powell, "The Iron Cage Revisited: Institutional Isomorphism and Collective Rationality in Organizational Fields," *American Sociological Review* 48 (1983): 147–160.

43. Fligstein concluded, "When an existing system of power is transformed, it requires a perceived crisis, either in the organization or field." Neil Fligstein, "The Structural Transformation of American Industry: An Institutional Account of the Causes of Diversification in the Largest Firms, 1919–1979," in *The New Institutionalism in Organizational Analysis*, ed. Walter W. Powell and Paul J. DiMaggio (Chicago: University of Chicago Press, 1991), 316.

44. George Thomas, "Cultural Analysis of Religious Change," *Sociological Inquiry* 66 (1996): 287.

45. Ibid.

46. One church advertisement makes this point in a humorous way. The picture features a man watching the Detroit Lions football game with the caption: Christianity's greatest competition has always been with the lions.

47. Robert Wuthnow, *Producing the Sacred* (Urbana and Chicago: University of Illinois Press, 1994), 30.

48. George Thomas, *Revivalism and Cultural Change* (Chicago: University of Chicago Press, 1989), 11.
49. Rice, *A Disease of One's Own*, 22.
50. Thomas, *Revivalism and Cultural Change*, 25.
51. Steven Brint and Jerome Karabel, "Institutional Origins and Transformations: The Case of American Community Colleges," in Powell and DiMaggio, *The New Institutionalism*, 350.
52. DiMaggio and Powell, "The Iron Cage Revisited," 148. Case studies mentioned by DiMaggio and Powell include: Lewis Coser, Charles Kadushin, and Walter W. Powell, *Books: The Culture and Commerce of Book Publishing* (New York: Basic Books, 1982); David Tyack, *The One Best System: A History of American Urban Education* (Cambridge: Harvard University Press, 1974); Michael B. Katz, *Class, Bureaucracy, and Schools: The Illusion of Educational Change in America* (New York: Praeger, 1975); and Erik Barnouw, *A History of Broadcasting in the United States*, 3 vols. (New York: Oxford University Press, 1966–68).
53. DiMaggio and Powell, "The Iron Cage Revisited."
54. DiMaggio and Powell, "Introduction," *The New Institutionalism*, 14.
55. Wuthnow, *Producing the Sacred*, 31.

Three   Ritual: Modern Liturgies for Skeptical Seekers

1. Walt Kallestad, *Entertainment Evangelism* (Nashville, Tenn.: Abingdon, 1996), 7.
2. James Barron, "A Church's Chief Executive Seeks the Target Audience," *New York Times*, 18 April 1995, A20.
3. Kallestad, *Entertainment Evangelism*, 26. While the term "imagineering" is closely related to the "imagineers" who design many of Disney's new products, Kallestad does not mention Disney's influence here.
4. Ibid., 73 and 81.
5. Bill Hybels and Lynne Hybels, *Rediscovering Church* (Grand Rapids, Mich.: Zondervan, 1995), 187.
6. Charles Trueheart, "Welcome to the Next Church," *Atlantic*, August 1996, 37.
7. See Willow Creek's Web site (Willowcreek.org), which lists the components of previous services at Willow Creek; the option to purchase messages, dramas, and sometimes songs; and the down-to-the-second timing of each aspect of the service.
8. Mary Douglas, *Natural Symbols* (New York: Pantheon, 1973), 1.
9. Ibid., 13.
10. Ibid.
11. See David Aberle, *The Peyote Religion among the Navaho* (London: Aldine, 1966).
12. Robert Wuthnow, *Meaning and Moral Order* (Berkeley and Los Angeles: University of California Press, 1987), 101.
13. Alan Wolfe, "Out of the Frying Pan into. . . What?" in *America at Century's End*, ed. Alan Wolfe (Berkeley and Los Angeles: University of California Press, 1991), 7–8.

14. Wuthnow, *Meaning and Moral Order*, 141.
15. Barry A. Kosmin and Seymour P. Lachman, *One Nation Under God: Religion in Contemporary American Society* (New York: Harmony Books, 1993), 237.
16. The relationship between denomination and display of religious symbols is statistically significant at the p = .00000 level. It is, however, a relatively weak relationship (lambda = .20000).
17. The relationship between display of symbols and year of establishment is statistically significant at the p = .00000 level. The relationship is quite strong (gamma = -.80072).
18. David L. Olsson, "Defining A Movement," *WCA Monthly*, June 1994, 2.
19. "1996 Church Leadership Conference Program Book" (South Barrington, Ill.: Willow Creek Community Church, 1996), 23.
20. Truehart, "Welcome to The Next Church," 38.
21. Paul Goldberger, "The Gospel of Church Architecture, Revised," *New York Times*, 20 April 1995, B1.
22. "The 1996 Church Leadership Conferences at Willow Creek," Willow Creek Community Church conference brochure, no date.
23. Session on planning seeker services, "Friday Forum," Willow Creek Community Church, South Barrington, Illinois, 27 March 1993.
24. A "vocal special" is what Willow Creek and other churches call a song performed by church singers for the attenders.
25. All of my interviews with seeker church pastors will be documented subsequently in the text only by denomination and the state in which the church is located.
26. *Program Book,* 1996 Church Leadership Conference (South Barrington, Ill.: Willow Creek Community Church, 1996), 23.
27. Kallestad, *Entertainment Evangelism*, 65.
28. Randall Balmer, *Mine Eyes Have Seen the Glory* (New York: Oxford University Press, 1993), 281.
29. Frank C. Senn, " 'Worship Alive': An Analysis and Critique of 'Alternative Worship Services,' " *Worship* 69 (May 1995): 222.
30. Truehart, "Welcome to the Next Church," 44.
31. Rick Warren, "How to Build a Purpose-Driven Church," Saddleback Seminar, Marietta, Georgia, 31 January 1995. Warren adds that "there is no such thing as Christian music. There are Christian lyrics, not tunes. [Thus] your music says nothing about your theology and everything about your culture. . . . There is no such thing as good music or bad music. To say so is thinly veiled racism. Bach is not better than pop." It is interesting that Warren should single out music as the major battleground for the church. In contrast to research that emphasizes the central place of moral issues such as abortion, homosexuality, and the ordination of women in religious conflict, such as James Davison Hunter, *Culture Wars* (New York: Basic Books, 1991), Warren places more emphasis on matters of cultural taste and style. One reason for this is that seeker churches are trying to appeal to "Unchurched Harrys" who are unlikely to hold conservative views on major social issues. As a result, seeker churches tend to de-emphasize these

controversial matters. Another reason that music may prove to be a major battleground for the church is that emotions run high whenever musical style is discussed—thereby proving the old adage that "all politics is local." Whereas issues such as abortion or welfare reform are removed in many ways from the weekly worship service, whether to sing favorite hymns such as "Just As I Am" or "The Old Rugged Cross" or to replace them with upbeat worship choruses will have an obvious and immediate effect on everyone's weekly church experience.

32. Respondents were asked to report the church's practices at its most seeker sensitive service.

33. Senn, "Worship Alive," 218.

34. The lyrics to these songs were listed at Willow Creek's Web site (Willowcreek. org). I selected every song available that was performed during a service for which I also had copies of the message (see chapter 4). In addition, I selected a random sample of songs from 1996 and 1997 services.

35. "From Here On Out," Willow Creek Music, Ever Devoted Music (ASCAP), copyright 1989 Greg Ferguson. Every song listed in Willow Creek's Web site is assessed for its style, tempo, and seeker sensitivity. This song was rated: style: pop; tempo: mid; seeker sensitivity rating: 8.

36. "Let the Lord Love You," Willow Creek Music (album: *A Place to Call Home*), copyright 1989, Rory Noland.

37. "Only by Grace," Willow Creek Music (album: *A Place to Call Home*), copyright 1993, Ever Devoted Music.

38. "Man of God," Willow Creek Music (album: *A Place to Call Home*), copyright 1995, Ever Devoted Music (ASCAP).

39. Milton J. Coalter, John M. Mulder, and Louis B. Weeks, *Vital Signs: The Promise of Mainstream Protestantism* (Grand Rapids, Mich.: Eerdmans, 1996), 67–68. See also Louis Schneider and Sanford M. Dornbush, *Popular Religion: Inspirational Books in America* (Chicago: University of Chicago Press, 1958).

40. Steve Pederson, "Introduction," *Sunday Morning Live: A Collection of Six Drama Sketches*, vol. 2, ed. Steve Pederson (South Barrington, Ill.: Willow Creek Resources, 1995).

41. These three dramas were performed at the 1996 Willow Creek Church Leadership Conference, 24 October 1996.

42. Nancy Beach, Programming Director, 1996 Willow Creek Church Leadership Conference, 24 October 1996.

43. Barbara Dolan, "Full House at Willow Creek," *Time*, 6 March 1989, 60.

44. Douglas, *Natural Symbols*, 14.

45. The two times that I have seen Warren he was wearing, true to his word, a Hawaiian shirt. I am unaware of what Warren wears to funerals.

46. Douglas, *Natural Symbols*, 14. Douglas suggests that the move away from ritualism consists of three phases. "First, there is the contempt of external ritual forms; second, there is the private internalizing of religious experience; third, there is the move to humanist philosophy. When the third stage is underway, the symbolic life of the spirit is finished." *Natural Symbols*, 7.

47. Senn, "Worship Alive," 194. Senn's article illustrates the accuracy of Mary Douglas's theories about the social conditions that foster informality.
48. Bill Hybels, "It's My Turn Now: The Significance of the Sacraments," Willow Creek M9024.
49. Senn, "Worship Alive," suggests that the trend towards subjective, emotional understandings of the sacraments is not new but is one of pietism's legacies to evangelicalism. The seeker church movement has enthusiastically adopted such an understanding.
50. Bill Hybels, "Developing Contagious Christian," talk given at the Willow Creek 1996 *Church Leadership Conference,* 24 October 1996.
51. Statement made at the 1996 Willow Creek Church Leadership Conference, 24 October 1996.
52. This relationship is statistically significant at the p = .00000 level and moderately strong (gamma = -.38731).
53. Gregory Pritchard, *Willow Creek's Seeker Services* (Grand Rapids, Mich.: Baker, 1996), 268.
54. Hybels noted that it is dangerous to associate the whole Christian message with any one symbol, such as the Cross. Bill Hybels, interview by Peter Jennings, *In the Name of God*, ABC news special, 16 March 1995.
55. In the Christian tradition, the Cross is offensive primarily because it is "foolishness to the Greeks.

Four   Messsage: Believe and Be Fulfilled

1. Harry Emerson Fosdick, "What Is the Matter with Preaching?" *Harper's Magazine*, July 1928, 135, cited in John MacArthur, *Ashamed of the Gospel* (Wheaton, Ill.: Crossway, 1993), 81.
2. Lee Stroebel, *Inside the Mind of Unchurched Harry and Mary* (Grand Rapids, Mich.: Zondervan, 1993), 213–214.
3. Doug Murren, *The Baby Boomerang* (Ventura, Calif.: Regal Books, 1990), 103.
4. Walt Kallestad, *Entertainment Evangelism* (Nashville, Tenn.: Abingdon, 1995), 75. In order to improve his preaching, Kallestad established a "Message Research and Evaluation Team," composed of members and nonmembers, that helps prepare messages that "speak to the real needs of people and to evaluate how we are doing."
5. Rick Warren, *The Purpose Driven Church* (Grand Rapids, Mich.: Zondervan, 1995), 294. Warren adds that "Today, 'preaching to felt needs' is scorned and criticized in some circles as cheapening the Gospel and a sellout to consumerism. I want to state this in the clearest possible way possible: Beginning a message with people's felt needs is more than a marketing tool! It is based on the theological fact that God chooses to reveal himself to man according to *our* needs!" *The Purpose Driven Church*, 295.
6. Cited in Gustav Niebuhr, "The Minister as Marketer: Learning from Business," *New York Times*, 18 April 1995, A20.
7. Bill Hybels and Mark Mittelberg, *Becoming a Contagious Christian* (Grand Rapids, Mich.: Zondervan, 1994), 208–209.

8. Marsha Witten, *All Is Forgiven: The Secular Message in American Protestantism* (Princeton, N.J.: Princeton University Press, 1993). Witten writes, "Since secularity may have a profound effect on the doctrines and ideologies of modern religion, the study of religious language may provide an important new direction for secularization research." *All Is Forgiven*, 18.

9. For other studies of evangelicalism and its relationship to modernity, see James Davison Hunter, *American Evangelicalism: Conservative Religion and the Quandary of Modernity* (New Brunswick, N.J.: Rutgers University Press, 1983), and Hunter, *Evangelicalism: The Coming Generation* (Chicago: University of Chicago Press, 1987).

10. John A. Schmalzbauer and C. Gray Wheeler, "Between Fundamentalism and Secularization: Secularizing and Sacralizing Currents in the Evangelical Debate on Campus Lifestyle Codes," *Sociology of Religion* 57 (Fall 1996): 245.

11. George Thomas, *Revivalism and Cultural Change* (Chicago: University of Chicago Press, 1989), 3–4.

12. Ibid., 13–14.

13. For example, one Baptist pastor in California noted that terms like "redemption" and "conversion" are more likely to refer to financial matters such as bonds than theological concepts to many seekers today.

14. George Barna, *Never on a Sunday* (Glendale, Calif.: Barna Research Group, 1990), 24–25, cited in Lee Stroebel, *Inside the Mind of Unchurched Harry and Mary* (Grand Rapids, Mich.: Zondervan, 1993), 211.

15. Bill Hybels, "The Narrow Way," Willow Creek message M9410. Willow Creek labels all messages in its *Seeds Resource Catalog* (South Barrington, Ill.: Willow Creek Community Church, 1995) by the year and week in which they were delivered. Thus, Hybels delivered "The Narrow Way" on the tenth Sunday of 1994. All subsequent references to Willow Creek messages will include the catalog number.

16. I know of several churches that use Willow Creek messages as the basis for their own seeker services. One church I visited was using the Willow Creek series on homosexuality, divorce, and abortion in its own services. At another church, a pastor had transcribed over a year's worth of Willow Creek messages and was adapting them for his own use.

17. One study of Willow Creek's messages found this exactly to be the case. Greg Pritchard found that seven out of ten messages during the course of a year focused on God's love, while only 7 percent of the messages stressed God's holiness. Greg Pritchard, "The Strategy of Willow Creek" (Ph.D. diss., Northwestern University, 1994), 769.

18. "Defining Family Values," Willow Creek messages M9242, M9243, M9244.

19. "Fixing Broken Relationships," M9342.

20. "Audience of One," M9348.

21. Isaiah 6:5, Revised Standard Version.

22. Hybels, "Averting Your Worst Nightmare," M9412.

23. Willow Creek message series M9502-9515. This series of messages has been turned into a book. See Bill Hybels, *The God You're Looking For* (Nashville,

Tenn.: Thomas Nelson, 1997). Hybels reduces the number of God's attributes he discusses from fourteen in the sermon series to eleven chapters in the book.

24. The paradox that the Christian God can be both transcendent and immanent is rooted in Scripture. The Hebrew prophets warned about the dangers of overlooking God's transcendence. For example, in Jeremiah 23:23–24, it is written " 'Am I only a God nearby,' declares the Lord, 'and not a God far away? Can anyone hide in secret places so that I cannot see him?' declares the Lord. 'Do I not fill heaven and earth?' declares the Lord."

25. Hybels, "God's Inclination," M9408.

26. Hybels, "Spiritual Eyesight," M9404.

27. Hybels, "God's Inclination," M9408.

28. Ibid.

29. Hybels, "Hang on for Heaven," M9339.

30. Hybels, "Simple Truth Telling," M9345.

31. Hybels, "Forming a Spiritual Foundation," M9417.

32. Lee Stroebel, "Salt and Light," M9430. Elsewhere, Hybels comments that he dislikes when he is compared with televangelist Jimmy Swaggart. See "Judge Not," M9407.

33. Stroebel, "What Would Jesus Say to Madonna?" M9331.

34. Hybels, "Divorce and Remarriage," M9344.

35. None of the women were senior pastors. Each female respondent indicated that her title in the church was "other member of the pastoral staff."

36. Bill Hybels and Lynne Hybels, *Rediscovering Church* (Grand Rapids, Mich.: Zondervan, 1995), 211.

37. Hybels, "Vision for the Church," M9421.

38. Hybels, "Secret Praying," M9350. Later, Hybels comments that Jesus gave the Lord's prayer "not to be recited" but instead to serve as a model for balanced prayer.

39. Hybels and Hybels, *Rediscovering Church*, book cover. In comparison, *Funk and Wagnalls Standard Collegiate Dictionary* offers several definitions of "church," including "a building for Christian worship," "religious services," and "ecclesiastical organization and authority." Max Weber's definition of "church" as "a hierocratic organization . . . which enforces its order through the psychic coercion by distributing or denying religious benefits" suggests a very different understanding. For the seeker church, the resort to the psyche is not for coercion but for coaxing. Weber, *Economy and Society*, ed. Guenther Roth and Claus Wittich (Berkeley and Los Angeles: University of California Press, 1968), 54.

40. Hybels, "The Narrow Way," M9410.

41. Hybels, "Judge Not," M9407.

42. Hybels, "God's Inclination," M9408.

43. Hybels, "The Beatitudes," M9337.

44. Hybels, "Spiritual Eyesight," M9404.

45. Hybels, "Hang on for Heaven," M9339.

46. This pastor adds, "We are not Bible-thumping fundamentalists who manipulate people into guilty trips to the altar. Instead, we would rather meet people where they are and do all that we can to try and lead them to Jesus Christ."
47. Hybels, "Watch out for Wolves," M9411.
48. Russell Chandler, " 'Customer' Poll Shapes Church," *Los Angeles Times*, 11 December 1989, A1.
49. Hybels, *Rediscovering Church*, 185. See appendix 1 for a discussion of the "train wreck" in Willow Creek's history that prompted major changes in Hybels's preaching style.
50. Hybels, "Simple Truth Telling," M9345.
51. Stroebel, "What Would Jesus Say to Michael Jordan?" M9329.
52. Harry S. Stout, *The Divine Dramatist: George Whitefield and the Rise of Modern Evangelicalism* (Grand Rapids, Mich.: Eerdmans, 1991), xviii.
53. Ibid., xx.
54. George Whitefield, "The Method of Grace," in *Select Sermons of George Whitefield* (Edinburgh: The Banner of Truth Trust, 1958), 78.
55. Ibid., 90.
56. Ibid., 94.
57. Ibid., 90. Whitefield's insistence that his hearers "beg of God" for faith reflects his Calvinist theology. According to Calvinist teaching, one cannot simply choose God; people do not have the capacity to follow Christ of their own free will. This is in marked contrast to the Arminianism prevalent in seeker churches (and much of contemporary Protestantism) today.
58. Whitefield, "The Lord Our Righteousness," in *Select Sermons of George Whitefield*, 134.
59. Author's visit to Cedar Run Community Church, Chantilly, Virginia, 16 October 1994.
60. Stroebel, "God's Wisdom Works," M9413.
61. Robert Wuthnow, *Christianity in the Twenty-first Century* (New York: Oxford University Press, 1993), 8.
62. See appendix A for a discussion of Schuller's influence on Willow Creek.
63. Robert Schuller, *Self-Esteem: The New Reformation* (New York: Jove Books, 1982), 146, 150.
64. Ibid., 12, 65, 98, 150, and 14–15.
65. Ibid., 100, 104–105.
66. Philip Rieff, *The Triumph of the Therapeutic* (Chicago: University of Chicago Press, 1966), 62.
67. James Davison Hunter, *Evangelicalism: The Coming Generation* (Chicago: University of Chicago Press, 1987), 71.
68. David Wells, *No Place for Truth* (Grand Rapids, Mich.: Eerdmans, 1993), 175.
69. Ibid., 178.
70. Rieff, *The Triumph of the Therapeutic*, 255.
71. See appendix A for a list of Willow Creek's ten core values.
72. Hybels, "Facing the Family Challenge, Part I," M9415.

73. The one example I encountered had to do with expelling staff members who were involved in clearly immoral behavior (i.e., adultery).
74. Thomas Luckmann, *The Invisible Religion* (New York: Macmillan, 1967), 110.

Five   Strategy: The Shopping Mall Church

1. Barry A. Kosmin and Seymour P. Lachman, *One Nation Under God: Religion in Contemporary American Society* (New York: Harmony Books, 1993), 239.
2. Charles Truehart, "Welcome to the Next Church," *Atlantic*, August 1996, 47
3. Interview by Lynn Neary, "All Things Considered," National Public Radio, 3 November 1994.
4. Thomas A. Stewart, "The Hottest Product is Brand X," *Fortune*, 25 September 1989, 128.
5. *Teaching Churches*, published by The Hendricks Group (Tyler, Tex.: Leadership Network: 1990), 6–7.
6. Robert David Sack, *Place, Modernity, and the Consumer's World* (Baltimore: The Johns Hopkins University Press, 1992). For a discussion of the geographical and moral significance of shopping malls and other modern places of consumption, see especially pages 134–148.
7. Ibid., 135.
8. Cited in Truehart, "Welcome to the Next Church," 40.
9. Rick Warren, "How to Build a Purpose-Driven Church," Saddleback Church Seminar, Atlanta, Georgia, 31 January 1995.
10. By "myth," I am referring to the cultural power or efficacy of an idea, not its level of veracity. Meyer and Rowan, for example, argue that the formal structure of organizations, especially their bureaucratic procedures, "reflect the myths of their institutional environments instead of the demands of their work activities." The myth that links bureaucracy with efficiency and rationality legitimates the form—even if the actual operation of the firm (informal structure) is substantially different. John Meyer and Brian Rowan, "Institutionalized Organizations: Formal Structure as Myth and Ceremony," in *The New Institutionalism in Organizational Analysis*, ed. Walter W. Powell and Paul J. DiMaggio (Chicago: University of Chicago Press, 1991), 41.
11. Robert Bellah et al., *Habits of the Heart* (Berkeley and Los Angeles: University of California Press, 1986).
12. Robert Wuthnow, "The Religion Industry: Further Thoughts on the Production of the Sacred," Society for the Scientific Study of Religion, Annual Meeting, Nashville, Tennessee, 9 November 1996.
13. George Barna, *Marketing the Church* (Colorado Springs: NavPress, 1988), 26.
14. Of the remaining respondents, 16.7 percent selected the response "neutral," and 13.5 percent disagreed with the statement.
15. Barna, *Marketing the Church*, 28.
16. Ibid., 12.
17. Pastor Marlon Vis, interview by Peter Jennings, "In the Name of God," ABC News special report, 16 March 1995.

18. See appendix A for more on Schuller's influence upon Willow Creek.

19. It is interesting to note that the results of this pastor's market research are virtually identical to those of Willow Creek's initial research. This pastor added, "We found that people considered church to be irrelevant, dull, and boring. We found it to be ineffective in their lives and they were seeking something but did not know how to describe it. We would hear them talk about the kind of clothing you had to wear to church, the kind of music that is constantly offered in the traditional church, the physical form of the church, the program content of the church. . . . And so we broke the mold a little bit with the way that we started our church."

20. Robert Wuthnow reports women are more likely than men to attend religious services, read the Bible, and give a lot of thought to developing their faith and are *less* likely than men to be without any religious affiliation. Wuthnow, *The Restructuring of American Religion* (Princeton, N.J.: Princeton University Press, 1988), 225.

21. Rick Warren, *The Purpose Driven Church* (Grand Rapids, Mich.: Zondervan, 1995), 170.

22. Interview by Peter Jennings, "In the Name of God."

23. *Church Leaders Handbook* (South Barrington, Ill.: Willow Creek Community Church, 1991), 4–5. See also Bill Hybels and Lynne Hybels, *Rediscovering Church* (Grand Rapids, Mich.: Zondervan, 1995), 167–182, for a more detailed discussion. Bill Hybels recalls that Willow Creek "pursued intuitively" its seven-step strategy. The strategy was only formalized after Hybels jotted it down on a napkin one day. *Rediscovering Church*, 169.

24. In chapters 3 and 4, I discussed the rituals and messages of seeker services (step 3). I will discuss small groups and evaluating one's spiritual gifts (steps 5 and 6) subsequently.

25. Warren, *The Purpose Driven Church*, 144.

26. Walt Kallestad, *Entertainment Evangelism* (Nashville, Tenn.: Abingdon, 1995), 110–113.

27. Milton J. Coalter, John M. Mulder, and Louis B. Weeks, *Vital Signs: The Promise of Mainstream Protestantism* (Grand Rapids, Mich.: Eerdmans, 1996), 112–113. Virtually everyone surveyed (96 percent) wanted "A sermon that relates Bible teachings to today's problems." The authors suggest that the most revealing response was elicited by a question posed to inactive Presbyterians: "If a good friend asked you to go along to church on Sunday, how likely would you be to go with your friend?" "Very likely" or "somewhat likely" was the response of 86 percent of the former Presbyterians.

28. Because of its size and flexible programming, the shopping mall church can retain the interest of the less committed (crowd)—as long as there is an energized core to serve in programs such as child care, small group leadership, and so on. One important area of future research is to assess how good a job seeker churches actually do of moving people from the crowd to the core. In other words, how many Unchurched Harrys become "fully devoted followers of Christ"? While Willow Creek understandably takes pride in how Lee Stroebel changed

from a cynical and irreligious newspaper reporter to a pastor of the church, such success stories may not be representative. In his interviews with Willow Creek staff members, Greg Pritchard found that the church estimates that up to two-thirds of the attenders at seeker services are "Churched Larrys" who are not advancing along the path to greater spiritual commitment in the ways that Willow Creek intends. Ideally, seekers who follow the steps in Willow Creek's strategy will become "fully devoted followers of Christ," defined by the five "Gs"" Grace, Growth, Group, Gifts, and Good Stewardship. See Greg Pritchard, "The Strategy of Willow Creek" (Ph.D. diss., Northwestern University, 1994), 790.

29. Kent R. Hunter, "Membership Integrity," in *Church Growth: State of the Art*, ed. C. Peter Wagner (Wheaton, Ill.: Tyndale House, 1986), 93.
30. Barna, *Marketing the Church*, 17.
31. George Barna, *User-Friendly Churches* (Ventura, Calif.: Regal, 1991), 107.
32. Kenneth Woodward, "A Time to Seek," *Newsweek*, 17 December 1990, 52.
33. Wade Clark Roof, *A Generation of Seekers* (San Francisco: HarperCollins, 1993), 110.
34. Carl George, *Prepare Your Church for the Future* (Grand Rapids, Mich.: Revell, 1991), 13.
35. This is step 6—"Serve in the body of Christ"—of Willow Creek's strategy.
36. Bruce Bugbee, *Network Serving Seminar: Equipping Those Who Are Seeking to Serve* (Pasadena, Calif.: Charles E. Fuller Institute, 1989), 3.
37. Pritchard, "The Strategy of Willow Creek," 99.
38. Leith Anderson, *Dying for Change* (Minneapolis: Bethany House Publishers, 1990), 130.
39. Ibid., 98.
40. "L ≥ C . . . The Law of Ecological Learning," *NetFax*, distributed by Leadership Network, Tyler, Texas, 11 December 1995, 1.
41. See step 5 of Willow Creek's outreach strategy.
42. See Hybels, *Rediscovering Church*, 191. The verse is Acts 2:42.
43. Paul Braoudakis, ed., *Church Leaders Handbook*, 3rd ed. (South Barrington, Ill.: Willow Creek Community Church, 1996), 120.
44. Hybels, *Rediscovering Church*, 178.
45. Don Cousins and Judson Poling, *Friendship with God* (Grand Rapids, Mich.: Zondervan, 1992).
46. George, *Prepare Your Church*, 22.
47. Robert Wuthnow, *Sharing the Journey* (New York: Free Press, 1994), 2.
48. Ibid., 3–4.
49. Ibid., 18.
50. Ibid., 358.
51. Robert Wuthnow, *Christianity in the Twenty-first Century* (New York: Oxford University Press, 1993), 215.
52. Wuthnow, *Sharing the Journey*, 7.
53. Hybels, *Rediscovering Church*, 212.
54. Cited in Truehart, "Welcome to the Next Church," 52.

55. Cited in "Church's 1-2 Punch a Knockout," *Chicago Tribune*, 21 May 1989, sec. 2, p. 2.

56. Rick Warren, "How to Build a Purpose-Driven Church," Saddleback Seminar, Atlanta, Georgia, 31 January 1995.

57. Barbara Stewart, ed., *Church Leaders Handbook*, 1st ed. (South Barrington, Ill.: Willow Creek Community Church, 1991), 3.

58. Interestingly, this exact series was given by a pastor at one of the seeker churches I visited. While only anecdotal, this example of the use of Willow Creek material does suggest the extent to which Willow Creek's philosophy shapes not only the style of seeker churches but also the content of their messages.

59. Conference brochure for the "Purpose-Driven Church," Saddleback Community Church, n.d.

60. John Seel, *The Evangelical Forfeit* (Grand Rapids, Mich.: Baker, 1993), 83.

61. Jim Mellado, "Willow Creek Community Church," Harvard Business School Case Study N9-691-102 (Cambridge: President and Fellows of Harvard College, 1991), 18.

62. Cited in *NetFax*, published by Leadership Network, Tyler, Texas, 17 April 1995, 1.

63. *Willow Creek Exchange*, June 1993.

64. Lyle Schaller, *The Seven-Day-a-Week Church* (Nashville, Tenn.: Abingdon, 1992), 30.

65. Mellado, "Willow Creek Community Church," 14.

66. Alasdair MacIntyre, *After Virtue*, 2nd ed. (Notre Dame, Ind.: University of Notre Dame Press, 1984), 30.

67. C. Peter Wagner, *Strategies for Church Growth* (Ventura, Calif.: Regal, 1987), 29.

68. MacIntyre, *After Virtue*, 74.

69. Ibid., 74, 86.

70. Ibid., 77.

71. Os Guinness, "Sounding Out the Idols of Church Growth," in *No God but God*, ed. Os Guinness and John Seel (Chicago: Moody Press, 1992), 173.

72. James Hunter, *Evangelicalism: The Coming Generation* (Chicago: University of Chicago Press, 1987), 195.

73. Willow Creek has started a new "Axis" service designed to reach baby-busters. Indeed, the "cutting edge" in the seeker church movement today is in developing services to reach "Generation X."

74. The diverse emphases of leading churches—Willow Creek, Saddleback, Crystal Cathedral, Houston's Exciting Second—suggests that while there are some shared philosophical or cultural approaches, there is not one distinct model of a seeker friendly church.

75. Robert Wuthnow, *Meaning and Moral Order* (Berkeley and Los Angeles: University of California Press, 1987), 145.

76. Ibid., 148.

77. Ibid., 151.

78. Ibid., 177.

79. Ibid., 184.

Six   Organization: The Postmodern Denomination

1. Interview by author, pastor of a nondenominational church in Georgia. Subsequent interviews will be noted in the text only.
2. Lyle Schaller, "Megachurch," *Christianity Today*, 5 March 1990, 22.
3. Blanchard quoted in *NetFax*, a publication of the Leadership Network, Tyler, Texas, 15 May 1995.
4. Interview by Diane Rehm, *The Diane Rehm Show,* National Public Radio (WAMU), Washington, D.C., 11 April 1995.
5. Norman Shawchuck, Philip Kotler, Bruce Wrenn, and Gustave Rathe, *Marketing for Congregations* (Nashville, Tenn.: Abingdon, 1992), 26.
6. Leith Anderson, *Dying for Change* (Minneapolis: Bethany House, 1990).
7. Actual figures are that 46 percent say the influence of religion is decreasing, 38 percent say it is increasing, and 16 percent say it is about the same.
8. John Dart, "It's Not All in a Name for Some Churches," *Los Angeles Times*, 22 December 1990, S4.
9. Jim Mellado, "Refocusing Our Mission and Strategy," *WCA Monthly*, October/November 1994, 1.
10. *1993 Church Associates Directory* (South Barrington, Ill.: Willow Creek Association, 1993), 4.
11. Bill Hybels, interview by Michael Maudlin, "Selling out the House of God?" *Christianity Today*, 18 July 1994, 25.
12. Jim Mellado, "Refocusing Our Mission and Strategy," *WCA Monthly*, October/November 1994, 2.
13. *NetFax*, 4 September 1995, 1.
14. Robert Wuthnow, *The Restructuring of American Religion* (Princeton, N.J.: Princeton University Press, 1988).
15. The Willow Creek Statement of Faith is one of several important Willow Creek documents.
16. David L. Olsson, "Defining A Movement, Part Two" *WCA Monthly*, June 1994, 1.
17. Ibid.
18. *WCA Monthly*, May-September 1994.
19. *WCA Monthly*, February 1993, 3.
20. "Ministering to Prevailing Churches," *WCA Monthly*, January/February 2000.
21. The countries are Australia, England, Germany, Ireland, Netherlands, Norway, Scotland, Spain, and South Africa.
22. Willow Creek Resources 1995–1996 catalog.
23. See the second part of the bibliography for a full citation of these works.
24. "Teaching Churches" (Tyler, Tex.: Leadership Network, 1990), 8 and 62.
25. Schaller, "Megachurch," 23. Schaller wonders, "who will perpetuate the orthodox Christian faith if the large churches do not depend on seminaries for future ministerial leadership?"
26. *The Exchange*, Willow Creek Association, September 1993.
27. James Mellado, "Harvard Business School Case Study of Willow Creek Com-

munity Church," Case Study N9-691-102 (Cambridge: Harvard University, 1991), 14.

28. Nancy T. Ammerman, "Denominations: Who and What are We Studying?" in *Reimagining Denominationalism*, ed. Robert Bruce Mullin and Russell E. Richey (New York: Oxford University Press, 1994), 111–133.

29. George Marsden, "Introduction: The Evangelical Denomination," in *Evangelicalism and Modern America*, ed. George Marsden (Grand Rapids, Mich.: Eerdmans, 1984), xi.

30. Wuthnow, *Restructuring*, 100–132.

31. Ibid., 121–122.

32. Ibid., 123.

33. Ibid., 125. Wuthnow adds that "special purpose groups constitute a valuable way of sustaining religious commitment. People can participate in these organizations for limited periods of time."

34. Russell E. Richey, "Denominations and Denominationalism: An American Morphology," in Mullin and Richey, *Reimagining Denominationalism*, 77.

35. Ibid.

36. Ibid.

37. Richey also notes that, with the shift to postdenominational confessionalism, the "grand cause of America" that once united Protestant denominations in their social and moral efforts no longer holds. Some conservative groups may press for a "Christian America" through specific moral campaigns on abortion, school prayer, homosexuality, and other issues, but "Christianizing" the social order is now more a source of division than of unity within Protestantism.

38. Ibid., 90.

39. William H. Swatos, Jr., "Beyond Denominationalism: Community and Culture in American Religion," *Journal for the Scientific Study of Religion* 20 (September 1981): 224.

40. Mark Chaves, "Denominations as Dual Structures: An Organizational Analysis," *Sociology of Religion* 54 (Summer 1993): 149.

41. Max Weber, *Economy and Society*, ed. Guenther Roth and Claus Wittich (Berkeley and Los Angeles: University of California Press, 1978), 54.

42. Chaves, "Denominations as Dual Structures," 154 and 159.

43. Thomas Luckmann, *The Invisible Religion* (New York: Macmillan, 1967), and Peter Berger, *The Sacred Canopy: Elements of a Sociological Theory of Religion* (Garden City, N.Y.: Doubleday, 1967).

44. Chaves, "Denominations as Dual Structures," 165.

45. Nancy Ammerman, "SBC Moderates and the Making of a Post-Modern Denomination," *The Christian Century*, 22–29 September 1993, 896.

46. Stewart R. Clegg, *Modern Organizations* (London: Sage, 1990), 21.

47. Jim Mellado, president, Willow Creek Association, interview by author, South Barrington, Illinois, 19 January 1996.

48. "Blazing New Trails," *WCA Monthly*, January/February 1996, 2.

49. Interestingly, Donald Luidens notes how the Reformed Church in America (RCA), the more liberal or Mainline counterpart to the Christian Reformed

Church, is in the midst of a "marketing struggle," which has it roots in the denomination's identity crisis. Should the RCA continue to stress its theological and ethnic distinctiveness, which seems only to have contributed to membership decline, or adapt with the times? The RCA "can be expected to continue to try various adaptive modes until it finds one which is perceived to reverse the membership trends—and thus lift the denomination out of the crisis mode." Luidens suggests that if the RCA does adapt to the times, the "new" RCA will be sharply different from the "old" RCA, "thereby divesting itself of any traditional underpinnings." The price of success, then, is a denomination or church that is unrecognizable to previous generations. Willow Creek has provided the adaptive model for the RCA's conservative counterpart the Christian Reformed Church. It remains to be seen whether Mainline denominations such as the RCA are willing and able to make the shift to seeker-sensitive ministry. See Donald A. Luidens, "Between Myth and Hard Data: a Denomination Struggles," in *Beyond Establishment: Protestant Identity in a Post-Protestant Age*, ed. Jackson Carroll and Wade Clark Roof (Louisville, Ky.: Westminster/John Knox Press, 1993), 264.

50. Mellado, interview.

Seven Translation and Tradition

1. Peter Jennings, "In the Name of God," ABC News Special, 16 March 1995.
2. Wade Clark Roof, *A Generation of Seekers* (San Francisco: HarperCollins, 1993), 110.
3. See Christian Smith et al., *American Evangelicalism: Embattled and Thriving* (Chicago: University of Chicago Press, 1998,) for such an argument.
4. Willy Welch, "Talkin' Episcopalian Blues," *Welcome the Light* (New York: Tamarisk Records, 1987).
5. There is good biblical precedence for this given Jesus's choice of earthy images in his parables.
6. This strategy is not unique to evangelical churches. See Randall Balmer's analysis of Mount Olivet Lutheran Church in Minneapolis for an example of a Mainline Protestant church using this strategy. Randall Balmer, *Grant Us Courage* (New York: Oxford University Press, 1996), 135–142.
7. George Thomas, *Revivalism and Cultural Change* (Chicago: University of Chicago, 1987), 162.
8. Roger Finke and Rodney Stark, *The Churching of America, 1776–1990* (New Brunswick, N.J.: Rutgers University Press, 1992), 16.
9. Nathan Hatch, *The Democratization of American Christianity* (New Haven, Conn.: Yale University Press, 1989), 9.
10. This refers to the title of Peter Berger's influential *The Sacred Canopy* (Garden City, N.Y.: Doubleday, 1967).
11. R. Stephen Warner, "Convergence Toward the New Paradigm," in *Rational Choice Theory and Religion*, ed. Lawrence A. Young (New York: Routledge, 1997), 88. Other key works in the new paradigm approach include: Warner, "Work in Progress toward a New Paradigm for the Sociological Study of Religion in the

United States," *American Journal of Sociology* 98 (1993): 1044–1093; Roger Finke and Rodney Stark, "Religious Economies and Sacred Canopies: Religious Mobilization in American Cities," *American Sociological Review* 53 (February 1988): 41–49; Roger Finke and Rodney Stark, "How the Upstart Sects Won America: 1776–1850," *Journal for the Scientific Study of Religion* 28 (1989): 27–44; and Laurence R. Iannaccone, "Why Strict Churches Are Strong," *American Journal of Sociology* 99 (1994): 1180–1211.

12. Donald Miller, *Reinventing American Protestantism* (Berkeley and Los Angeles: University of California Press, 1997), 181–182.

13. Ibid., 183–184. Because Miller develops a very helpful summary of the connections between new paradigm churches and the new paradigm in the sociology of religion, I will only briefly summarize these here. I will focus subsequently on how this research might also inform neosecularization theory, which is quite different from the new paradigm approach but not necessarily incompatible with it. Some of the differences in our approach may be due to different types of data. Miller used rich ethnographic research on congregational life and individuals, while this data is focused on leaders and institutions.

14. Nancy Ammerman, *Congregation and Community* (New Brunswick, N.J.: Rutgers University Press, 1997), 362–367.

15. Smith et al., *American Evangelicalism*, 77.

16. Warner, "Work in Progress toward a New Paradigm,"1080.

17. Robert Bellah wonders whether "the balance of American religious life [is] slipping away from those denominations that have had a historic concern for the common good toward religious groups so privatistic and self-centered that they begin to approach the consumer cafeteria model of Luckmann's invisible religion." Bellah, "Civil Religion: The American Case," in *Varieties of Civil Religion*, ed. Robert Bellah and Phillip Hammond (San Francisco: Harper and Row, 1980), 20

18. Starke and Finke, *The Churching of America*.

19. David Yamane, "Secularization on Trial: In Defense of a Neosecularization Paradigm," *Journal for the Scientific Study of Religion* 36 (January 1997): 113–115.

20. Mark Chaves, "Secularization as Declining Religious Authority," *Social Forces* 72 (March 1994): 768.

21. Peter Beyer, *Religion and Globalization* (London: Sage, 1994), 80.

22. Ibid., 80.

23. Miller, *Reinventing American Protestantism*, 23–26.

24. Ibid., 190. This formula is a revised version (updated for the new millennium) of the classic Anglican formulation of Scripture, tradition, and reason.

25. Robert Wuthnow, *Sharing the Journey* (New York: Free Press, 1994), 29.

26. Ibid., 358.

27. Richard Ostling, "Superchurches and How They Grow," *Time*, 5 August 1991, 62.

28. Recognizing the challenge of reaching a different generation, Willow Creek has created a new service, called Axis, that is designed to reach Generation X. It meets in Willow Creek's gymnasium, can feature harder-edged music, and stresses the importance of relationships even more than the original Willow

Creek model. For example, attenders are often seated at round tables during the service to facilitate interaction.

29. Lee Stroebel, "Inside the Mind of Unchurched Harry and Mary," *WCA Monthly*, October 1993, 2.
30. David L. Olsson, "Defining A Movement, Part Two" *WCA Monthly*, June 1994, 2.
31. Interview by Peter Jennings, "In the Name of God."
32. For a more detailed argument, see the last third of Gregory Pritchard, *Willow Creek's Seeker Services* (Grand Rapids, Mich.: Baker Books, 1996), in which he argues that Willow Creek has accommodated itself to the therapeutic ethos of contemporary culture.
33. Robert Wuthnow, *Christianity in the Twenty-first Century* (New York: Oxford University Press, 1993), 48. See also Robert Wuthnow, *After Heaven: Spirituality in American since the 1950s* (Berkeley and Los Angeles: University of California Press, 1998), for a discussion of how a practice-oriented spirituality might combine the best of the rootedness of traditions with the individual responsiveness of spirituality.
34. Alasdair MacIntyre, *After Virtue* (Notre Dame, Ind.: University of Notre Dame Press, 1984), 221–222.
35. Marva J. Dawn, *Reaching Out without Dumbing Down* (Grand Rapids, Mich.: Eerdmans, 1995), 256.
36. See for example Thomas Howard, *Evangelical Is Not Enough* (Nashville, Tenn.: Thomas Nelson, 1984); Frederica Mathewes-Green, "In the Passenger Seat: From Canterbury to Constantinople," *Regeneration Quarterly*, 1 (Spring 1995): 7–10; Jeffrey Sheler, "From Evangelicalism to Orthodoxy," *U.S. News and World Report*, 15 January 1990, 58–59; Timothy Ware, *The Orthodox Church* (Harmondsworth, Middlesex, England: Penguin, 1967); and Robert Webber, *Evangelicals on the Canterbury Trail* (Harrisburg, Penn: Morehouse Publishing, 1989). For the stories of eleven evangelical converts to Catholicism, see *Surprised by Truth*, ed. Patrick Madrid (San Diego: Basilica Press, 1995).
37. Cited in John Seel, *The Evangelical Forfeit* (Grand Rapids, Mich.: Baker, 1993), 50.
38. For example, evangelical minister and author John MacArthur argues that the seeker church movement embraces a flawed conception of revival because it is too dependent upon modern techniques, rather than God's action. MacArthur argues that the influential methods and assumptions of nineteenth-century revivalist Charles Finney undergird the seeker church movement—and that these assumptions are as flawed today as they were a century ago. Finney's emphasis on the ability of the right methods to spark a revival reflected an inadequate understanding of God's sovereignty in the salvation of the elect, according to MacArthur. Despite his considerable success (or because of it), "Finney's approach to ministry thus foreshadowed and laid the foundation for modern pragmatism. . . . The modern market-driven ministry is simply a culmination of the movement Finney began." MacArthur adds "the church in our generation is still seething with the leaven Finney introduced, and modern Evangelical pragmatism is proof of that." See John MacArthur, *Ashamed of the Gospel: When the*

Church Becomes Like the World (Wheaton, Ill.: Crossway Books, 1993), 159 and 235.

39. The problem with the seeker churches, according to Os Guinness, is not their innovations *per se* but that many of these innovations, such as the application of managerial and communications techniques to the church, are not accompanied by a corresponding rededication to evangelical truth and theology. Though Guinness praises innovative churches for their commitment to "mission, renewal, and reformation," he suggests that the seeker church movement's "theological understanding is often superficial, with almost no element of biblical criticism." Guinness goes on to argue that "[t]heology is rarely more than marginal in the church growth movement and discussion of the traditional marks of the church is virtually nonexistent." As an example, Guinness cites one Christian leader who returned home from a church growth conference puzzled because there had been "literally no theology" and "no serious reference to God at all." Modern tools and techniques make it possible to proclaim the Christian message so effectively that "there no longer appears to be any need for God." Guinness cautions that "we modern Christians are literally capable of winning the world while losing our own souls." Os Guinness, *Dining with the Devil* (Grand Rapids, Mich.: Baker, 1993), 24, 53, 29, 43. Similarly, John Seel argues that the uncritical use of managerial, therapeutic, and technological languages and techniques, which he finds in abundance at Willow Creek's Church Leadership Conference, tends to reshape expectations about the role of pastors and churches. Eminent pastors do not achieve their prominence as a result of their exposition of biblical texts but instead as a result of their expertise in "management, marketing, drama, and counseling." Seel argues that doctrinal orthodoxy is not sufficient because modernity poses the greatest challenge not to formal beliefs but to informal assumptions about what is true and what makes sense. "Long before modernity changes the doctrinal content of belief," writes Seel, "it alters one's assumptions about how life is to be organized day to day. Before theology is diluted, every other aspect of social life is transformed. The new is celebrated while the traditional is ridiculed." See Seel, *The Evangelical Forfeit*, 93 and 110.

Appendix A   A Brief History of Willow Creek Community Church

1. Bill Hybels and Mark Mittelberg, *Becoming a Contagious Christian* (Grand Rapids, Mich.: Zondervan, 1994), 208–209.
2. "Welcome," *Willow Creek Community Church*, no date.
3. "Church History," *Welcome to Willow Creek*, Willow Creek Community Church, 14.
4. Bill Hybels and Lynne Hybels, *Rediscovering Church* (Grand Rapids, Mich.: Zondervan, 1995), 101.
5. This figure is taken from the book jacket of Bill Hybels, *Too Busy Not to Pray* (Downers Grove, Ill.: InterVarsity Press, 1988).
6. While the church's success could not have been predicted, it was not altogether surprising to the early leaders of Willow Creek. One of the early members of the

church who has since left for another church recalls that "one of the questions that sometimes gets asked . . . is, 'Could you have ever dreamed that Willow Creek could become a ministry like this?' And not in an arrogant or egotistical way at all, but more in a way of God speaking to people back then, I tell them, 'we did dream that this would happen.' There were times when we were out for coffee and we would talk about Willow Creek community church the way it is now, and we would believe it's going to be a reality. We'd just say, 'I believe that God is going to do this. There is going to be a place where literally thousands of people come together and worship and find Christ.' We actually talked about that."

7. Hybels and Hybels, *Rediscovering Church*, 53.
8. Rob Wilkins, "An Inside Look at The Early Years," *Church Leaders Handbook* (South Barrington, Ill.: Willow Creek Community Church, 1991), 27.
9. Bill Hybels and Rob Wilkins, *Descending into Greatness* (Grand Rapids, Mich.: Zondervan, 1993), 206. The following section draws heavily from pages 206–212.
10. Hybels and Hybels, *Rediscovering Church*, 26.
11. Rob Wilkins, "An Inside Look at The Early Years," 28. This section draws extensively from pages 28–30.
12. Hybels and Hybels, *Rediscovering Church*, 29–30.
13. Wilkins, "An Inside Look at the Early Years," 29.
14. Ibid., 33.
15. Hybels and Wilkins, *Descending into Greatness*, 207.
16. Wilkins, "An Inside Look at the Early Years," 30.
17. Ibid. 35.
18. Interview with a former Willow Creek pastor, who adds, "What happened was that Bill and myself and a couple of other people at South Park Church reached a point where we said there's probably not a lot further to go here in just a high school ministry. The only step to be taken now is to consider a church, an adult ministry that doesn't define itself in just high school terms. We kept talking about that more and more until we just finally made the break and we just moved to Palatine."
19. Bill Hybels, "Passages that Pump Me Up, Part One," Willow Creek Community Church, Tape M9421.
20. Ibid.
21. Hybels and Wilkins, *Descending into Greatness*. The dedication reads "To Dr. Gilbert Bilezikian, whose life has been a nonstop testament to what this book is about. Thanks Gil . . . You started teaching me these lessons twenty years ago, and you're finding new ways to teach them all the time."
22. "The Man Who Saw Willow Before It Was Willow," *Willow Creek Monthly*, July 1995, 1.
23. Interview with a former Willow Creek pastor.
24. Hybels and Hybels, *Rediscovering Church*, 69.
25. See Gregory Pritchard, "The Strategy of Willow Creek" (Ph.D. diss., Northwestern University, 1995). Pritchard documents that the staff at Willow Creek is unusually reluctant to mention Schuller's influence upon the church because Schuller is perceived by many evangelicals as having watered down the Gospel

through an overemphasis on psychological categories. For example, Schuller argues that Christians must recast traditional theology in terms of self-esteem and avoid using Christian terminology, such as sin, that might alienate the unchurched. Willow Creek, in contrast, does talk about sin directly to its audience. See Robert Schuller, *Self-Esteem: The New Reformation* (New York: Jove Books, 1982). Lynne and Bill Hybels are the most forthright about Schuller's influence upon Willow Creek in *Rediscovering Church*, 68–70.

26. Schuller mentions this in an interview with Gregory Pritchard. See Pritchard, "The Strategy of Willow Creek," 186.
27. Wilkins, "An Inside Look at the Early Years," 41.
28. Ibid., 43.
29. Hybels and Hybels, *Rediscovering Church*, 87.
30. "The Theater Days," *Willow Creek*, Special Anniversary Issue (South Barrington, Ill.: Willow Creek Community Church, n.d.), 38.
31. Hybels and Hybels, *Rediscovering Church*, 98.
32. This section draws primarily from ibid., chapter 6.
33. Pritchard, "The Strategy of Willow Creek," 165.
34. Hybels and Hybels, *Rediscovering Church*, 101.
35. Ibid., 134.
36. Ibid., 136.
37. Ibid., 119.
38. Cited in Pritchard, "The Strategy of Willow Creek," 619.
39. George Barna, *Marketing the Church* (Colorado Springs: Navpress, 1988), 7–8.

Appendix B   Methodology and Survey Information

1. Funding for the survey was provided by the University of Virginia's Institute for Advanced Studies in Culture.
2. Don A. Dillman, *Mail and Telephone Surveys: The Total Design Method* (New York: John Wiley, 1978).
3. By 9 May 1995, the final date for entering the data from returned surveys, 448 had been returned. Shortly after this date, I received five more surveys, which I added to the data set. Later in the summer, after I had completed most of my data analysis, I received 7 more surveys. These 7 are included as part of the total response rate. The Center for Survey Research conducted a data entry reliability report on the 448 surveys received by 9 May. CSR found a per field error rate of 0.25 percent. Ten percent of the surveys were checked for data entry reliability (46 out of 448). An average of 120 fields of data were entered in each survey. Fourteen total errors were found.
4. John B. Williamson et al., "Content Analysis," *The Research Craft* (Boston: Little, Brown, 1982).
5. Marsha Witten, *All Is Forgiven: The Secular Message in American Protestantism* (Princeton, N.J.: Princeton University Press, 1993).
6. The conferences I attended were: Willow Creek's Friday Forum, South Barrington, Illinois, 27 March 1993; "How to Build a Purpose-Driven Church," sponsored

by Rick Warren, pastor of Saddleback Valley Community Church, Atlanta, Georgia, 31 January 1995; and George Barna's "What Effective Churches Have Discovered," Richmond, Virginia, 1 June 1995.

7. Some of the books critical of seeker churches include: Marva J. Dawn, *Reaching Out without Dumbing Down* (Grand Rapids, Mich.: Eerdmans, 1995); Os Guinness, *Dining with the Devil: The Megachurch Movement Flirts with Modernity* (Grand Rapids, Mich.: Baker Books, 1993); John F. MacArthur, *Ashamed of the Gospel: When the Church Becomes Like the World* (Wheaton, Ill.: Crossway Books, 1993); Kenneth Myers, *All God's Children and Blue Suede Shoes* (Wheaton, Ill.: Crossway, 1989); John Seel, *The Evangelical Forfeit* (Grand Rapids, Mich.: Baker Books, 1993); Bruce Shelley and Marshall Shelley, *The Consumer Church* (Downers Grove, Ill.: InterVarsity Press, 1992): Douglas D. Webster, *Selling Jesus: What's Wrong with Marketing the Church?* (Downers Grove, Ill.: InterVarsity Press, 1992); David Wells, *No Place for Truth* (Grand Rapids: Eerdmans, 1993); and Wells, *God in the Wasteland* (Grand Rapids, Mich.: Eerdmans, 1994).

8. Funding for travel to West Coast seeker churches and to Willow Creek was provided by the Institute for Advanced Studies in Culture.

Selected Bibliography

Scholarly Sources

Ahlstrom, Sydney. *A Religious History of the American People*. New Haven, Conn.: Yale University Press, 1972.

Ammerman, Nancy. "SBC Moderates and the Making of a Postmodern Denomination." *The Christian Century*, 22–29 September 1993, 896–899.

———. "Denominations: Who and What are We Studying." In *Reimagining Denominationalism*, edited by Robert Bruce Mullin and Russell E. Richey. New York: Oxford University Press, 1994.

———. *Congregation and Community*. New Brunswick, N.J.: Rutgers University Press, 1997.

Balmer, Randall. *Mine Eyes Have Seen the Glory*. New York: Oxford University Press, 1993.

———. *Grant Us Courage*. New York: Oxford University Press, 1996.

Beckford, James. "Religious Organizations." In *The Sacred in a Secular Age*, edited by Phillip E. Hammond. Berkeley and Los Angeles: University of California Press, 1985.

Bedell, Kenneth B., ed. Yearbook of American and Canadian Churches. Nashville, Tenn.: Abingdon, 1995.

Bellah, Robert. *Beyond Belief: Essays on Religion in a Post-Traditional World*. New York: Harper and Row, 1970.

———. "Civil Religion: The American Case." In *Varieties of Civil Religion*, edited by Robert Bellah and Phillip Hammond. San Francisco: Harper and Row, 1980.

Berger, Peter L. "The Market Model of Ecumenicity." *Social Research* 30 (Spring 1963): 77–93.

———. *The Sacred Canopy: Elements of a Sociological Theory of Religion*. Garden City, N.Y.: Doubleday, 1967.

———. *A Far Glory.* New York: Free Press, 1992.

Beyer, Peter. *Religion and Globalization.* London: Sage, 1994.

Bibby, Reginald W. "Why Conservative Churches *Really* Are Growing: Kelley Revisited." *Journal for the Scientific Study of Religion* 17 (June 1978): 129–137.

Bibby, Reginald W., and Merlin B. Brinkerhoff. "The Circulation of the Saints." *Journal for the Scientific Study of Religion* 12 (September 1973): 273–283

———. "Circulation of the Saints Revisited." *Journal for the Scientific Study of Religion* 22 (September 1983): 253–262.

Blumhofer, Edith, and Randall Balmer. "Introduction." In *Modern Christian Revivals.* Champaign, Ill.: University of Illinois Press, 1993.

Caplow, Theodore, Howard M. Bahr, and Bruce A. Chadwick. *All Faithful People.* Minneapolis: University of Minnesota Press, 1983.

Carpenter, Joel A. *Revive Us Again: The Reawakening of American Fundamentalism.* New York: Oxford University Press, 1997.

Carroll, Jackson W. and Wade Clark Roof. "Beyond Establishment, but in Which Direction?" In *Beyond Establishment: Protestant Identity in a Post-Protestant Age,* edited by Jackson W. Carroll and Wade Clark Roof. Louisville, Ky.: Westminster/John Knox Press, 1993.

Chaves, Mark. "Secularization *and* Religious Revival: Evidence from U.S. Church Attendance Rates, 1972–1986." *Journal for the Scientific Study of Religion* 28 (December 1989): 464–477.

———. "Family Structure and Protestant Church Attendance: The Sociological Basis of Cohort and Age Effects." *Journal for the Scientific Study of Religion* 30 (December 1991): 501–514.

———. "Denominations as Dual Structures: An Organizational Analysis." *Sociology of Religion* 54 (Summer 1993): 147–169.

———. "Intraorganizational Power and Internal Secularization in Protestant Denominations." *American Journal of Sociology* 99 (July 1993): 1–48.

———. "Secularization as Declining Religious Authority." *Social Forces* 72 (March 1994): 749–774.

Chaves, Mark, and David E. Cann. "Regulation, Pluralism, and Religious Market Structure: Explaining Religious Vitality." *Rationality and Society* 4 (July 1992): 272–290.

Chaves, Mark, and James C. Cavendish. "More Evidence on U.S. Catholic Church Attendance," *Journal for the Scientific Study of Religion* 33 (December 1994): 376–381.

Clegg, Stewart R. *Modern Organizations.* London: Sage, 1990.

Coalter, Milton J., John M. Mulder, and Louis B. Weeks. *Vital Signs: The Promise of Mainstream Protestantism.* Grand Rapids, Mich.: Eerdmans, 1996.

Dawn, Marva J. *Reaching Out without Dumbing Down.* Grand Rapids, Mich.: Eerdmans, 1995.

Demerath, N. J., III, Peter Dobkin Hall, Terry Schmitt, and Rhys H. Williams, eds. *Sacred Companies: Organizational Aspects of Religion and Religious Aspects of Organizations.* New York: Oxford University Press, 1998.

DiMaggio, Paul J., and Walter Powell. "The Iron Cage Revisited: Institutional Isomorphism and Collective Rationality in Organizational Fields." *American Sociological Review* 48 (April 1983):147–160.

Douglas, Mary. *Natural Symbols*. New York: Pantheon, 1973.

Durkheim, Emile. *The Elementary Forms of Religious Life*. 1915; reprint, New York: Free Press, 1965.

Eiesland, Nancy L. "Mapping Faith: Choice and Change in Local Religious Organizational Environments." In *Re-Forming the Center: American Protestantism, 1900 to the Present*, edited by Douglas Jacobsen and William Vance Trollinger, Jr. Grand Rapids, Mich.: Eerdmans, 1998.

Finke, Roger, and Rodney Starke. "Religious Economies and Sacred Canopies: Religious Mobilization in American Cities, 1906." *American Sociological Review* 53 (February 1988): 41–49.

———. "How the Upstart Sects Won America: 1776–1850." *Journal for the Scientific Study of Religion* 28 (1989): 27–44.

———. *The Churching of America, 1776–1990*. New Brunswick, N.J.: Rutgers University Press, 1992.

Flanagan, Kieran. *Sociology and Liturgy*. New York: St. Martin's Press, 1991.

Fligstein, Neil. "The Structural Transformation of American Industry: An Institutional Account of the Causes of Diversification in the Largest Firms, 1919–1979." In *The New Institutionalism in Organizational Analysis*, edited by Walter W. Powell and Paul J. DiMaggio. Chicago: University of Chicago Press, 1991.

Friedland, Roger, and Robert R. Alford. "Bringing Society Back In: Symbols, Practices, and Institutional Contradictions." In *The New Institutionalism in Organizational Analysis*, edited by Walter W. Powell and Paul J. DiMaggio. Chicago: University of Chicago Press, 1991.

Gallup, George, Jr., and Jim Castelli. *The People's Religion: American Faith in the 90's*. New York: Macmillan, 1989.

Geertz, Clifford. "Religion as a Cultural System" In *The Interpretation of Cultures*. New York: Basic Books, 1973.

Glock, Charles Y. "The Role of Deprivation in the Origin and Evolution of Religious Groups." In *Religion and Social Conflict*, edited by R. Lee and M. Marty. Oxford: Oxford University Press, 1964.

Guinness, Os. "Sounding Out the Idols of the Church Growth Movement." In *No God but God*, edited by Os Guinness and John Seel. Chicago: Moody Press, 1992.

———. *Dining with the Devil: The Megachurch Movement Flirts with Modernity*. Grand Rapids, Mich.: Baker, 1993.

———. *The American Hour*. New York: Free Press, 1994.

Hadaway, C. Kirk, Penny Long Marler, and Mark Chaves. "What the Polls Don't Show: A Closer Look at U.S. Church Attendance." *American Sociological Review* 58 (1993): 741–752.

Hammond, Phillip E. *Religion and Personal Autonomy*. Columbia: University of South Carolina Press, 1992.

Handy, Robert T. *A Christian America*. New York: Oxford University Press, 1971.

Hannan, Michael T. and John Freeman. "Structural Inertia and Organizational Change." *American Sociological Review* 49 (April 1984): 149–164.

Harrison, Paul. *Authority and Power in the Free Church Tradition*. Princeton, N.J.: Princeton University Press, 1959.

Hatch, Nathaniel. *The Democratization of American Christianity*. New Haven: Yale University Press, 1989.

Herberg, Will. *Protestant, Catholic, Jew.* New York: Anchor Books, 1960.

Hoge, Dean R., and David A. Roozen, eds. *Understanding Church Growth and Decline: 1950–1978*. New York: The Pilgrim Press, 1979.

Hudnut-Beumler, James. *Looking for God in the Suburbs: The Religion of the American Dream and Its Critics, 1945–1965*. New Brunswick, N.J.: Rutgers University Press, 1994.

Hughes, Richard T., and C. Leonard Allen. *Illusions of Innocence: Protestant Primitivism in America, 1630–1875*. Chicago: University of Chicago Press, 1988.

Hunter, James Davison. *American Evangelicalism: Conservative Religion and the Quandary of Modernity*. New Brunswick, N.J.: Rutgers University Press, 1983.

———. "Religion and Political Civility: The Coming Generation of American Evangelicals." *Journal for the Scientific Study of Religion* 23 (December 1984): 364–380.

———. *Evangelicalism: The Coming Generation*. Chicago: University of Chicago Press, 1987.

Iannacone, Lawrence. "Religious Practice: A Human Capital Approach." *Journal for the Scientific Study of Religion* 29 (September 1990): 297–314.

———. "The Consequences of Religious Market Structure." *Rationality and Society* 3 (April 1991): 156–177.

———. "Why Strict Churches Are Strong." *American Journal of Sociology* 99 (1994): 1180–1211.

Inglehart, Ronald. *Culture Shift in Advanced Industrial Societies*. Princeton, N.J.: Princeton University Press, 1990.

Johnson, Benton, Dean R. Hoge, and Donald A. Luidens. "Mainline Churches: The Real Reason for Decline." *First Things*, March 1993, 13–18.

Kelley, Dean. *Why Conservative Churches are Growing*. New York: Harper and Row, 1972.

Kellstedt, Lyman A., and John C. Green. "Knowing God's Many People: Denominational Preference and Political Behavior." In *Rediscovering the Religious Factor in American Politics*, edited by David C. Leege and Lyman A. Kellstedt. Armonk, N.Y.: M. E. Sharpe, 1993.

Kosmin, Barry A., and Seymour P. Lachman. *One Nation Under God: Religion in Contemporary American Society*. New York: Harmony, 1993.

Kuhn, Thomas S. *The Structure of Scientific Revolutions*. 2nd ed. Chicago: University of Chicago Press, 1970.

Lawrence, Paul R., and Jay W. Lorsch. *Organization and Environment*. Cambridge: Harvard University Press, 1967.

Luckmann, Thomas. *The Invisible Religion*. New York: Macmillan, 1967.

Luecke, David S. "Is Willow Creek the Way of the Future?" *Christian Century* 14 (May 1997): 479–485.

Luidens, Donald A. "Between Myth and Hard Data: A Denomination Struggles." In *Beyond Establishment: Protestant Identity in a Post-Protestant Age,* edited by Jackson W. Carroll and Wade Clark Roof. Louisville, Ky.: Westminster/John Knox Press, 1993.

MacArthur, John F. *Ashamed of The Gospel: When the Church Becomes Like the World.* Wheaton, Ill.: Crossway, 1993.

MacIntyre, Alasdair. 2d ed. *After Virtue.* Notre Dame: University of Notre Dame Press, 1984.

Marsden, George. *Fundamentalism and American Culture.* New York: Oxford University Press, 1980.

Marsden, George. "The Evangelical Denomination." In *Evangelicalism and Modern America,* edited by George Marsden. Grand Rapids, Mich.: Eerdmans, 1984.

Maudlin, Michael G., and Edward Gilbreath. "Selling Out the House of God?" *Christianity Today,* 18 July 1994, 21–25.

McKinney, William, and Dean R. Hoge. "Community and Congregational Factors in the Growth and Decline of Protestant Churches." *Journal for the Scientific Study of Religion* 22 (March 1983): 51–66.

McLoughlin, William G., Jr. *Revivals, Awakenings, and Reform: An Essay on Social Change in America, 1607–1977.* Chicago: University of Chicago Press, 1978.

Meyer, John W., and Brian Rowan. "Institutionalized Organizations: Formal Structure as Myth and Ceremony." *American Journal of Sociology* 83 (1977): 340-363.

Meyrowitz, Joshua. *No Sense of Place: The Impact of Electronic Media on Social Behavior.* New York: Oxford University Press, 1985.

Miller, Donald. *Reinventing American Protestantism.* Berkeley and Los Angeles: University of California Press, 1997.

Moore, R. Laurence. *Selling God: American Religion in the Marketplace of Culture.* New York: Oxford University Press, 1994.

Mouw, Richard J. *Consulting the Faithful: What Christian Intellectuals Can Learn From Popular Religion.* Grand Rapids, Mich.: Eerdmans, 1994.

Myers, Kenneth. *All God's Children and Blue Suede Shoes.* Wheaton, Ill.: Crossway, 1989.

Niebuhr, Gustav. "Mighty Fortresses: Megachurches Strive to Be All Things to All Parishioners." *Wall Street Journal,* 13 May 1991.

————. "Where Shopping-Mall Culture Gets a Big Dose of Religion." *New York Times,* 16 April 1995, A1, A14.

Niebuhr, H. Richard. *The Social Sources of Denominationalism.* New York: Meridia, 1929.

Nolan, James Lawry. *The Therapeutic State.* New York: New York University Press, 1998.

Noll, Mark. *A History of Christianity in the United States and Canada.* Grand Rapids, Mich.: Eerdmans, 1992.

————. *The Scandal of the Evangelical Mind.* Grand Rapids, Mich.: Eerdmans, 1994.

Ostling, N. "Superchurches and How They Grow." *Time,* 5 August 1991, 62.

————. "The Church Search." *Time,* 5 April 1993, 44–49.

Postman, Neil. *Amusing Ourselves to Death*. New York: Viking Penguin, 1985.

Primer, Ben. *Protestants and American Business Methods*. Ann Arbor, Mich.: UMI Research Press, 1979.

Pritchard, Gregory. *Willow Creek's Seeker Services*. Grand Rapids, Mich.: Baker, 1996.

Rice, John Steadman. *A Disease of One's Own*. New Brunswick, N.J.: Transaction Publishers, 1996.

Richey, Russell E. *Denominationalism*. Nashville, Tenn.: Abingdon, 1977.

———. "Institutional Forms of Religion." In *Encyclopedia of the American Religious Experience*, vol. 1, edited by Charles H. Lippy and Peter W. Williams. New York: Scribner's, 1988.

———. "Denominations and Denominationalism: An American Morphology." In *Reimagining Denominationalism*, edited by Robert Bruce Mullin and Russell E. Richey. New York: Oxford University Press, 1994.

Rieff, Philip. *The Triumph of the Therapeutic*. Chicago: University of Chicago Press, 1966.

Roof, Wade Clark, and William McKinney. *American Mainline Religion: Its Changing Shape and Future*. New Brunswick, N.J.: Rutgers University Press, 1987.

Roof, Wade Clark. *A Generation of Seekers*. San Francisco: HarperCollins, 1993.

———. "God is in the Details: Reflections on Religion's Public Presence in the United States in the Mid-1990s." *Sociology of Religion* 57 (summer 1996): 149–162.

Roozen, David, and C. Kirk Hadaway. *Church and Denominational Growth*. Nashville, Tenn.: Abingdon, 1993.

Sack, Robert David. *Place, Modernity, and the Consumer's World*. Baltimore: The Johns Hopkins University Press, 1992.

Scherer, Ross P. "A New Typology for Organizations: Market, Bureaucracy, Clan and Mission, with Application to American Denominations." *Journal for the Scientific Study of Religion* 27 (December 1988): 475–198.

———. Introduction. In *American Denominational Organization*, edited by Ross P. Scherer. Pasadena, Calif.: William Carey Library, 1980.

Schmalzbauer, John A., and C. Gray Wheeler, "Between Fundamentalism and Secularization: Secularizing and Sacralizing Currents in the Evangelical Debate on Campus Lifestyle Codes." *Sociology of Religion* 57 (Fall 1996).

Seel, John. *The Evangelical Forfeit*. Grand Rapids, Mich.: Baker, 1993.

———. "Modernity and Evangelicals: American Evangelicalism as a Global case Study." In *Faith and Modernity*, edited by Philip Sampson, Vinay Samuel, and Chris Sugden. Oxford: Regnum, 1994.

Senn, Frank C. *Christian Worship and its Cultural Setting*. Philadelphia: Fortress Press, 1983.

———. " 'Worship Alive': An Analysis and Critique of 'Alternative Worship Services.'" *Worship* 69 (May 1995): 194–224.

Shawchuck, Norman, Philip Kotler, Bruce Wrenn, and Gustave Rath. *Marketing for Congregations*. Nashville, Tenn.: Abingdon, 1992.

Sheler, Jeffrey. "From Evangelicalism to Orthodoxy." *U.S. News and World Report*, 15 January 1990, 58–59.

———. "Spiritual America." *U.S. News and World Report*, 4 April 1993, 53–54.

Shelley, Bruce, and Marshall Shelley. *The Consumer Church*. Downers Grove, Ill.: InterVarsity Press, 1992.

Shils, Edward. *Tradition*. Chicago: University of Chicago Press, 1981.

Smith, Christian, et al. *American Evangelicalism: Embattled and Thriving*. Chicago: University of Chicago Press, 1998.

Stark, Rodney. "Rational Choice Theories of Religion." *The Agora* 2 (Winter 1994): 1–5.

Stark, Rodney, and Laurence R. Iannacone. "Rational Choice Propositions about Religious Movements." In *Religion and the Social Order: A Handbook on Cults and Sects in America*, edited by David G. Bromley and Jeffrey K. Hadden. Greenwich, Conn.: JAI Press, 1993.

Stout, Harry S. *The Divine Dramatist: George Whitefield and the Rise of Modern Evangelicalism*. Grand Rapids, Mich.: Eerdmans, 1991.

Swatos, William H., Jr. "Beyond Denominationalism?: Community and Culture in American Religion." *Journal for the Scientific Study of Religion* 20 (September 1981): 217–227.

Thomas, George. *Revivalism and Cultural Change*. Chicago: University of Chicago Press, 1989.

———. "Cultural Analysis of Religious Change and Movements." *Sociological Inquiry* 66 (August 1996): 285–302.

Truehart, Charles. "Welcome to the Next Church." *Atlantic*, August 1996.

Wacker, Grant. "Uneasy in Zion: Evangelicals in Postmodern Society." In *Evangelicalism and Modern America*, edited by George Marsden. Grand Rapids, Mich.: Eerdmans, 1994.

Warner, R. Stephen. *New Wine in Old Wineskins*. Berkeley: University of California Press, 1988.

———. "Work in Progress toward a New Paradigm for the Sociological Study of Religion in the United States." *American Journal of Sociology* 98 (March 1993): 1044–1093.

———. "Convergence toward the New Paradigm." In *Rational Choice Theory and Religion*, edited by Lawrence A. Young. New York: Routledge, 1997.

Watt, David Harrington. *A Transforming Faith: Explorations of Twentieth-Century American Evangelicalism*. New Brunswick, N.J.: Rutgers University Press, 1991.

Weber, Max. *Economy and Society*. Edited by Guenther Roth and Claus Wittich. Berkeley: University of California Press, 1978.

Weber, Timothy P. "Fundamentalism Twice Removed: The Emergence and Shape of Progressive Evangelicalism." In *New Dimensions of American Religious History*, edited by Jay P. Dolan and James P. Wind. Grand Rapids, Mich.: Eerdmans, 1993.

Webster, Douglas D. *Selling Jesus: What's Wrong with Marketing the Church?* Downers Grove, Ill.: InterVarsity Press, 1992.

Wells, David. *No Place for Truth*. Grand Rapids, Mich.: Eerdmans, 1993.

———. *God in the Wasteland.* Grand Rapids, Mich.: Eerdmans, 1994.
White, James F. *Introduction to Christian Worship.* Nashville, Tenn.: Abingdon, 1980.
Whitefield, George. *Select Sermons of George Whitefield.* Edinburgh: Banner of Truth Trust, 1958.
Woodward, Kenneth L. "A Time to Seek." *Newsweek,* 17 December 1990, 50–56.
———. "Dead End for the Mainline?" *Newsweek,* 9 August 1993, 46–47.
Williamson, John B., et al. "Content Analysis." *The Research Craft.* Boston: Little, Brown, 1982.
Witten, Marsha. *All Is Forgiven: The Secular Message in American Protestantism.* Princeton, N.J.: Princeton University Press, 1993.
Wolfe, Alan. *One Nation, After All.* New York: Viking, 1998.
Wuthnow, Robert. *Meaning and Moral Order.* Berkeley and Los Angeles: University of California Press, 1987.
———. *The Restructuring of American Religion.* Princeton, N.J.: Princeton University Press, 1988.
———. "Introduction." In *Vocabularies of Public Life,* edited by R. Wuthnow. London: Routledge, 1992.
———. *Christianity in the Twenty-first Century.* New York: Oxford University Press, 1993.
———. *Sharing the Journey.* New York: Free Press, 1994.
———. "The Small-Group Movement in the Context of American Religion." In *I Come Away Stronger,* edited by R. Wuthnow. Grand Rapids, Mich.: Eerdmans, 1994.
———. *Producing the Sacred.* Urbana and Chicago: University of Illinois Press, 1994.
———. *After Heaven: Spirituality in America since the 1950s.* Berkeley and Los Angeles: University of California Press, 1998.
Yamane, David. "Secularization on Trial: In Defense of a Neosecularization Paradigm." *Journal for the Scientific Study of Religion* 36 (January 1997): 113–115.

Seeker Church Movement Sources

Anderson, Leith. *Dying for Change.* Minneapolis: Bethany House Publishers, 1990.
Barna, George. *Marketing the Church.* Colorado Springs, Colo.: Navpress, 1988.
———. *Never on Sunday.* Glendale , Calif.: Research Group, 1990.
———. *User Friendly Churches.* Ventura, Calif.: Regal, 1991.
Bugbee, Bruce. *Network Serving Seminar: Equipping Those who are Seeking to Serve.* Pasadena, Calif.: Charles E. Fuller Institute, 1989.
Church Leaders Handbook. 3d ed. Edited by Paul Braoudakis. South Barrington, Ill.: Willow Creek Community Church, 1996.
George, Carl. *Prepare Your Church for the Future.* Grand Rapids, Mich.: Revell, 1991.
Heinecke, Paul T., Kent R. Hunter, and David S. Luecke. *Courageous Churches.* St. Louis: Concordia, 1991.
Hybels, Bill. *Who You Are When No One's Looking.* Downers Grove, Ill.: InterVarsity Press, 1987.

————. *Too Busy Not to Pray*. Downers Grove, Ill.: InterVarsity Press, 1988.
————. *The God You're Looking For*. Nashville, Tenn.: Thomas Nelson, 1997.
Hybels, Bill, and Lynne Hybels. *Fit To Be Tied*. Grand Rapids, Mich.: Zondervan, 1991.
————. *Rediscovering Church*. Grand Rapids, Mich.: Zondervan, 1995.
Hybels, Bill, and Mark Mittelberg. *Becoming A Contagious Christian*. Grand Rapids: Zondervan, 1994.
Hybels, Bill, and Rob Wilkins. *Descending into Greatness*. Grand Rapids, Mich.: Zondervan, 1993.
Kallestad, Walt. *Entertainment Evangelism*. Nashville, Tenn.: Abingdon, 1995.
Leadership Network. *Teaching Churches: A Study of Ten Models of Church-To-Church Instruction*. Arlington, Tex.: The Hendricks Group, 1990.
McGavran, Donald. *Effective Evangelism: A Theological Mandate*. Phillipsburg, N.J.: Presbyterian and Reformed Publishing Company, 1988.
————. *Understanding Church Growth*. Rev. ed. Edited by C. Peter Wagner, Grand Rapids, Mich.: Eerdmans, 1990.
McGavran, Donald, and Winfield C. Arn. *Ten Steps for Church Growth*. New York: Harper and Row, 1977.
Murren, Doug. *The Baby Boomerang*. Ventura, Calif.: Regal Books, 1990.
Schaller, Lyle. *Growing Plans*. Nashville, Tenn.: Abingdon, 1983.
————. *The Seven-Day-A-Week Church*. Nashville, Tenn.: Abingdon, 1992.
Shawchuck, Norman, Philip Kotler, Bruce Wrenn, and Gustave Rathe. *Marketing for Congregations*. Nashville, Tenn.: Abingdon, 1992.
Schuller, Robert. *Your Church Has Real Possibilities*. Glendale, Calif.: Regal, 1975.
————. *Self-Esteem: The New Reformation*. New York: Jove, 1982.
Stroebel, Lee. *Inside the Mind of Unchurched Harry and Mary*. Grand Rapids, Mich.: Zondervan, 1993.
Sunday Morning Live: A Collection of Drama Sketches from Willow Creek Community Church. Vols. 1 and 2. Edited by Steve Pederson. Grand Rapids, Mich.: Zondervan Publishing House and Willow Creek Resources, 1992.
Towns, Elmer L. *10 of Today's Most Innovative Churches*. Ventura, Calif.: Regal, 1990.
Vaughan, John N. *The World's 20 Largest Churches*. Grand Rapids: Baker Book House, 1984.
Wagner, C. Peter. *Our Kind of People: The Ethical Dimensions of Church Growth in America*. Atlanta: John Knox Press, 1979.
————, ed. *Church Growth: State of the Art*. Wheaton, Ill.: Tyndale House Publishers, 1986.
————. *Strategies for Church Growth*. Ventura, Calif.: Regal, 1987.
Warren, Rick. *The Purpose Driven Church*. Grand Rapids, Mich.: Zondervan, 1995.
Willow Creek Association. *Church Associates Directory*. South Barrington, Ill.: Willow Creek Association, 1993.
Willow Creek Community Church. *Seeds Resource Catalog*. South Barrington, Ill.: Willow Creek Community Church, 1993.

Index

George, Carl, 116, 199

God, analogies for, 85; authority of, 85; belief in, 44; benevolent image of, 88; contact with, 41; culturally appealing characteristics of, 86; defining, 83–86; direct devotion to, 71; domesticated, 121; encounters with, 86–88, 170; existence of, 79; as Father, 83, 86; free choice and, 33; imitating, 100; immanence of, 84, 87; as internal presence, 121; knowing, 100; loving, 100; need for, 229n. 39; omnipresence of, 85; paternal love of, 79, 83; perceptions of, 121; personal relationship with, 44, 79, 108; presence in communion, 72–73; reality of, 100; redemption and, 21; search for, 98; transcendent attributes of, 84–85; trust in, 67; vulnerability of, 86

Gospel, contextualization of, 78; transformation of, 104; translation of, 104, 182; truth, 99

Grace, awareness of, 32

Graham, Billy, 1, 32, 151

Great Awakening, 1

Guerin, Dave, 183

Guinness, Os, 130, 229n. 39

Habitat for Humanity, 200

Hammond, Philip, 40

Hatch, Nathan, 170

"Have I Told You that I Love You," 2

Heartland Community Church (Kansas), 7

Heidelberg Catechism, 162

Hell, 93, 98

"He Won't Let Me Down," 17

Holiness churches, 27

Holmbo, Dave, 191, 192, 193, 194, 197

Holy Spirit, 84

Houston, Whitney, 66

Hunter, James, 103, 130

Hybels, Bill, 4, 10, 19, 30, 31, 55, 70, 72, 78, 82, 84, 88, 91, 93, 94, 96, 103, 104, 112, 116, 119, 120, 123, 124, 127, 128, 130, 139–140, 143, 162, 163, 181, 192, 193, 194, 195, 196, 199, 201, 207n. 1, 218n. 39

Hybels, Lynne, 92, 163, 181, 198, 199, 200

identity, ascriptive, 76; based on choice, 11; Christian, 185; common, 153; community, 155–156; competition for, 50; cultural, 150, 161; denominational, 7, 28, 51, 59–61, 131, 138, 141, 150, 152, 163; ethnic, 162; evangelical, 153–156; individual, 185; institutional, 176; national, 162; religious, 30, 38, 152, 164; shared, 152, 185; subcultural, 173

ideology, 130–133

individualism, 31, 185; cultural, 40, 45; expressive, 109; growth of, 76; utilitarian, 109; values and, 45

Inglehart, Ronald, 46

innovation, 78; reasons for, 47–49; results of, 49–52; in seeker churches, 38, 47–52

Institute for Church Leadership, 195–196

In the Name of God (television), 9

isomorphism, 52, 53, 165

Jennings, Peter, 2

Joel, Billy, 66

judgment, divine, 99

justice, divine, 44

Kadel, Paula, 10

Kallestad, Walt, 48, 54, 55, 65, 78, 136

Kensington Community Church (Michigan), 5

Kuhn, Thomas, 48

Lasch, Christopher, 120

Leadership Network, 47, 107, 140, 148, 149

About the Author

Kimon Howland Sargeant is an officer in the Religion Program at The Pew Charitable Trusts. Previously, Sargeant was the Sorokin Post-Doctoral Fellow at the University of Virginia's Institute for Advanced Studies in Culture. He received his Ph.D. in sociology from the University of Virginia and has published articles on religion, education, and cultural conflict in the United States.